Shoot First

AND ASK QUESTIONS LATER

Sut Jhally & Justin Lewis
General Editors

Vol. 7

PETER LANG
New York • Washington, D.C./Baltimore • Bern
Frankfurt am Main • Berlin • Brussels • Vienna • Oxford

JUSTIN LEWIS, ROD BROOKES,
NICK MOSDELL, TERRY THREADGOLD

Shoot First
AND ASK QUESTIONS LATER

Media Coverage of the 2003 Iraq War

PETER LANG
New York • Washington, D.C./Baltimore • Bern
Frankfurt am Main • Berlin • Brussels • Vienna • Oxford

Library of Congress Cataloging-in-Publication Data

Lewis, Justin.
Shoot first and ask questions later: media coverage of the 2003 Iraq war /
Justin Lewis, Rod Brookes, Nick Mosdell, Terry Threadgold.
p. cm. — (Media and Culture; vol. 7)
Includes bibliographical references and index.
1. Iraq War, 2003—Journalism, Military. 2. Iraq War, 2003—Mass media and the
war. 3. Iraq War, 2003—Press coverage. I. Lewis, Justin.
II. Series: Media & culture (New York, N.Y.) ; v. 7.
DS79.76.S56 2006   070.4'4995670443--dc22   2005029798
ISBN 0-8204-7418-5
ISSN 1098-4208

Bibliographic information published by **Die Deutsche Bibliothek**.
Die Deutsche Bibliothek lists this publication in the "Deutsche
Nationalbibliografie"; detailed bibliographic data is available
on the Internet at http://dnb.ddb.de/.

Cover design by Sophie Boorsch Appel

The paper in this book meets the guidelines for permanence and durability
of the Committee on Production Guidelines for Book Longevity
of the Council of Library Resources.

© 2006 Peter Lang Publishing, Inc., New York
275 Seventh Avenue, 28th Floor, New York, NY 10001
www.peterlangusa.com

Contents

CHAPTER ONE

Models of War Reporting

AS WE FINISHED THIS BOOK, footage of frontline armed conflict in Iraq returned to the world's television screens to a degree unparalleled since George Bush declared that "major combat operations have ended" on 2 May 2003. Journalists from the main American and British broadcasters accompanied U.S. divisions leading a major assault on Fallujah. From positions outside the city, U.S. artillery mortars and phosphorous shells were televised raining down on Fallujah like fireworks across the night sky. Handheld video cameras appeared to give a soldier's-eye view of the fight to clear the city, house by house, mosque by mosque. Reporters filed live reports by videophone against a soundtrack testifying to the devastating return of force by U.S. helicopter gunships, mortars, and missiles against rebel snipers. Their reports were not completely in favor of the U.S. military they shadowed. Journalists could and did introduce a note of caution about U.S. claims regarding rebel positions, could and did indicate concern about the casualties civilians were likely to sustain from the launch of all of this firepower.

Indeed, it was an embedded cameraman who found himself in a position to film an American soldier shooting an injured Iraqi insurgent; if he had not been there, an incident that for many amounts to a war crime would not have been filmed. But whereas in the campaign against Saddam

Hussein, footage filmed by news crews accompanying U.S.-led units was balanced, to some extent, by footage filmed by crews in Baghdad, there was no footage of the battle for Fallujah from the other side at all. Al-Jazeera, who had an office in Fallujah and who on their past record may have been expected to provide such footage, had been prohibited from covering Iraq from within Iraq.[1] For other journalists, even Iraqis, many more of whom had been killed than Westerners, it simply was not safe.

Broadcast coverage of the battle of Fallujah was nowhere near as extensive as the coverage of the March–April 2003 campaign. Fallujah did not saturate television schedules in the same way and indeed had to compete for headlines with domestic news stories. Nevertheless, it is a significant indication of how Western television broadcasters may cover future conflicts. The battle for Fallujah marked the return of embedded journalism, the program of barracking journalists with frontline units devised by the Pentagon in late 2002.[2] Some journalists had been embedded with military units at different times since the original campaign, but for the battle of Fallujah, most of the major broadcasters had reporters back in the front line (if not on the same scale). The return of embedded journalism meant more pictures from Iraq than there had been for months. Already a dangerous place for Western journalists, increasing murders and kidnappings of journalists and Westerners in general meant that those reporters who stayed were largely reduced to covering Iraq from within the heavily fortified International Zone in Baghdad.

But if the battle of Fallujah marked the return of embedded reporting, there was a significant difference this time round. During and after the Iraq War 2003, considerable concern arose in political and media circles about the implications of embedded reporting. Would embedded journalists end up "in bed with" the military units on which they depended for transport, rations, and protection? Admittedly, the concern was more apparent in mainstream media circles in the United Kingdom than in the United States. In London, for example, immediately following the war, a number of public seminars had been organized in which most of the embedded journalists and their editors participated.[3] The rights and wrongs of embedded journalism became a key part of a public debate around the media coverage of the war. In the United States, too, it provided a key focus for critics of the media coverage of the war (see Schechter 2003 and Tim Robbins's off-Broadway satire *Embedded*).

By contrast, when we examine the coverage of and response to the battle for Fallujah, it is very difficult to find examples of any comparable concern (even allowing that the news media treated it as an important story but not one worth clearing the schedules for). Embedded reporting seems, by that point, to have been taken for granted as, if maybe not perfect, the only safe and practical way in which news organizations can cover wars. A practice that on its introduction was controversial at least has now become almost routine. If there is now a consensus to accept embedded reporting, what are the implications for future media coverage of Iraq and other armed conflicts?

The research that forms the basis of this book was the product of the initial climate of concern about embedded reporting in the British news media during and just after the war in Iraq; we were commissioned by the BBC to produce a report on the implications of embedding. Our report included interviews with thirty-seven key actors in the war coverage, twenty-seven journalists and editors, and ten key personnel in the Ministry of Defence and the Pentagon (Lewis et al. 2004, and see also Threadgold and Mosdell 2004). It included a thorough qualitative and quantitative content analysis, other versions of which have been published (Lewis 2003; Lewis and Brookes 2004a, 2004b). Our assessment of embedded reporting was mixed. We were unable to find evidence that substantiated the argument, made by a number of critics, that embedding turns reporters into public relations officers for the military—indeed, we were able to find examples in which embedding enabled journalists to subject military claims to critical scrutiny in a way that they wouldn't have been able to do if they were dependent on the U.S. military's briefing operation at Central Command (CentCom) in Qatar. Many journalists praised their unprecedented access to frontline personnel and the lack of censorship. Nevertheless, our conclusions made an important qualification:

> Both broadcasters and the public are in emphatic agreement that a multiplicity of sources and perspectives is essential for objective and balanced war coverage.... Embedded reporting may be a useful addition to the mix, but...it should remain part of a picture that also includes independent reporting. (Lewis et al. 2004, 5)

Just a year after our original report was produced, our concern about embedded reporting becoming the only form of reporting seems to have been realized in the case of Fallujah.

Besides developing the original research and making it more widely available, the aim of this book is to situate embedded reporting within the recent history of military news management. The Pentagon and many of its critics share a belief that the embedded program represents a revolutionary approach to military news management. For the Pentagon, embedding is a mutually beneficial system that gives the journalists what they need (access, stories) whilst enabling the military to get their point of view across. For its critics, it's a propaganda weapon that exploits all the latest techniques of Hollywood action movies and reality television,[4] and shows how sinister and sophisticated the Pentagon has become.

Our aim is to challenge the widely, although by no means universally, held assumption that embedded reporting is radically new. Undoubtedly, significant aspects of the embedded program are new, and we aim to identify those, but important continuities exist from previous conflicts. If, then, we are to assess the novelty of the embedded program, we need first to set up a model of recent military news management policies against which to evaluate it.

The U.S./UK Military News Management Model between the Falklands Conflict and Afghanistan

Since the Falklands conflict, U.S./UK military news management policy has been formulated as a response to the "myth of Vietnam" (Tumber and Palmer 2004, 2). According to this myth, unsympathetic coverage produced by journalists with unlimited access to the battlefield and the help of technology turned public opinion against the war. Although Hallin (1989) showed this not to be the case (media coverage was only unsympathetic at the end of the war, after American public opinion had already turned), the myth has fulfilled a useful function for the military in the United States and in Britain: it legitimized increasing control over the media.

The Falklands conflict of 1982 was the first major campaign in which the United States or United Kingdom had been publicly involved since Vietnam. Decisions about how reporters were accommodated on the expedition, or even whether they would be accommodated at all, were left by the Ministry of Defence (MoD) to the very last minute. Journalists' relationships with their minders and with navy personnel on the three ships to which they were assigned were characterized by varying degrees of antagonism. From the news organizations' perspective, it was disastrous. No television footage got back until it was too old to use, journalists felt ill-prepared, badly treated, and heavily censored and restricted. Morrison and Tumber describe the MoD's "inability to plan sophisticated news control" (1988, 19). And yet despite the apparently chaotic, last-minute, and adhoc manner with which the MoD appears to have dealt with this situation, the Falklands campaign introduced many of the elements that have characterized the model of restrictive military news management which has underpinned the American and British approach since[5] (Knightley 2003, 484; Carruthers 2000, 131).

When U.S. forces invaded Grenada in 1983, the military initially completely excluded the media, on occasion by force. The public justification was that they could not guarantee the safety of journalists. On the third day of the campaign, the military introduced a limited television pool consisting of the three major American networks—reports had to be filed through military channels and were heavily censored (Young and Jesser 1997, 127–132). News chiefs representing most of the major news organizations made strident complaints about the exclusion and censorship of journalists. The manager of CBS complained, "I would like to protest the attitude expressed by your public affairs office that we learned lessons from the British in the Falklands. This is the United States, not Britain" (cited in Young and Jesser 1997, 132). As a result, a commission was set up under Major General Winant Sidle to make recommendations regarding the handling of the media in future operations, although explicitly not to review the Grenada campaign. The ensuing report (the Sidle report) has become a touchstone for subsequent U.S. campaigns. It asserts the media's responsibility to inform the American public on the progress of wars involving U.S. forces and the military's responsibility to support the media in this task. It makes eight recommendations, the most important of which can be summarized as follows: that public-affairs planning in advance of a campaign should be coordinated with military planning; that the implementation of a pool system is the only way in which journalists can be accommodated in a military campaign, but that this system should be used only for as long as is necessary; that an ongoing pool should be implemented for use in unforeseen crises; that membership in pools requires journalists' compliance with guidelines, contravention of which results in loss of accreditation; that escorts should be provided to assist journalists; and that adequate communications and transport be provided (Young and Jesser 1997, 135–6).

But despite these recommendations, when U.S. troops invaded Panama City in December 1989, the same history of exclusion and restriction repeated itself. For the first day, the pool that had been established—twelve reporters and camera operatives—was grounded at Howard Air Force Base, well away from the capital, while three hundred journalists who had flown in to Panama City airport were either stranded there or advised to fly back out. Afterward, a curfew and travel restrictions severely curtailed the ability of journalists to report (Young and Jesser 1997, 146–8).

By the time of the 1991 Gulf War, experience in the Falklands, Grenada, and Panama had led the Pentagon and the MoD to develop a model of news management that severely restrained the media's ability to report. They imposed restrictions both on news content and on access to the war zone, despite the recommendation in the Sidle report that the military should support the media in its key role of informing the American public. The Gulf War, however, provided a different challenge. First, the number of journalists covering the conflict was greater—estimates of the number of journalists in the region account for about 1,600. Second, interest was more international.

In order to assess the degree to which embedded reporting marked a radical break from previous U.S./UK military news management strategies, we need to identify the key components of the post-Vietnam model. Clearly, the specific character of each conflict produces some differences. There may well have been differences between how the Pentagon and the MoD envisaged strategies and how those strategies were implemented on the ground, both as a response to changing circumstances and as influenced by the decisions and performance of individual military personnel. Implementation may have been uneven, with some journalists experiencing much stricter censorship and restrictions on movement than others. Nevertheless, we believe we can identify eight common elements.

1. *Reporting restrictions.* For each of the conflicts in which they were involved, the MoD and the Pentagon have published guidelines on what journalists cannot report in the interests of protecting operational security. Both the MoD and Pentagon are concerned about the enemy monitoring news reports for information that would help identify the positions of forces, predict their tactics, or identify any weaknesses. They argue that content restrictions only go as far as is necessary to protect operational security. The MoD has asserted on a number of occasions that these guidelines are not an attempt to censor reporting on matters of "taste or tone." Before the Gulf War, the Pentagon stated that "material will be examined solely for its conformance to the…ground rules, not for its potential to express criticism or cause embarrassment" (Williams 1992, 8).

During the Falklands campaign, guidelines sent to task-force commanders outlined that officers and crews were to be "specifically briefed to avoid discussing with [reporters] or in their hearing the following:

a. Speculation about possible future action.
b. Plans for operations.
c. Readiness state and details about individual units' operation capability, movements, and deployment.
d. Details about military techniques and tactics.
e. Logistical details.
f. Intelligence about Argentinian forces.

g. Equipment capabilities and defects.
h. Communications" (Harris 1983, 26).

During the Gulf War, the Pentagon introduced a single sheet with twelve restrictions on reporting:

> For US or coalition units, specific numerical information on troop strength, aircraft, weapons systems, on-hand equipment or supplies...
> Any information that reveals details of future plans, operations or strikes...
> Information, photography or imagery that would reveal the specific location of military forces...
> Rules of engagement details.
> Information on intelligence collection activities...
> During an operation, specific information on friendly force troop movements, tactical deployments, and dispositions that would jeopardise operational security or lives...
> Identification of mission aircraft points of origin...
> Information on the effectiveness or ineffectiveness of enemy camouflage, cover, deception, targeting, direct and indirect fire, intelligence collection or security measure.
> Specific information on missing or downed aircraft or ships while search and rescue operations are planned or underway.
> Special operations forces' methods, unique equipment or tactics.
> Specific operating methods and tactics...
> Information on operational or support vulnerabilities that could be used against US forces. (Williams 1992, 5–6).

In addition, light-discipline restrictions—prohibitions against the use of visible light at night—were imposed on journalists based with military units to avoid giving away their position.

However, guidelines restricting reporting in the interests of operational security can also restrict journalists from carrying out their legitimate role in conveying information to the public during wartime, as recognized in the Sidle report. For example, guidelines restricting information on the specific location of military forces could hamper journalists' ability to report the actual progress of units, as opposed to claims made by MoD and Pentagon officials.

The Gulf War also introduced restrictions on reporting casualties. The potential for transmitting live or near-live visual footage from the front entailed the risk that next of kin might learn of the death of a relative through news reports rather than through official notification by a uniformed representative of the military. As far as the Pentagon was concerned, "the anguish that sudden recognition at home can cause far outweighs the news value of the photograph, film or videotape" (Williams 1992, 8). Once again, though, this can be seen as a constraint on journalists' ability to report on the progress of the war, if the real cost of the war in terms of friendly-force casualties is effectively rendered invisible.

Occasionally, there have been attempts to extend restrictions on journalists beyond those strictly necessary for the protection of operational security or to protect next of kin from learning about the death of a relative through news reports. Two weeks before the Gulf War, the Pentagon attempted to introduce restrictions on spontaneous or off-the-record interviews with service personnel, images of soldiers in "agony or severe shock," and images of patients with severe disfigurements (Taylor 1992, 35). Although the second of these does relate to the issue of reporting casualties, there seems little justification for the others except to restrict journalists from submitting potentially negative coverage from the front. However, in this instance, the Pentagon withdrew these restrictions under the threat of legal action from U.S. news organizations (Taylor 1992, 36).

The Pentagon and the MoD have presented restrictions on journalistic reporting as a legitimate exemption from what they would argue is an otherwise supportive role of journalists covering wars. Even though these restrictions do inhibit journalists in covering major aspects of armed conflicts, news organizations have largely accepted them—as long as they are justified, in terms of operational security or the need to protect the next of kin of service personnel killed in action. By contrast, news organizations have resisted attempts to restrict reporting beyond this rationale.

2. *Minders (escorts)*. A second key component of the post-Vietnam model is the assignment of minders (called "escorts" in the United States) to journalists accompanying military units. Their role has been to brief reporters, to keep reporters under constant supervision, and to act as the first link in a chain of "security review." For the Falklands conflict, five civilian public relations officers were assigned as minders. As part of their duties, they were required to go though journalists' copy and remove passages that broke the guidelines (Morrison and Tumber 1988, 14, 146–9; Harris 1983, 28). During the Gulf War, Public Affairs Officers (U.S.) and Public Relations Officers (UK) were assigned to the Media Response Teams as an essential part of the pool system.

Journalists' experience of dealing with minders has often depended on the individual minder concerned: one American journalist during the Gulf War recalled, "You could get an angel or a devil" (Taylor 1992, 52). Nevertheless, the system has ensured that the ability of journalists to do their jobs *depends heavily* on their individual minder. Minders have had the power to provide information or withhold it; to escort journalists to where the action is, or, by contrast, to restrict them to locations where nothing is happening; to interpret ground rules in whatever way they see fit; and to help journalists get their stories back, or to hinder or even block them.

3. *"Security review."* A third key component of the post-Vietnam model is a system of security review to check that journalists' copy does not break the ground rules. During the Falklands campaign, copy was subjected to a chain of review, from the civilian minders at the front to the military censors at the MoD back in London, before it was released for use by news organizations. In the Gulf War, American journalists with the Media Response Teams assigned to frontline units were required to submit their copy, photos or videos to a forward transmission unit at the Joint Information Bureau (JIB) in Dhahran; unlike the British, they were not allowed to uplink them directly (Taylor 1992, 51; Carruthers 2000, 135). In contentious cases, reports could be submitted back to the Pentagon for final approval.

4. *Restrictions on journalists' access to communications.* In the Falklands, journalists were wholly dependent on military communication systems partly because portable means of transmitting copy or pictures were not available. In the Falklands campaign, while onboard ships, journalists could get their copy out only by using ships' communications systems, and thus depended on the ship's captain for the ability to file their stories. When on land, journalists who traveled with the troops depended on helicopter pilots to get copy back to the minders, who had remained on ship. Although the technology to transmit copy or pictures from a portable unit was available during the Gulf War, the Pentagon insisted that copy, video, and photos be sent back to the JIB so that they could be subject to "review."

5. *The pool system.* Ostensibly, the pool system was introduced as a means of dealing with two problems in accommodating journalists on military expeditions: that the number of media personnel needing to cover a particular conflict vastly exceeds the capacity of the military to accommodate them, given the high newsworthiness of this type of story; and that the need of journalists to compete amongst themselves for exclusives may lead to conduct likely to endanger themselves or the unit with which they are based.

In the pool system, the military first sets a limit on the number of journalists accommodated, including limits for the different types of journalists (TV, photo, pencil). Mindful of being accused of selecting sympathetic journalists, the military may leave decisions as to the appointment of specific media personnel to the news organizations themselves. Second, copy, photos, and video are available for use by participating news organizations. Finally, journalists may have to agree in writing to obey their minders and to submit their copy for security review (as in the Gulf War).

The pool system was introduced in the United Kingdom during the Falklands conflict as a response to the logistics of that particular campaign. Copy filed by journalists was made freely available to all news organizations. In addition, journalists formed informal pools on each of the three vessels on which they were accommodated.

The Pentagon developed its version of the pool system based on the recommendations of the 1984 Sidle report. A Pentagon Department of Defense pool was set up to cover unforeseen conflicts. During the Gulf War, the Pentagon initiated a two-tier pool system, assigning a privileged two hundred (mainly) U.S. and British journalists to Media Reporting Teams (MRTs). Closely supervised by Public Affairs Officers (called Public Relations Officers in the United Kingdom), these MRTs were then assigned to frontline units in the desert (Taylor 1992; MacArthur 1993). Journalists in MRTs were required to sign a set of guidelines declaring that they would not conduct off-the-record interviews with military personnel, that they would submit their copy for "review," and that they would remain with and obey their minders at all times (MacArthur 1993, 19; Carruthers 2000, 134).

6. *Briefing operations.* In the Falklands campaign, it was the MoD back in London who was responsible for providing press briefings: there was no briefing operation anywhere near the conflict zone. By contrast, during the Gulf War, a briefing operation was set up to manage those of the 1,600 journalists not assigned to MRTs whose employers wanted them to report from the war zone. This second-tier pool system consisted of the "hotel warriors" based in Riyadh and at the home of the coalition Joint Information Bureau (JIB) in Dhahran. These journalists were entirely reliant on regular daily briefings by Public Relations Officers and the main briefing by General Norman Schwarzkopf. Most journalists reporting on NATO's conduct of the 1999 campaign in Kosovo or on the U.S. campaign in Afghanistan were similarly dependent on this type of briefing operation.

7. *Privileged access.* During the Falklands and Gulf War conflicts membership of the pools was restricted by military authorities in the Britain and the United States mainly to news organizations based in those same coun-

tries. During the Falklands conflict only British media organizations were represented (with the exception of one Reuters journalist). During the Gulf War, the two hundred MRT positions were restricted to members of the elite news organizations of the nations participating in the coalition: Britain, France, and the United States. Journalists from neutral countries were restricted to access to the briefings in Riyadh and Dhahran.

8. *Exclusion of "unilaterals" from the war zone.* The converse of the military granting access to the war zone as a privilege has been their exclusion of so-called unilateral journalists through force or the threat of force (the term "unilateral" was coined by the military). Ten journalists attempting to land in Grenada during the invasion of 1983 were intercepted, arrested, and had their film and reports confiscated by U.S. forces (Young and Jesser 1997, 129). In the Gulf War, journalists were threatened with detention by coalition forces, deportation by the Saudi authorities, or, on one occasion, being shot by U.S. soldiers (Taylor 1992, 60).

While media coverage of all of these operations during the period of the campaigns themselves has largely been sympathetic, media organizations, bureau chiefs, and professional associations (such as the American Society of Newspaper Editors during the Gulf War) have been strident in their criticisms of military handling of journalists behind the scenes during the campaigns and openly afterward. Criticisms focused on restrictions on movement, lack of understanding of journalists' needs (i.e., to have access to material for stories and to be able to return them as quickly as possible before they are out of date and therefore worthless) and the lack of technological and/or logistical provision to meet those needs, excessive censorship, and dissemination of false information. Such criticism led to the institution of official inquiries in the case of the Falklands and Grenada (which resulted in the Sidle report).

During and after each conflict, official media statements reveal unfavorable comparisons, bordering on hyperbole, with military handling of the media in previous wars. In August 1990, when U.S. troops were being stationed in Saudi Arabia in preparation for the Gulf War, the bureau chiefs of the main press and television news organizations wrote to President Bush complaining that the U.S. military wasn't doing enough to ensure that the Saudi government would grant visas for U.S. journalists:

> Never in American history has this country been faced with as large a commitment of manpower and equipment with as little opportunity for the press to report. (cited in MacArthur 1993, 10)

The author of a hard-hitting report on military news handling of the Afghanistan campaign conducted for *Columbia Journalism Review* concluded:

> Journalists have been denied access to American troops in the field in Afghanistan to a greater degree than in any previous war involving US military forces. Bush administration policy has kept reporters from combat units in a fashion unimagined in Vietnam, and one that's more restrictive even than the burdensome constraints on media in the Persian Gulf. (Hickey 2002, 26)

And yet, if complaints from media organizations and journalists might seem to testify to the dominant position of the military within the post-Vietnam model, government and military complaints about the media during wartime also abound. To some extent, the loud public expression of complaints about the media during wartime can reasonably be interpreted as a means of ensuring they are kept in line. Nevertheless, complaints have tended to coalesce around two main concerns: news coverage from "behind enemy lines" and the media's use of military experts and retired service personnel to interpret the progress of the war and to speculate on future tactics.

News coverage from "behind enemy lines" was the result of either maintaining correspondents in major cities (such as the CNN and British television news organizations had done in Baghdad during the Gulf War), or using material originating from broadcasters based in "enemy" or neutral nations (such as al-Jazeera in Afghanistan). Typically, this material might include coverage of news conferences and statements from official sources on the enemy side, as well as footage of the devastation caused by American or British military action on civilians, or in the case of conflicts purportedly motivated by humanitarian concerns, footage of civilians protesting against the military action ostensibly carried out in their interests. The use of this type of material in the Gulf War led to both the BBC and CNN being denounced as the "Baghdad Broadcasting Corporation."

The anxiety about the use of military experts and retired service personnel to interpret the progress of the war and to speculate on future tactics parallels that behind "operational security" restrictions; even if these experts are not privy to the actual tactics pursued by military commanders, the thinking goes, they may yet reveal valuable information to an enemy monitoring the media.

To sum up, a military news management model has developed between the conflicts in the Falklands and Afghanistan that favors the military, in terms of its control and restrictions. Widespread complaints from journalists, editors, and media organizations attest to their frustration with journalistic dependence on the military when producing war reports. And yet, if complaints about the media by governments and the military are taken at face value, the model isn't working for them, either. The reason for this, we suggest, is that the post-Vietnam military model is *restrictive*. It has been very effective at imposing restrictions on what journalists can report from the side of the American or British military but does not control the material from elsewhere. At times when broadcasters tend to clear the schedules in recognition of what they see as extraordinarily newsworthy events, the post-Vietnam model's restrictions on news content also restricted news *quantity*, forcing broadcasters to go elsewhere to fill the airtime. This was a problem for the British government during the Falklands conflict, when they complained about the BBC's use of reports from Buenos Aires and their use of "armchair generals." But with the proliferation of twenty-four-hour rolling news services during the 1990s on cable, satellite, and digital platforms, alongside the emergence of al-Jazeera and other Arabic news channels, and the development of cheap and portable cameras and satellite dishes, both the amount of airtime to be filled and the range of material that could be used to fill that airtime expanded exponentially (Thussu 2003).

In this context, the relative lack of criticism of embedded reporting in the 2003 Iraq War contrasts sharply with the previous Gulf conflict. On the side of media organizations, the criticism of military news management that characterized previous campaigns has been largely absent. Individual experienced correspondents working as unilaterals, however, offered much criticism of embedding reporting (Simpson 2003; Omaar 2004). The *New York Times* and the *Washington Post* have apologized for their "cheerleading" coverage on Iraq—but their apologies were for insufficient critical coverage of official claims linking Saddam Hussein and Al Qaeda and asserting Iraqi possession of weapons of mass destruction *preceding* the war, not for their coverage of the actual war. And as far as we are aware, no other media organization has felt the need to apologize for their role in covering the war itself, nor has there been any organizational, formal, or institutional criticism of the military's management coming from journalists or the media. Certainly anxieties about aspects of the embedding policy remain amongst journalists, but there seems to have been a consensus that embedded reporting, if not perfect, is the best available option, and that subject to minor revisions, it will form the basis for future relations between media and military.

In this book, we will argue that embedded reporting needs to be assessed in this context. Does it represent a radical revision of previous military practice, finally taking into account newsworkers' criticisms by providing for their needs and supporting them in their role of informing the public? Or does it simply represent a self-serving modification of the post-Vietnam model, ensuring for the military that by locating so many journalists near to the front line, producing so much exciting action footage, broadcasters will no longer have to go elsewhere—where they might find stories less sympathetic to the military—simply to fill airtime?

To address these questions, we begin with the military itself. Through interviews with all the key figures responsible for the military presentation of the 2003 Iraq War (our own and those conducted by the Select Committee on Defence in Britain), the next three chapters examine how the Pentagon and the MoD planned and implemented their news management strategies and the links between them.

In Chapter 5, we look at how British and Arab journalists—from those embedded to news editors and directors—viewed the experience of covering the 2003 Iraq War. Chapters 6 and 7 analyze the actual coverage of the war, focusing mainly on British television, although Chapter 7 includes al-Jazeera and American coverage on ABC and NBC for points of comparison.

In Chapter 8, we turn to the way people in Britain viewed the war, drawing upon surveys and focus groups with British television viewers in late summer 2003. This completes our analysis of the production, content, and reception of the media coverage of the war, and on that basis, in the final chapter we offer some broad conclusions about the future of media coverage of military conflict.

CHAPTER TWO

The Background to Embedding

IN THE SUMMER OF 2003 we interviewed personnel from both the Pentagon and the Ministry of Defence (MoD) who were involved directly in the implementation of the respective embedding programs in the United States and the United Kingdom. They belonged to units called Public Affairs at the Pentagon and Media Operations at the MoD.

This chapter locates the policy of direct media involvement and apparently transparent (and uncensored) media access, managed by Media Operations at the MoD and Public Affairs at the Pentagon, and described in their interviews with us, within the wider perspectives of military strategic information operations [info ops]/psychological operations [psyops], information warfare, public diplomacy, and political communications involving both advertising and public relations techniques.[1] Our first aim is to provide some insight into the political and philosophical similarities and differences between the two nations' public affairs/media operations activities, and to provide some of the essential context for reading our own interviewees' responses in chapters 3 and 4. Our second aim is to question approaches taken since Iraq 2003 which have characterized the whole exercise as lies, propaganda, and media distortion (e.g., Miller 2004a) and to tease out the complex strands of information/communication that were actually involved.

We have relied on a number of sources in putting this chapter together. All of this material is easily available. Some of it is U.S. material exploring, for example, the relations between the Pentagon's Public Affairs strategy and public relations. Some of it explores the structure of coalition communications before and during Iraq 2003. Some of it is published on official U.S. and UK government websites. In particular we have referred to the work of the United Kingdom Parliament Select Committee on Defence Third Report (16 March 2004) and available online with its two attached Volumes of Minutes of Evidence.[1] The Select Committee was a House of Commons Committee appointed to report to the House on the management of Iraq 2003 (includi ng the management of information). It took evidence from a wide range of witnesses (listed at the beginning of Volumes 2 and 3 of the Minutes of Evidence) between May 2003 and February 2004, beginning with the Secretary of Defence. We focus later in this chapter on the evidence of Air Vice Marshall Mike Heath and Wing Commander Ian Chalmers who were called to give evidence (16 December 2003) on the UK approach to Information Operations and the extent to which it had become influential at a cross-government level. We do this in conjunction with some U.S. materials on information and psychological operations in order to understand how practitioners of these disciplines understand and define the information they produce as "truth" not lies.

We also explore the evidence of Mr. A. Pawson and Colonel Paul Brook (12 November 2003) from the MoD, whom we interviewed ourselves in August 2003 (see Chapter 4 for the detailed account of those interviews). Pawson and Brook were called before the Select Committee to give evidence on the media strategy for Iraq 2003. The evidence they give to the Select Committee adds important information about the relationship between Media Operations and Information Operations in the UK context, information that our own interviews did not access so clearly.

We use these materials in this chapter because of the anxiety that has been expressed by journalists and academics, both before Iraq 2003 and since, about the blurring of Information Operations and Media Operations or Public Affairs (Miller 2004a). This anxiety is based on seeing the two as binary opposites, the former (info ops) as "deception" (of enemies), the latter as "truthful" (to home and friendly audiences). If they begin to blend, the worry is that practices of deception usually directed at enemies begin to be used to deceive audiences at home and even coalition partners. While there is some truth in this understanding of the issues, we believe it is more complex than this, and we aim here to explore some of that complexity.

Information Warfare

In an age of increasingly sophisticated, digital and satellite communications, the use of information as a weapon is becoming a dominant feature of modern warfare. Information and the management of it are also globally increasingly important parts of government and foreign policy. Much has been written concerning the use (and abuse) of information and intelligence in the buildup to, and justification of, the 2003 invasion of Iraq (Snow 2003; Rampton and Stauber 2003; Miller 2004a; Short 2004; Pilger 2004). In this book we focus primarily on how embedded journalists covered overt combat operations, not on the historical or political background to the conflict; nonetheless, the "tools of influence" outlined by Brown in the U.S. context below, and paralleled in the UK, cannot be unrelated, as we will see, to the construction of particular "versions of reality" in Iraq once battle had commenced and the media had become involved in the embeds policy.

Within the context of the "war on terror" in the United States, Brown (2003) makes some careful distinctions relevant to understanding the background of embedding. He describes three different paradigms of communication that the United States has used "as a tool of influence." The first, info ops, "the attempt to make sense of warfare as an exercise in information processing," encompasses "any effort to attack or defend the information necessary for the conduct of operations." In the American context, he argues, this has meant bringing together "'psychological operations' (PsyOps), deception, public affairs—that is, the military-press interface—and civil military affairs with computer network operations" (Brown 2003, 90). This fusion has been controversial and continues to be so because it begins to blur, as discussed above, the traditional distinction between psychological operations (commonly understood as permissible deception of an enemy, discussed at more length later) and the public affairs/military-press interface (designed to transmit honest messages to home audiences). Embedding in both countries emerges as part of this interface.

The second "tool of influence" in the United States is public diplomacy, which brings together international broadcasting, educational exchanges, cultural diplomacy, and overseas information activities. The third tool, political news management or "spin," is apparently the newest but actually reflects what are, according to Brown, in fact "very long-term responses to the mediation of political life by television and media coverage" (Maltese 1992; Brown 2003, 90–91). Brown attempts to reconcile the relationship between these three paradigms as follows:

> Given the way in which spin has become a reflex and the fact that the most prominent spokespersons for any country are its political leaders, it is not surprising that political communications techniques are being imported into international politics. The techniques of the spin-doctors stand between the manipulation implied in IO [information operations] doctrine and the "objec-

tivity" advocated by public diplomacy [and public affairs] practitioners. On the one hand spin-doctors insist that they deal in truth because the mass media are their channel for reaching their target audiences and the loss of credibility with journalists [if they tell lies] will prevent them from doing this.... On the other hand they see "truth" as plural. Their job is to persuade their media that one version of reality rather than another is the "real" story and that the way they tell it is the correct one. This approach seeks to balance an active approach to shaping the media environment with a broader commitment to some rules of the game. (Brown 2003, 91–2)

There are some noticeable differences in the ways in which the work of those whom we interviewed, people primarily involved in the policy and implementation of embedding at the Pentagon and in the United Kingdom, was implicated in, or affected by, the three "tools of influence" outlined by Brown. This chapter will provide the background to the parallels and the differences discussed in chapters 3 and 4, but it will also emphasize the important fact that information—its collection, use, and dissemination—was an overarching focus of an integrated political and military strategy employed by both principal coalition partners during Iraq 2003. Moreover, from a global, political perspective, the embeds program played a small but integral, and above all, highly visible, part in this strategy. Indeed, we would suggest that the overall philosophy of the embedding policy was precisely designed—in both countries—to detract public attention from the historical, political, and ideological justification of this particular conflict, and deliberately to focus public attention, opinion, and, crucially, empathy (public support), in a concerted and personal way, on the conduct and situation-specific outcomes of the combat operations, and the narrow three-week time frame of the "media war." We discuss the media war in Chapter 7, looking at the way the very nature of embedding produced a narrative which focused on the progress of the war to the exclusion of other issues, a narrative of "winning the war" to which the toppling of the statue of Saddam Hussein at the end of three weeks was the obvious and dramatic climax. The "end" of the war was an artefact of the nature of the media coverage. In fact the conflict continued but the embeds went home. Indeed, insurance costs alone would probably have mitigated against a media war of very much longer duration than this.

Information Dominance

Miller analyzes the related issue of the concepts of "full spectrum dominance" and "information dominance" in U.S. military strategy and foreign policy (Miller 2004b, 3; Miller 2004c; Snow 2003, 7–8). Together, he argues, the two concepts imply "that US forces are able to conduct prompt, sustained and synchronised operations with combinations of forces tailored to specific situations and with access to and freedom to operate in all domains—space, sea, land, air and information" (quoted from Pentagon's Joint Vision 2020 in Miller 2004b, 3). Information, Miller argues, has "become an element of combat power" (2004b, 4). Miller appears to be referring here to what Taylor (2003) calls information warfare. Taylor identifies the first Gulf War as "the first information war" because "it embraced this new thinking by taking out Iraqi air defense systems on the opening nights of the conflict, conducted precision strikes against enemy command and control facilities and even extended into shaping the global media perception about the progress of war in the coalition's favor" (103).

As Miller points out, two new elements here do not occur in conventional propaganda models: "the integration of psychological operations into a much wider conception of information war" and "the integration of information war into the core of military strategy" (2004b, 5; see also Snow 2003). In Britain, the MoD and the Foreign and Commonwealth Office, according to Miller, also now use the term "information dominance" (2004b, 6), which is the theory driving "information operations" in both offices. Miller believes that this is the logical result of "the close integration of the US and UK global propaganda" effort in and around Iraq 2003 (2004b, 6). The difference between this and traditional propaganda, which involved "crafting the message and distributing it via government media or independent news media," is what Miller calls *interoperability*, where "information systems talk to and work with each other" (Miller 2004b, 5–6).

Information dominance has two goals: "building up and protecting friendly information" and developing the "ability to deny, degrade, destroy and/or effectively blind enemy capabilities" (Miller 2004b, 6, 8). Miller points out that "these refer not simply to military information systems but also to propaganda and the news media" (Miller 2004b, 10). In relation to Iraq 2003, Miller sees the embeds policy as a strategy of the first kind, citing both Clive Myrie and Gavin Hewitt as embedded journalists who "crossed the line from reporting to engaging in combat" or "picking out targets for the military." Such journalists, he argues, were indeed "in bed" with the military, and in those cases the military strategy to constrain and control the media worked "by protecting friendly information" (Miller 2004c, 10–11).

However, there are several key points to note when thinking of the embedding policy as a practical consequence of the theory of information dominance. Information dominance appears to be a theory of military dominance that drives information operations at the overall strategic level. It affects "propaganda and news media" to the extent that information is used to construct favorable images abroad (with the aim of avoiding conflict) and to the extent that it is used to destroy enemy media capabilities. The attack on al-Jazeera in Baghdad may be a case in point, as Miller (2004c) suggests. However, this differs from the use of information intended (or indeed "crafted") for a public audience by public affairs and media operations, and these uses should not be easily conflated.

It is also worth noting that British armed forces are considerably behind the American in terms of the technical interoperability of their communication systems—something they are seeking to address at the moment. When asked by the Chairman of the Select Committee on Defence,[2] "Were you satisfied that the technology for decision making was compatible with American systems?" Air Marshall Brian Burridge (UK National Contingent Commander for the Iraq operation) replied, "No. One of my significant lessons is about that very thing, CIS [Command Information Systems] generally. We are just about to launch into the defence information infrastructure project, which I hope will be the beginning of putting this right. The US are considerably ahead of us in their command and control technology and they use a single secure system for operations and intelligence and for all participating agencies such as CIA, DIA, etc." (response to Question 229). Interoperability as a concept, then, may not immediately transfer to the UK context where it refers to information infrastructure. In Miller's other sense of "the integration of propaganda and media institutions into the war machine" (2004b, 6) interoperability is relevant to both contexts, but works differently in each.

Psychological Operations

Particularly relevant to embedding and the "integration of the media into the war machine," as we have seen above, are the various levels of psychological operations (called psyops in the United Kingdom, psyop in the United States) that are involved. Psychological operations has a long and varied history but has only developed as an acknowledged discipline relatively recently, with the rapid advancement of mass communication technologies. Though the term may conjure associations with deceit and perhaps even some form of brainwashing, it is in fact a nonlethal tool to gather intelligence and information, and the use of this information, according to practitioners, is based ultimately on truth. The U.S. Joint Chiefs of Staff's *Doctrine for Joint Psychological Operations* (Joint Publication 3-53) gives the following definition:

Psychological operations (PSYOP) are planned operations to convey selected information and indicators to foreign audiences to influence the emotions, motives, objective reasoning, and ultimately the behavior of foreign governments, organizations, groups, and individuals. (2003, ix[3])

Significantly, these operations see "foreign audiences" as the target for this information; such audiences are either adversaries or those in areas likely to affect the outcome of operations—the term does not refer to multinational (coalition) partners. The principal aim of psychological operations is conflict avoidance, an aim repeated often in our interviews with media operations personnel at both the Pentagon and at the MoD (see, for example, the discussion of "force on mind" operations in the interviews at the MoD). The doctrine further states:

When properly employed, PSYOP can save lives of friendly and/or adversary forces by reducing adversaries' will to fight. By lowering adversary morale and reducing their efficiency, PSYOP can also discourage aggressive actions and create dissidence and disaffection within their ranks, ultimately inducing surrender. (I-1)

The doctrine does contain echoes of the philosophy behind information dominance in that one of its stated aims is to counter "adversary propaganda, misinformation, disinformation, and opposing information to correctly portray friendly intent and actions, while denying others the ability to polarize public opinion and affect the political will of the United States and its multinational partners within an operational area" (x). However, the doctrine makes an important distinction between the use of psychological operations in a military context and its use within the domain of public affairs or media operations. It is worth quoting at length from the section dealing with public affairs (PA) and psychological operations:

PA provide accurate and timely information without attempting to influence or sway the audience. As open sources to foreign countries and the United States, PA channels can be used to disseminate international information. *To maintain the credibility of military PA, care must be taken to protect against slanting or manipulating such PA channels.* PA channels can be used to provide facts that will counter foreign propaganda, including disinformation, directed at the United States.

(a) PA operations and activities shall not focus on directing or manipulating public actions or opinion.

(b) PA and PSYOP products should provide a timely flow of information to external and internal audience. *Based on policy, PA and PSYOP must be separate and distinct even though they reinforce each other and involve close cooperation and coordination.*

(c) PA and PSYOP products must be coordinated and deconflicted early in the planning process and during execution. *Although PA and PSYOP generated information may be different, they must not contradict one another or their credibility will be lost.*

Although each has specific audiences, information often will overlap between audiences. This overlap makes deconfliction crucial. Under no circumstances will personnel working in PA functions or activities engage in PSYOP activities. (I-9, emphasis in original)

A Joint Warfare Publication on Media Operations published by the MoD and seen by the researchers at the MoD in London exactly parallels the definitions of, and distinctions between, these functions. Some accounts of the history of British psychological operations relate the concept back to earlier conceptions of "white," "gray," and "black" propaganda, distinctions also worth noting. "White" propaganda refers to messages truthfully attributed to their source. Those falsely attributed to another party are considered "gray," while those planted to appear as the product of the target adversary are considered "black."[4]

It is necessary to separate the complexity of information dominance as a military/foreign policy strategy and theory from the complementary but very different roles of government and military media management (with and without a PR or advertising component), the broad sweep of public diplomacy and the again very different information operations (including psychological operations) aspect of military activities.

While there was undoubtedly an element of "gray" propaganda in the public debate concerning the justification of the war in Iraq—for example, the use of material plagiarized from a Ph.D. thesis in the "dodgy dossier"—we would suggest that the linguistic connotations evoked by Miller's concerns about the use of psychological operations are misleading when referring to its role in the media operations. The emphasis expressed in the doctrine above, and in our interviews with media operations personnel, is very much on absolute and demonstrable truth for the sake of continued credibility. This is "white" propaganda but with a crucial addition to the previous paradigms: the careful crafting of messages and their delivery, drawing upon public relations expertise.

Coalition Political News Management

Literature published since Iraq 2003 reveals the closely linked nature of British and American political communications and news management strategies, both at home and abroad, in the fifteen years or so leading up to Iraq 2003 (Miller 2004a; Short 2004; Kampfner 2004). There can be no doubt, despite the claims of our MoD interviewees (see Chapter 4), that the "key messages" of the 2003 Coalition's media operations in Iraq were carefully crafted and presented to the global public by teams of professionals skilled in the arts of perception management, and that considerable effort was put into the presentation of a united front at the more strategic level.

Coalition Information Centers (CIC) and the Office of Global Communications (OGC)

Alastair Campbell, former UK press secretary, played a large role in NATO media operations in the 1999 war against Yugoslavia, operations in which Short believes that Blair and Campbell were able to "hone their PR machine and Blair's image as a humanitarian war leader" (Short 2004, 93; Curtis 2004, 77). Campbell also played a key role in managing public opinion around the Afghanistan war, persuading the White House that the United States and Britain should coordinate their messages more effectively, and setting up the Coalition Information Centers (CIC) in London, Washington, and Islamabad "to get the message across at all times of the news cycle," to enable more efficient responses to propaganda from the other side (Kampfner 2003, 134).

In Washington, the CIC became the Office of Global Diplomacy, later of Global Communications, and "a permanent feature of the national security organization of the White House," "seeking to coordinate foreign information activities across the entire government" (Maltese 1994; Brown 2003, 92). Miller (2004d, 80) believes that this drew on British government propaganda expertise and describes it as "sitting at the top of the global pyramid" of information coordination. Brown relates its development to a different history. In 2001, the now infamous Office of Strategic Influence was established in Washington at the Department of Defense to coordinate "all means of influencing foreign audiences" and in doing so, to use "instruments including deception and 'truth projection'" (Brown 2003, 92). News of its existence was leaked to the American press in February 2002. Secretary of Defense Donald Rumsfeld closed it down overnight as a result of fierce criticism both from the press, who feared that they might be the targets of the deception, and from the presidential communications staff, who feared loss of credibility if they were seen to be deceiving media organizations (Brown 2003, 92). Brown's argument is that the OGC, whatever its origins in British propaganda models, or perhaps because of them (see below), actually took on all the functions of the proposed Office of Strategic Influence by another name. Thus information operations became a key tool of government communications strategy, influencing not only public diplomacy (through the State Department) but also political news management in an international context.

In practice, as in theory (see above), the White House Press Office and Public Affairs at the Pentagon, both of which are subordinate to the OGC, continue claiming they have no knowledge of such activities and are explicitly opposed to them (Rampton and Stauber 2003, 65–6). Like Media Operations at the MoD in the United Kingdom, they define and construct themselves as very much apart from both psychological operations and "propaganda." Nonetheless, the distinctions and their apparent blurring have come to be a matter of concern for the U.S. Defense Science Board Task Force on Strategic Communication who, in relation to the war on terror, do not themselves appear to have been satisfied that psychological operations and public diplomacy are always kept separate:

> The creation of the Office of Strategic Influence (OSI) in October of 2001, and its subsequent implosion four months later, produced a bow wave of effects in the strategic communication arena. The renewed emphasis by the White House and DOD for the need to maintain a firewall between operational and tactical influence efforts (PSYOP) and broader influence efforts like Public Diplomacy (PD), produced a bifurcated interagency process. Two NSC Policy Coordination Committees on information strategy and a new White House Office of Global Communication have proven ineffective thus far in producing an NSC-approved strategic information campaign for the War on Terror.[5]

The Defense Science Board does not question whether public diplomacy (media operations) and psyop should be kept separate.

The OGC at the top of this "pyramid" was concerned with the agreeing and "crafting" of the daily messages to be distributed globally and locally around coalition activities: the day's message was set "with an early morning conference call to British counterpart Alastair Campbell, White House communications director Dan Bartlett, State Department spokesman Richard Boucher, Pentagon spokesperson Torie Clarke, and White House Office of Global Communications (OGC) director, Tucker Askew—a routine that mirrors the procedure during the conflict in Afghanistan" (Miller 2004d, 81; see also Tumber and Palmer 2004, 64).

Thus the threat of Saddam Hussein, weapons of mass destruction, links with terrorism, and the language and narratives that dominated both British and American reporting of the case for war were jointly constructed and coordinated globally by the OGC and the Campbell group at Downing Street, and then transmitted down through the rest of the American (Miller 2004d, 81) and British "information warfare" apparatuses. As we now know, these were also linked to what Miller calls "faked and spun intelligence information supplied by the United Kingdom and by the secret Pentagon intelligence operation, The Office of Special Plans" (2004d, 81). The blending of "tools of influence" at work here supports Brown's (2003) arguments above and requires further deconstruction below.

Public Relations and Advertising

Perhaps the major difference between the two coalition partners was the earlier and more significant involvement of the public relations and advertising industries in the United States, which has "a one-hundred-year history of marrying commerce with politics and tapping public relations to 'brand' America abroad" (Snow 2003, 25; see also Taylor 1990; 1992). Nor was this involvement in any way secret. The *Washington Post* (30 July 2002) reported the establishment of the OGC "to co-ordinate the administration's foreign policy message and supervise America's image abroad," and the *Times* of London reported in September 2002 that the OGC "would spend $200 million on a 'PR blitz against Saddam Hussein' aimed 'at American and foreign audiences' and using 'advertising techniques to persuade crucial target groups that the Iraqi leader must be ousted'" (cited in Rampton and Stauber 2003, 38). Notably, the press here seems to pick up on the PR/advertising nexus but makes no overt mention of the information operations identified by Brown (above).

Public relations and advertising have a long history in the U.S. State Department's Office of Public Diplomacy, which is broadly responsible for the management of overseas public perceptions of the United States and its activities. Through this office, "overseas propaganda," public relations and advertising, and the tools of the media industry (radio, television, newspapers) enter government service together as one branch of "information warfare." In 2001, three weeks after 9/11, Colin Powell appointed Charlotte Beers as Undersecretary for Public Diplomacy. She had worked at the public relations firm Ogilvy and Mather from 1992–1997; her speciality from her work in the private sector was "brand stewardship." Before Beers resigned for health reasons in March 2003 (Snow 2003, 24), she undertook the biggest public relations effort in the history of U.S. foreign policy to sell the United States to the world as a tolerant and open society, and to win international support for American policies. Rampton and Stauber, who deal at length with the details of the campaign she mounted, attribute her resignation to "the abject failure of the campaign," (2003, 34) which cost more than $500 million.

Public relations is also very much implicated in the U.S. embedding process, through the key figure of Victoria Clarke. She belonged to two different groups reported by Rampton and Stauber (2003, 38ff.) as having played important PR and lobbying roles in the lead-up to Iraq 2003. Dan Bartlett, White House Communications Director, reported in September 2002 that the "band" was being brought together again in readiness for Iraq. This, according to *Newsweek's* Martha Brant, was the same group who had produced the public relations campaign for Afghanistan. The group included Bartlett; Tucker Askew, communications director of the OGC; James Wilkinson, a former deputy communications director at the White House who later served as spokesperson to General Tommy Franks at CentCom in Qatar; Victoria Clarke from the Pentagon; Richard Boucher, spokesperson for Secretary of State Colin Powell; and Cheney adviser Mary Matalin. They met daily via conference call "to plan media strategy" with the aim of "controlling the message within the administration" so that no one "freelances on Iraq" (Rampton and Stauber 2003, 39). This "cross-government" group brought together the representatives of what once would have been the distinct agendas of military/media strategy (truth), image control abroad (selective selling and branding), and psychological operations (manipulation of truth for reasons of national security), a union that reveals not only how the OGC "crafted" its national and global messages, but also how blurred these different agendas had already become at an institutional level and still further, discursively, in that "crafting." This blurring is also evident in the Campbell group in the United Kingdom (see below).

The second group was reported in *PR Week* (26 August 2002), a leading trade publication for the PR industry, as an "informal 'strategic communications' group" which Secretary Rumsfeld is said to have relied on. Victoria Clarke is said to have "assembled" this group, which consisted of lobbyists, PR people, and Republican insiders, including Republican PR executive and lobbyist Sheila Tate (quoted in Rampton and Stauber 2003, 39). Before she joined the Pentagon, Victoria Clarke had run the Washington office of the public relations firm Hill and Knowlton, "which had run the PR campaign for the government-in-exile of Kuwait during the build-up to Operation Desert Storm a decade earlier" (Rampton and Stauber 2003, 184–5). Part of the function of this Clarke/Rumsfeld group was to convince the public of the link between the antiterrorism cause and the need "to engage 'rogue states'—including Iraq—that are likely to harbor terrorists" (*PR Week*, 16 September 2002, quoted in Rampton and Stauber 2003, 39–40). It is interesting in relation to this that Clarke, Whitman, and Blair, in interviews with us, all articulated this same "key message."

Clarke's association with Hill and Knowlton is also significant. Rampton and Stauber explore in depth the implication of public relations and advertising in the development of the Pentagon's communications strategies from the time of the first Gulf War (2003, 42 ff.), and in particular of Hill and Knowlton's involvement in the buildup to that operation:

> Hill and Knowlton, then the world's largest PR firm, served as mastermind for a massive PR campaign to persuade Americans that they should support a war to reclaim the country [Kuwait] from Iraq. Much of the money for the pro-war marketing campaign came from the government-in-exile of Kuwait itself, which signed a contract with H&K nine days after Saddam's army marched into Kuwait. (Rampton and Stauber 2003, 70)

Hill and Knowlton appears to have been responsible for the "babies torn from incubators story," delivered by a fifteen-year-old Kuwaiti girl to a Congressional Human Rights Caucus in October 1990 as part of a presentation of Iraqi human rights violations. The story has "become infamous within the PR community itself" (Rampton and Stauber 2003, 70) and was not finally disproved until after the war. The story was cited by the president, "in congressional testimony, on TV and talk shows, and at the U.N. Security Council" (72), and "Amnesty International repeated the claim in a December 1990 human rights report" (71). What Hill and Knowlton failed to reveal at the Caucus was that the teller of this tale was a member of the Kuwaiti royal family, and that the vice-president of the company had "coached" her testimony (73).

Hill and Knowlton are not the only PR firm to have been involved. After the end of Operation Desert Storm, George H. W. Bush ordered a covert CIA operation to unseat Saddam Hussein. The CIA employed public relations consultant John W. Rendon to organize "anti-Saddam propaganda campaigns inside Iraq." Rendon has acted as a campaign consultant to Democrats but now specializes in American military operations. The Rendon Group, which he heads, has worked in Argentina, Colombia, Haiti, Kosovo, Panama, and Zimbabwe. During the buildup to Desert Storm, he was paid $100,000 a month for media work on behalf of the Kuwaiti royal family. His postwar contract with the CIA involved spending "more than $23 million producing videos and comic books ridiculing Saddam," among other things (Rampton and Stauber 2003, 43). The Rendon Group also helped organize the Iraqi National Congress in 1992 and channeled $12 million of CIA money into it between 1992 and 1996 (Rampton and Stauber 2003, 43).

Rendon was contracted to handle the PR aspects of the U.S. war in Afghanistan in 2001, and the *New York Times* reported in 2002 that the Rendon Group had been appointed to assist the new Pentagon propaganda agency, the Office of Strategic Influence (OSI). The *Times* report included the information that the OSI would provide foreign reporters with possibly false news items, and the backlash (see above) forced its closure: but Rendon's contract with the Pentagon was not canceled (Rampton and Stauber 2003, 49).

It is worth noting here that the source for Rampton and Stauber's (2003) account of these events is often public-relations trade publications and mainstream media. The events were not secret, nor were the strategies of information warfare and management. Yet there was no media (or indeed academic) outcry, and apparently no connection made between these strategies and the embedding policy. This history and this particular story tell us that once one starts "crafting messages to target audiences" in a global media context, there is a very fine line between truth and fiction, information and deception, information operations and media management, and psychological operations. The messages are also hard to control. They develop, largely because of the nature of new information technologies, a life of their own. It was, we must remember, a Hill and Knowlton–trained professional, working in a cross-government context, who constructed the embeds program and managed the media in the United States in the 2003 Iraq War. It is hard to imagine that she did not know how to utilize that fine line between truth and fiction in the crafting of messages and the management of news. That very specific kind of PR knowledge would explain much of what she and others at the Pentagon told us in interviews (see Chapter 3) about their approach to embedding.

The Coalition Information Center in the United Kingdom

The work on the Pentagon and the history of the construction of Iraq 2003 reviewed above tend to suggest that the complex of global news management, the selling of culture via public diplomacy, and the use of information warfare and information and psychological operations is an American phenomenon. And yet there is clear evidence of a process of influence, collaboration, and consultation between the American and British systems of public perception management and, as we have seen above, the United Kingdom seems to be the model for the United States, rather than vice versa. Less has been published (either by the media or the academy) about the way the British system itself operates, even though Brown (2003) thought that then its model of cross-government implementation was one that the United States could usefully imitate.

Britain's CIC, on which America's OGC was modeled, was reactivated by Alastair Campbell for the 2003 Iraq War, and functioned among other things to "keep selling the message" about Saddam Hussein's crimes, largely, according to Kampfner, to divert the media from growing tensions between the United States and Britain over the second UN resolution (2003, 264). Once the war was actually under way, Campbell intended the CIC to coordinate and sell whatever the message was to be: "The twenty-four hour media day would start in the field, move to London and end in Washington" (Kampfner 2004, 314), presumably to make sure the coalition was on message for the next day. Miller (2004d) has given one account of that complex process.

It is the function of the cross-departmental committee known as the Communication (later Coalition) Information Center (CIC) to coordinate the information operations of the MoD and the Foreign Office. In the context of Iraq 2003, the CIC was chaired by Alastair Campbell and run from Downing Street, although located in the Foreign Office Information Directorate. Campbell also chaired the Iraq Information Group at Number 10, and there was an "alternative diplomatic policy center" there which linked straight into the centers of power in Washington (Miller 2004d, 82). Miller identifies four other main elements of what he calls the "propaganda apparatus" for Iraq 2003, noting the low-level activity of the embeds program but also its success as a public relations "coup" (2004d, 89).

First, Miller points out, the Foreign Office Public Diplomacy Policy Department is the equivalent of the State Department Office of Public Diplomacy in the United States in function, method, and tools, and is responsible for managing public perceptions of the United Kingdom overseas. Second, the newly established Civil Contingencies Secretariat coordinated out of the Cabinet Office and focusing, among other things, on the alleged "terrorist threat," parallels the Clarke/Rumsfeld group discussed above. Third in Miller's account, and very much subordinate to the command-and-control "propaganda" systems in Washington and London, was the operation "in theater"—the stage for the crushing of Iraq. This was Central Command in Qatar, the Forward Press Information Center in Kuwait, and the embedded reporters with their military minders. Last, there were the U.S. and UK military psychological operations teams undertaking overt and covert operations inside Iraq, which are said to target only enemy opinion to break resistance. All of these operations have their own contribution to make to the attack on Iraq, although most public debate has focused on the CentCom/embed system and latterly (in the United Kingdom) on the Downing Street operation overseen by Campbell (Miller 2004d, 82; Tumber and Palmer 2004).

Miller does not actually address the military/media interface at the MoD, nor does he deal with the other arms of the UK information warfare arsenal central to Britain's information campaign. Our interviews with MoD personnel make clear that campaign is, in theory, directed by the Cabinet Office CIC, coordinated across the Foreign and Commonwealth Office, the Department of Trade and Industry, the Department for International Development, and the MoD. Representatives of these departments, much like the first group above, the "band" in which Victoria Clarke is involved, collectively produce the "messages" passed on to other groups, who then release them to the media. Within the MoD, Media Operations and Information Operations, at least in theory, meet regularly to determine the broad themes and messages to be released by the Press Office to the media. What is not clear, as we shall see below, is whether in the UK context there was any single figure, like Victoria Clarke, who integrated all of this with the embeds program. Alastair Campbell is the most likely candidate, but his involvement at media ops level is opaque (see below), and he was, of course, despite his influence in the United States, a journalist by training, not a Hill and Knowlton professional.

UK Information Operations

Miller does not examine the cross-government implementation strategy that attempts to bring all this together and to coordinate across government departments, nor does he disentangle the strands of information and psychological operations, public relations, and media management which seem to have been at stake in the MoD Media Operations unit's management of the embeds program. These issues, like the relations between the media and intelligence services discussed by Keeble (2003), are difficult to access and complex to understand but they are, like so much else, actually openly available in various documents reflecting and reporting on the war on the UK Parliament website[6–7] The most instructive of these as discussed in the introduction to this chapter, are the minutes of evidence given by Air Vice Marshall Mike Heath and Wing Commander Ian Chalmers on information operations and by Mr. A. Pawson and Colonel Paul Brook on media operations These minutes tell us much more than the Select Committee on Defence's published and more often read *Third Report* (2004) that draws from them. What also emerges from the questions asked by the members of the Select Committee of these witnesses is the fact that members of the Select Committee themselves are having as much difficulty understanding how the various bits of government/military/MoD/public relations communications fit together as those who have written about the process since Iraq 2003 (Miller 2004d; Curtis 2004).

The starting point in questioning both info ops and media ops witnesses is not the Vietnam War, which is so often the starting point for discussions of embedding (see Chapter 1), but the failures of information operations and military/media interactions in the Falklands and in the first half of the NATO operations in Kosovo (Questions 1361, 1575, 1581). The first question asked of Heath and Chalmers by the Chairman of the Committee is about how far information operations have achieved a cross-government approach, which departments are actually involved in it, and how it is defined in the UK context (Question 1571). The Chairman then asks what documents about it are available to be read (Question 1573). Air Vice Marshall Heath responds:

> Information Operations is co-ordinated actions undertaken to influence an adversary or potential adversary in support of political and military objectives by undermining his will, cohesion and decision-making ability through affecting his information, information-based processes and systems, whilst protecting one's own decision makers and decision-making process. (Response to Question 1571)
>
> A large element of Information Operations is, of course, Classified. It comes under several disciplines and those include electronic warfare, psychological operations, operational security, deception, computer network operations, and information insurance. (Response to Question 1573)

It is very clear in Heath's evidence that the cross-government approach does indeed affect a whole range of actors and groups, and that info ops is conceived as a process of deterrence as well as a way of managing conflict and postconflict restoration and reconstitution. These are seen as different stages in a process, and all that happens in moving from one to the other is that "the style of the messages changes" as they are "crafted" for different audiences and purposes (response to Question 1578). The starting point is "a positive statement of national intent from the government" (as we will see in Chapter 4 in our interviews with the MoD, the absence of this "positive intent"]made the Iraq 2003 conflict particularly difficult to manage in the United Kingdom).

Asked about the "departmental structure of taking a genuinely inter-departmental approach" (Question 1579), Heath's answer is complex. He names the Foreign Office as the "major interlocutor," working with the Cabinet Office and the Campbell group, and, "on an ad hoc basis," the Department for International Development and the Home Office. The Foreign Office is said to have been too "regionally rather than information focussed" in the past but to have recently changed. Wing Commander Chalmers provides the information that the Foreign Office now has an information directorate that used to be part of the Public Diplomacy Department. He does not mention the Department of Trade and Industry, which our MoD contacts included in this wider implementation group. He also names the Information Campaign Co-ordination Group, which functions to "agree that the themes and messages we propose are agreeable to other departments" and within the MoD to decide how information and media operations will develop their "lines of attack."

There are also indications of anxieties about the blurring of information operations and deception as the coordination of activities across government proceeds. Heath recalls, "We spent considerable effort persuading the Foreign Office that we were not their enemies...and we shared a common goal in terms of defence diplomacy and the delivery of war avoidance," and comments that it was a "slightly more difficult tussle with the media ops folks" (response to Question 1581, referring here to media operations within the MoD).

He is then asked about the role of Downing Street, who were "obviously extremely central to media operations and the campaign together" (Question 1583). At this point Heath insists that people outside information operations do not understand it, and that it is all "based on truth," except the bit where they try to "lie or dissuade or persuade military commanders."

Heath then reveals the role played by info ops in relation to Downing Street in the cross-government information campaign:

> We forced our way into the Campbell group because we felt that if there was going to be cross-government ownership of an information campaign it had to be led from the very top....We demonstrated that there were key messages that should not be released as soon as you had them, they needed to be crafted to be released at certain times, and that is I think the strength we brought to the Campbell group. (Response to Question 1584)

When asked about others involved in the overall info ops campaign, Heath refers to the recruitment of a number of Iraqi exiles, specifically academics and medical professionals: "We looked everywhere to understand inside the Iraqi psyche and mentality. It was up to us to decide how that could be crafted into action" (response to Question 1629).

This acknowledges activities in the United Kingdom of a kind that directly parallel those reported by Rampton and Stauber (2003) and Snow (2003) in the United States. Notably, in this reply, the distinction Heath maintains carefully elsewhere between "influence" operations at home and internationally breaks down. Later he refers to this group of Iraqi exiles again as having been a part of "a department called human factors" who were all civilians (response to Question 1643). He goes on to talk of how Information Operations paid "people on a casual basis for support" (response to Question 1630), referring to the Rendon Group: "We used the Rendon Group quite considerably over the last five years to provide us with input at that level." His description of the Rendon Group is perhaps an example of the "crafting" for different audiences which he speaks of at every turn during his evidence: "The Rendon Group is a bespoke academic group that is freelance but does a considerable amount of work for the Pentagon and State Department." The Rendon Group is referred to elsewhere as a public relations firm; its own website describes it as a "Global Strategic Communications Consultancy."[8] It is consistently portrayed as having contributed significantly to the Pentagon's ten-year preparation for Iraq 2003, and to the construction of the three-week media war in 2003 (Rampton and Stauber 2003, 4–5, suggest that Rendon may have stage-managed the fall of the statue of Saddam Hussein). Yet the members of the Select Committee ask no further questions about this connection.

It seems clear that Britain's cross-government implementation plan looks very like the structures and processes the American media has recently been resisting as a further intrusion of information/psychological operations into the normal processes of military/media and political communication processes. Perhaps the greatest PR coup of all in relation to the enormous attention paid to the embedding of journalists (see Chapter 1) has been to keep the focus of media and academic inquiry away from these very issues. But when we turn to the role of media operations within the MoD, the picture Heath constructs under examination above seems to require some further adjustments. It is certainly not clear from the evidence of Pawson and Brook to the Select Committee that media operations are always "on message" in relation to the agenda of information operations.

UK Media Operations

In the United Kingdom, the MoD's media operations used its existing media staff both in the MoD headquarters and in the armed forces to staff the Iraq 2003 operation. From the MoD's perspective, the Cross-Government Implementation Group receives guidance from the Cabinet Office and consists of representatives of the Foreign and Commonwealth Office (FCO), Department for Trade and Industry (DTI), Department for International Development (DfID), and the Ministry of Defence itself. This group produces an Information Campaign, part of what the News Release Group (an adhoc meeting giving overall direction for MoD media operations and sometimes referred to in our interview materials as "the daily prayer meeting") considers in its formulation of themes and messages for release to the media through the Director of News and the Press Office. The News Release Group involves both Media Operations and Information Operations personnel, who must work together because their activities are closely related, but who must also be seen as distinct so that the media will not feel that they are being manipulated or used for misinformation purposes. The News Release Group normally includes representatives of Permanent Joint Headquarters (PJHQ) and may include NATO (if involved).[9]

The position taken by the representatives of MoD Media Operations before the Select Committee on Defence is very different to that taken by Heath in his evidence before the same Committee and attempts, on cue, to distinguish itself from information and psychological operations at every turn. Mr. A. Pawson, Director General of Corporate Communications, and Colonel Paul Brook, Assistant Director, Media Operations Policy, gave evidence. Pawson (response to Question 1360) describes the MoD media plan as being developed as an integral part of the overall military plan "under the chapeau of the senior military and ministerial exchanges that were taking place," including exchanges with PJHQ and CentCom. Asked when politicians were brought into the process, Pawson replies that both he and Brook had only joined the MoD in January of 2003 and do not really know the answer to this question. He continues, however, that "the media operation planning was conducted in the framework of overall military planning and it was the same people right at the top involved" (response to Question 1362). The Chairman then asks explicitly what role Number 10, "reputed to have had a controlling hand over media relations across government," had had on "media operations planning for Op Telic [UK operations in Iraq] and at what stage" (Question 1364). Pawson's reply is the same one we received in our interviews: the plan, including embedding, was the MoD's plan, designed to "put accurate information in the public domain," and media/military engagements had operated according to the *Green Book* (the British military's published code of practice for dealing with the media in times of emergency, tension, conflict, or war).

Asked by a member of the Select Committee whether what they were trying to do was "news management," (Question 1373) Pawson replies, "We are quite clear to separate out media operations from, if you like, information and deception type of work. There is some American doctrine that tends to see the world as a global whole"—a "doctrine" from which Pawson distances himself. Brook's response, asked for his perceptions of the same issue (Question 1375) is more muddied by the whole business of coordination across government and close interaction between information and media operations within the MoD itself. He again makes a real distinction between "perception management" and the "presentation of information," but qualifies it by insisting that the latter must never "cut across anything that might have a detrimental effect on perceptions." He talks of the need for coordination between those who deliver psychological operations and those who "conduct military activities which also send a message" and, while maintaining the distinction Pawson had articulated, refuses to divorce what is done completely "from the American approach" (response to Question 1375).

What seems clear in these exchanges is that Pawson, at least, does not talk the info ops/PR talk that Heath and Brook do. Perhaps this is why when we interviewed Pawson, Brook sat in on the interview. But all of this may also have to do with what appears to be the relatively quick turnover of staff in this section of the MoD; there is no institutional memory. Of those we ourselves interviewed in 2003, Lieutenant Colonel Taverner, Pawson, and Pam Teare (Director of News) had left by mid-2004. The differences in the way people perceive and discuss the issues may also be related to the different kinds of training and background of staff in the corporate communications/media operations area in the MoD, where those entrusted with media operations seemed to come from military or media rather than PR backgrounds. The same is true of Campbell at Downing Street. Two of our key interviewees at the MoD were completing academic degrees in Public Relations in 2003–4, but did not have the degrees when they were involved in managing the embeds program. . The tendency for "career civil servants," often from the Government Information and Communication Service, to be operating in these areas of the MoD, with no specific training in PR, is a feature of media relations that Harris commented on in the Falklands conflict (1983, 95–98) and was still the case in 2001 (see the Ministry of Defence's *How the Directorate General Communications [DGCC] Works*, notes from an induction pack for new staff, 2001). Our attempts to interview the MoD about these details in the late summer of 2004 were unsuccessful.

Many questions remain unanswered in the Minutes of Evidence given to the Select Committee about the role of Downing Street in the embedding policy, and about the effect of the cross-government information campaign on media operations. The whole area seems somewhat awkwardly placed between the centrality of information operations at every level in the model outlined by Heath and the insistence on the provision of accurate information intended to distinguish media operations from information operations within the MoD. But to the extent that those who gave evidence to the Select Committee, and those who were interviewed for our research, are *incompletely* incorporated into the "global American model," or indeed into information operations or the cross-government information campaign, and perhaps because they emerge from different interpretive communities from those who manage the latter, they actually do seem to have attempted to carry out their task—that is, to provide accurate information and to position themselves between the MoD and the media as "a valve in both directions," persuading the MoD to help the media and at the same time "getting what the department wants us to put out to the media" (Pawson, response to Question 1349, Minutes of Evidence to the Select Defence Committee).

Accordingly, we cannot simply brand all of these operations as propaganda or lies. This is not simply propaganda in any of its older senses, and the meanings of truth and lies are very flexible, constantly shifting with the operations of power and influence in these institutional contexts. Miller's "lies and deception" (2004) framework is not complex enough to account for this new communications context. That said, Miller is probably alone to date in actually beginning to map and draw attention to the workings of this complicated new machinery across the American and British contexts.

CHAPTER THREE

The Pentagon Perspective

ALTHOUGH THE PHENOMENON of reporters traveling with combat units is not new, its manifestation during the 2003 Iraq War differs significantly from earlier conflicts. The new terminology, for example— "embedded reporter" rather than "war correspondent"—is not as trivial as it may first appear, arising as it does from the huge Pentagon initiative that brought accredited journalists to the American frontline forces. Victoria Clarke, Assistant Secretary of Defense for Public Affairs, was widely credited as the architect of the embeds policy, at least in terms of American coverage, and has given numerous interviews since the official end of hostilities. Her reasoning for the policy ran as follows:

> In previous conflicts, including Afghanistan, we made the best effort possible to provide access to the media. Iraq was different for a lot of reasons, and so there was an extraordinary evolution of what we were already doing, and it had to do with the factors. It had to do with the fact that we knew if we went to war, we'd have a lot more people out there, a lot more soldiers, sailors, airmen and marines. It had to do with the fact that we knew the more people saw the U.S. military, the more they would understand the mission and how they're going about their jobs, and the more the people saw of the Iraqi regime.[1]

Putting a human face on combat operations was a key idea, particularly coming as it did from a highly experienced public relations practitioner, as we shall discuss in more detail throughout this chapter.

As well as Victoria Clarke, we also interviewed her deputy at the Pentagon, Bryan Whitman; Rear Admiral "T" McCreary, responsible for the strategic organization of the program from the military side; and Major Tim Blair, responsible at the tactical level of placing embeds with their units. The first three of these interviews took place in Washington, D.C., in October 2003, while Major Blair was interviewed via telephone in the same month.

For both Pentagon and Ministry of Defence interviews we constructed a semistructured interview schedule that aimed to investigate similar issues but also allowed a degree of flexibility according to each individual's particular role in the process. Several broad themes were consistent across these interviews:

- The individual's role in the planning and execution of the embedding process.
- Their thoughts on the philosophy and wider objectives of the use of embeds.
- The practical details of the process and how well it worked.
- Issues concerning dealing with journalists who were not embedded (the so-called "unilaterals").
- The future of conflict coverage and media operations.

Objectives and Background

American preparations for the media operation began as early as September 2002. Simultaneous but independent discussions were taking place within the Pentagon and the media communities; Admiral McCreary began to confer with military representatives about how operational coverage would work in practice, while Victoria Clarke was polling journalists and bureau chiefs on their perceived requirements. These discussions resulted in the Public Affairs Guidelines[2] (PAG), a negotiated agreement between the Pentagon and the media industry about interactions in war when journalists were embedded. The PAG was specifically developed for the Iraq context and was part of a concerted and extensive program of preparation for the "information war" in the conflict in Iraq.

The PAG articulates the "problem" that the whole embedding project was designed to solve and makes clear that the policy was designed to address a number of publics: within the United States, around the globe, and in Iraq. It also assumes that that a "transparent" flow of information will necessarily show American forces in a favorable light, since embedding will facilitate "telling our story":

Media coverage of any future operation will, to a large, extent, shape public perception of the national security environment now and in the years ahead. This holds true for the US public; the public in allied countries whose opinion can affect the durability of our coalition; the publics in countries where we conduct operations, whose perceptions of us can affect the cost and duration of our involvement. Our ultimate strategic success in bringing peace and security to this region will come in our long-term commitment to supporting our democratic ideals. We need to tell the factual story—good or bad—before others seed the media with disinformation and distortions, as they most certainly will continue to do. Our people in the field need to tell our story. (2.A)

The entire public affairs team, civilian and military, worked very closely together to implement this policy: upward to Secretary Donald Rumsfeld and Chairman Richard Myers, and downward through the services to unit commanders and Public Affairs Officers (PAOs) on one hand and to bureau chiefs, reporters, and editors on the other. What comes across in our interviews is a very clear sense of an integrated public affairs plan and a shared mission. In fact, in interviews, it was sometimes hard to break through the heavily rehearsed discourse. This sense of the well-oiled architecture of the plan, buttressed by everyone, is in marked contrast to the impression one gets from the MoD interviews in the following chapter (in which the media were not assumed to be part of a shared mission). Thus Victoria Clarke followed the PAG when she told us:

The strategy was pretty simple—if good things are happening, you want people to see it. And I knew that if people could see, both in the U.S. and abroad, the men and women of our U.S. military, they would be impressed—they are the most committed, the best trained. On the other hand, bad things happen—the best way to put bad things behind you is to put a big spotlight on them—so the same strategy was best for positive and negative things.

In our interview, Major Tim Blair also followed the PAG, explaining:

The main mind-set was the Iraqi regime and Saddam had a history of misinformation and disinformation and propaganda, if not outright lies; we knew as one of the components of the war that counteracting that disinformation was going to be a large task. And what better way than to have eyes on the ground, unbiased opinions from mainstream news media to put out factual information of what they actually saw on the ground—that was the main driving force.

A key characteristic of the way the Pentagon approached embedding seems to lie in Victoria Clarke's management of the public affairs process and her involvement and integration across political and military levels. She argued that the reason she was capable of taking a pragmatic view of the "bad news" or "misinformation" aspects of the consequences of embedding was her central role in the war planning process:

> One of the smartest things Rumsfeld did was from the very earliest days—I was part of the war planning. I was involved in every single meeting and planning session, I was just there start to finish, every day. I had, with very few exceptions, all the information he had—and so I felt comfortable, I knew how things were going strategically. If I hadn't been privy to all that information, I may have gotten more nervous or upset by individual stories.

Our interviews with the team makes explicit that all had been trained to respond in exactly the same way to questions, from the media or the military or from interviewers like us, about the way the process worked. In each interview, the same questions receive sometimes almost verbatim answers. These are often followed by elaboration and detail, but the conforming answers are always present.[3] This has interesting consequences for assessing the information provided by unit commanders and civil briefings to embedded reporters and others during the war. The PAG emphasizes the whole exercise in terms of operational security being dependent on "security at the source" (3.R, 6.A, 6.A.1): "Media products will not be subject to security review or censorship except as indicated in Par 6.A.1. Security at the source will be the rule." The military will need, in short, to remain "on message." This applies as well to interviews with service members: "All interviews with service members will be on the record. Security at the source is the policy" (4.A). We must assume that all service members had had some training in the meaning of "security at the source," and that this involved "boundaries in talking to the media."

The very different nature of the media's embedded relationship produced a lot of very detailed "off-the-record" information—precisely the material (dealt with in 6.A.1 of the PAG) not directly usable without military clearance. This is the context in which we must read the Pentagon team's desire to get "our story across," to have "direct eyewitnesses," and to produce "transparency."

Embeds as the Focus

The objectives of the PAG, and the interviews above, make clear that reports from the front lines were always intended to be the focus of media coverage, with two primary goals: to counter any disinformation from the Iraqi regime, and to demonstrate the professionalism of U.S. forces via maximum exposure of individual combatants.

The sheer volume of frontline footage from embeds was designed to avoid any "news vacuum" into which less favorable pieces of analysis or counterresponses from the Iraqi regime might seep. On occasions when negative footage did appear—scenes of civilian casualties from marketplace bombings, or of coalition casualties or POWs, images taken by Iraqi TV and broadcast by al-Jazeera—a concerted effort was made to undermine it, either by displays of moral outrage that such scenes be transmitted or by protracted denials and then promises of full investigations (designed to diffuse the news value of the events by allowing them to be replaced with additional, instantly more "newsworthy" action footage). Second, the embed footage provided "independent" rebuttal of the claims of the Iraqi information minister, Mohammad Said al-Sahhaf, quickly nicknamed "comical Ali" after some of his more optimistic statements about the Iraqi response. Victoria Clarke told us:

> I think the classic case of how we didn't have to rebut too much of what they were saying is the days before the fall of Baghdad. There's the Iraqi information minister standing up saying: "There are no coalition forces at the airport, we've wiped them out, we've killed a thousand of them," and there the airport was [on television] under coalition control or the tanks were going through the streets in Baghdad.

The second aspect of the vast embedding exercise involved providing positive images of U.S. troops. Once again, the volume of compelling frontline footage contributes to its execution here, with the emphasis on the hometown unit and the individual soldier as the face of the war (discussed below), personalizing the reports and detracting focus from the overall policy of the campaign. This is perhaps partly aided by the different audiences for which the American and British products were intended, something that was of far greater concern to those at the MoD whom we interviewed than to their American counterparts. Colonel Paul Brook (Media Operations at the MoD) suggested that:

> The American approach was simply the provision of an ability to spectate. And they were completely satisfied with simply providing the spectacle. In other words, putting in maybe six hundred embeds, making sure they were able to provide their stuff, and that's all they needed, because they, in public support terms, did not have the public support issues that we started the war. I mean, they were delivering messages to a convinced audience, whereas we were not.

In our interview, Victoria Clarke was adamant that the American public would be able to find context for the embedded reports from the diversity of news sources available to them:

> I disagree with those who say that there was no context behind it, my experience was, and this is purely U.S., was especially for the first several weeks, people watched a lot. The average American watched a lot, they read a lot, they read more newspapers than they usually do, which is good. They listened to the coverage of the war in their cars on their radio, they'd go on line during the day.

This places the responsibility for context firmly in the hands of the public, rather than the military media operation. While this may have some support from the responses to our focus groups, as we'll discuss in Chapter 8 (although those groups mostly refer to UK coverage), it was mainly in the initial stages of the war that people claimed to have increased and diversified their news-seeking behavior. After some time, it appears, the volume of uncontextualized dramatic footage and conflicting or repetitive reports made the picture *more* confusing, and our respondents, at least, reverted to evening news bulletins to try to get a condensed, overall picture. Although polls taken in the United Kingdom during and after the war lend some support for the increase in news viewing (e.g., the Independent Television Commission's *Conflict Around the Clock* [4]), their figures are primarily for evening bulletins. Victoria Clarke acknowledged that the volume of reports was a problem for news editors themselves:

> The television bureau chiefs here in town told me that in the early days and weeks their biggest problem was that they had so much product coming back, both live and taped, and they couldn't, it wasn't that it was redundant, it was that there was so much of it.

Interestingly, in our interview with her, Victoria Clarke also gave something of a contradictory anecdote. Referring to the earlier point that erroneous news stories rarely caused upset because she was privy to the wider picture, she mentioned the infamous quote by Lieutenant General William Scott Wallace. On 27 March 2003, the *New York Post* carried a story referring to a lull in the progress of combat operations and the response of Fedayeen fighters, in which the senior U.S. commander is quoted as saying, "The enemy we're fighting is different from the one we'd wargamed against." In fact, in the full article on another page, the reporter further quoted Wallace as having expected this response from the Iraqi forces. Clarke remarks:

> I have pointed out that General story to several people, so first of all, the context of the lead was wrong, but then if you went to the jump page, which not many people do, you have an entirely different take.... Headline writers, and the ones who write the little bits at the bottom, they do more damage than anything else.

Providing Context: CentCom

In late 2002, as part of Exercise Internal Look, as many as a thousand non-combat U.S. military personnel were deployed from U.S. Central Command in Tampa, Florida, to a new, multibillion-dollar air base at Camp as-Saliyah, Qatar (CentCom). The purpose of this part of the exercise was ostensibly to test mobile communications capabilities from a "forward-deployed" location, but there was clear speculation within the American media that this was in preparation for a military campaign in Iraq.[5]

In the exercise, CentCom Qatar functioned as the headquarters of the American-led operation, and from there daily briefings took place. These were scheduled for 2 p.m. local time—in time for the daily agenda setting for the morning bulletins on the American news networks. It seems clear that this press center was designed specifically for the benefit of these televised bulletins and far less for the benefit of the thousand or so accredited correspondents who spent much of their time in air-conditioned warehouses watching events unfold on the multiple television sets installed there:

> They passed through exceptional security (including scanners that let the technicians see them naked) to wait for news in front of a $200,000 stage assembled by *Good Morning, America*'s art director, George Allison. The backdrop was a powder-blue-and-white world map and seven plasma video screens so high-quality that networks could film the action onscreen and broadcast it directly. *Army Times* called it "glitzy." It looked damned good on TV.[6]

However, the glamorous Hollywood set in Qatar quickly lost credibility with journalists and was slow to provide the necessary information, perhaps reflecting the different media approaches of the United Kingdom and United States, given the differences in domestic public opinion (see the following chapter). As our research shows, less than 4 percent of the reports in our quantitative analysis of the coverage of the entire war came from Qatar.

Unlike the first Gulf War, and deliberately so on the part of the Americans, there was no charismatic "Stormin' Norman" Schwarzkopf to provide inspirational briefings. General Vincent Brooks gave competent, factual briefings but was subordinate to General Tommy Franks, the most senior officer at CentCom. To some journalists, this was akin to being briefed by middle management in a manufactured press center that was designed for a television audience rather than a pack of journalists. When *New York* magazine writer Michael Wolff asked General Brooks, "Why are we here? Why should we stay? What's the value of what we're learning at this million-dollar press center?" he was met with some derision from fellow American journalists and outright hostility from American PAOs. In the United States he faced accusations of a lack of patriotism.[7]

In our interviews, Victoria Clarke rejects such criticisms, suggesting that they are a product of something akin to jealousy of the embeds, rather than valid concerns about the lack of timely and comprehensive information from CentCom. It is clear that she always considered the embed footage to be the real story of the war, and that briefing material to provide the wider context would always be secondary:

> There were plenty of individuals, and they didn't tend to be regular national security correspondents, would come to me in the weeks and months leading up to the war and saying to me, "Well, I'm thinking I should be in Qatar, because that's the centerpiece and that is where all the action is going to be," and they tended to be people interested in one thing, always trying to win prizes, thinking they are going to write a book. And I would say, "I can't make these decisions for you, but there isn't going to be one place that dominates, it's just not the way it works, and if this embedding works out, that is going to be the most amazing stuff and that is going to be the coverage that everybody pays attention to that will be the news of the war."

James Wilkinson, director of strategic communications to General Franks, was no less disparaging in his dismissal of the criticisms, nor any less overt about the anticipated role of the embeds: "Qatar was never designed to be the font of all news; the font of all news was designed to be the front lines and their embeds and it worked out. We couldn't be happier."[8]

Attitudes toward Independent Reporters

The safety of journalists in future conflicts has become a matter of serious debate within the industry and the subject of review at the Ministry of Defence. What McCreary admitted was a "shoot-first-and-ask-questions-later" approach meant that many independent journalists were killed by U.S. forces. The apparent flexibility with which individual unit commanders dealt with the "embedded for life" policy has also come in for considerable criticism. The U.S. Public Affairs Guidance document mentions nonembedded reporters only once and includes no other specific guidelines on how to deal with them. Indeed, at the recent Newsworld International Conference in Dublin, Bryan Whitman stated that the media "does not have the right" to be on the battlefield.[9] In briefings before the war with bureau chiefs, there is little mention of nonembedded journalists:

I don't want a misperception here. When you're talking about chem/bio gear, that's only the embedded media. That is not the three thousand media that show up at Qatar for covering the news center. Just so there's no misunderstanding. It's only the guys out with the operating forces.[10]

Whitman certainly made it very clear in the February briefing to bureau chiefs that safety would be a major issue for unilaterals:

The battlefield's a dangerous place to be, and it's going to be a dangerous place, even embedded with our forces. It will be an even more dangerous place for reporters that are out there not in an embedded status, that are moving around the battlefield, running to the sounds of the guns. And I guess we can't caution you enough as to the dangers that presents to a U.S. military force in combat, moving across the ground, coming across reporters that may or may not have armed guards for their own security out there. [11]

John Simpson recounts an incident that demonstrates precisely this policy, describing how his armed Kurdish bodyguards were pulled out of their vehicle and forced to the ground at a checkpoint manned by American marines in a heightened state of fear of attack: "You do not feel safe around American soldiers who think their lives and those of their comrades are in danger."[12]

In the same February briefing, Whitman further warned of the dangers for journalists stationed in the Iraqi capital: "We don't believe Baghdad is a safe place to have reporters"—a point Victoria Clarke followed up:

Journalists operating independently of embedding status. We cannot guarantee their safety...and Baghdad specifically. It's not a good place to be now, and it will not be a good place to be if there is indeed military action.... This will not be anything like 1991.... For instance, communication targets in Baghdad are obviously something we would take out.[13]

Later Whitman responded to a question about independent journalists operating in northern Iraq by saying that such reporters would be unlikely to be taken on as embeds and "would be treated just like any other civilian person found on the battlefield."

In our interviews, members of the Pentagon team reiterated these positions. Tim Blair said, "It is difficult to discern valid military targets with [unilateral] media all over—roaming on the battlefield. The best solution was to take the media with us—a great level of safety for the media." Admiral McCreary, when asked about unilaterals, told us:

Without embedding more would have got killed—maybe even by us, inadvertently—because when that camera goes up on the shoulder and you don't know who that is—that might be a missile—you're going to shoot first and ask questions later. That wasn't necessary, because so many media were embedded. The unilaterals that were behind you, were coming to you—meant a lot less issues on the battlefield where you had to identify so many. If there'd been five hundred or six hundred people trying to come at you, I'm sure we would have made a lot more mistakes in shooting people and unfortunately killing them.

Victoria Clarke gave a similar response, although with more effort to put a softer edge on the policy:

> It's a matter of reality. We said to them: "Do not think just because the Iraqi regime went out of its way to help news media twelve years ago that they were going to do so this time. There are plenty of indications that it's just the opposite. We cannot guarantee your safety—you're not with us—you're not traveling with us—we cannot guarantee your safety." Now 99 percent of the news organizations understood and supported that.... There's a Marine who got badly injured going out after some unilateral reporter, and that happened again and again because at the end of the day our people are very decent humane people and they don't want someone to get hurt.... Some really, really annoying circumstances. Dan Rather and a crew decided they were going to drive in from Jordan to Baghdad, and we called them and encouraged them—and begged them—and said: "Please, please don't do this. This is a bad idea." And two days of arguing and they decided to do it and guess what? Two dozen U.S. forces had to stop what they were doing and baby-sit them overnight in the desert because they got into hot water.

Clarke's comment to us that "it is a fact of life to have unilaterals" was followed by:

> Oh—that happened a lot—there was back and forth—unembedded would latch onto a unit and then disappear again—my feeling was—that's up to the unit commander—if he wants to do that, that's up to him.

Whitman indicated that "it was never the intent for news organizations to cover only from an embedded standpoint—we knew there would be unilateral journalists out there," but he suggests that the place for these was in locations "where news organizations would need to get an appropriate level of context" to frame the embedded reports—the Pentagon itself and the CentCom Press Center, rather than on the battlefield.

Training

In the United States, the training program for embeds was part of the integrated public affairs approach that characterized Victoria Clarke's management. The training was planned well in advance in the form of week-long boot camps, attended by fifty to sixty people at a time and aimed at the military as well as the media. Unlike at the MoD, training was not an official requirement for embedding. "It was," according to Clarke, "a decision for news organizations to make." After going through it, "some people said: 'This isn't for me.'" It was designed to "increase the comfort levels on both sides"—on the part of the news media and on the part of the military. The military would understand that the media were taking it seriously and "do not want to get in [their] way," and the media would understand "that the military were prepared to make this commitment." According to Whitman, they trained 232 journalists, "not nearly as many as we sent in." Victoria Clarke explained the importance of training in promoting mutual respect among media and military:

> It is hard to explain how the development of this was such a constant pro-cess but when I tell a three-star [general] that these fifty news organizations have pulled some of their best correspondents out of work for a week—they are taking this seriously. They were impressive programs—some very impressive live-fire exercises and things like that—a five-mile hike with twenty-five-pound packs and simulated attacks.... This was important for some people to have gone through—to be sufficiently trained and self-aware—how hard it was, how dan-gerous.

This description, as we shall see in the next chapter, contrasts starkly with MoD comments on military attitudes to embedding and on the difficulties of getting journalists to commit to the limited training available when it was still not clear that there was going to be a war.[14]

Technology

The PAG details technical and other kinds of support for journalists with troops (2.C.2, 2.C.3, 2.C.4). Units are instructed, for example, to "plan lift and logistical support to assist in moving media products to and from the battlefield so as to tell our story in a timely manner" (2.C.3); the PAG states explicitly that units will be able to nominate local/regional media to be embedded with them (3.B). This support was an important factor in the very positive feedback in interviews from British journalists embed-ded with U.S. troops, and the fact that American war coverage contained significantly more "human interest" stories than in the United Kingdom.

There seems little doubt from all the evidence we have that, in terms of technical support, the Pentagon offered much more than the Ministry of Defence. Admiral McCreary explained this in ways that also shed light on the whole logic of embedding and the PAG ground rules about operational security:

> We were actually way ahead of everybody, because we started thinking about live technology on the battlefield ten years ago, after Desert Storm. We all saw where the technology was going because of the independents, the unilaterals (in Baghdad during that time), that you would have the chance to see war live—and the proliferation of commercial satellites that could look down and see a location and maybe show things. We've kind of adopted an attitude in the past ten years—both the war fighter and those who deal with information—that strategic surprise probably doesn't exist any more. So the only thing you can garner is tactical surprise. Therefore, if you have live technology on the battlefield, you only have to control it for the period of time to garner your tactical surprise—after that it doesn't make any difference.

This may also have been why commanders on the ground were more flexible (than the briefings with bureau chiefs would have suggested) about allowing news organizations to bring more with them than they could carry:

> ADM. McCREARY: A couple of organizations brought trucks with them, and we let them travel—five or six miles behind the convoys—and then they were able to shoot back.... This was more flexibility than we wanted back here because we were worried about friendly fire—not knowing what these trucks would look like.

Major Tim Blair discussed other kinds of help U.S. troops gave embedded reporters:

> We had encouraged it—you take what you need to produce your product. Public Affairs Officers on the ground wanted to help the media. They recharged batteries, transported videos.

Bryan Whitman recalled even earlier preparations for logistical support:

> Very early on, we took all the cameramen and technical people from the networks into the Pentagon parking lot, and we said, "You'll have to be able to power everything from Humvee vehicles." We practiced. We got some typical generators—like military units would have—and figured out how to use those. The emphasis was on innovation—there was a lot of collaboration to find things that worked—we shared knowledge. Some devices couldn't be used—and we found that out—and they shared technical resources.[15]

As a consequence, there were no technical surprises for the Pentagon when the embeds began to report back from the battlefield. As James Mates, an ITV correspondent embedded with the U.S. Marines, said to us: "They were thrilled to have a dish with them in which they could be seen to be winning the war."

Allocation of Slots

The allocation of embedded slots clearly had a U.S./UK bias. Whitman told us that he had discussed with his counterparts at the Ministry of Defence that he had wanted to reserve some of the U.S. slots for international media for the United Kingdom and "wanted to make sure they were doing the same for the U.S. media," and suggested that it had been a "collaborative, not directive" process from his end. The PAG ground rules were negotiated with the military and the media, and the news organizations, as in the United Kingdom, were given embedding slots and had the responsibility of allocating their reporters to these.

While they had different motivations, the media in both the United Kingdom and the United States were complicit with the media operations and public affairs agendas of the Ministry of Defence and the Pentagon. The project was, in that sense, a mutual production. Major Tim Blair, who managed the actual process of offering slots to the media in the United States, told us:

> Everybody wanted access. We had to try to spread it around equitably and to ensure the widest dissemination of information.... Everybody wanted to be on the tip of the spear. There was immense pressure from the prima donnas, the premier reporters—they all wanted embeds where the action was going to be—and it didn't work that way. It was not how we had designed the program.... There was pressure throughout. Later there were attempts at horse-trading—to get better positions—but we were hard to bend.

According to Victoria Clarke, "the stars thought Qatar would be the place to be," but in the actual events embeds produced the more immediate and compelling footage. This added to the pressure later to move people around.

Embed placements with U.S. forces were "for life," as they were with the Ministry of Defence. The major difference between the way the MoD and the Pentagon went about embedding was in relation to foreign and local/regional news. For the United States, foreign embeds were a central part of the exercise precisely because of the global context in which the United States saw itself as waging the war. Whitman was the architect of this part of the American plan, which he connected to the war on terror:

Iraq was part of the global war on terror. The need to have a significant amount of international coverage was tough—to reach the Arab, Asian, Latin American populations. There are large ungoverned areas of Latin America ripe for terrorists to go to. Africa, of course, is ripe for terrorism.

Nonetheless, the bulk of the embedded program—80 percent—was reserved for American reporters. All those we interviewed at the Pentagon said that at another time, they would increase the proportion of foreign to national news agencies represented. Tim Blair admitted that none of his team, himself included, "had a great depth of knowledge about international media going into this" and included ways of rectifying that in his account of lessons learned for next time. In response to a question about whether she cared about world coverage of the war, Victoria Clarke replied:

Oh, a lot. One of the biggest concerns if you went to war with Iraq was what would happen in that region of the world. Would governments be overthrown? We were very, very concerned. Public support around the world is important—you gotta do it—devote slots to foreign news organizations—our news organizations complain, but we need to do more.

Blair also told us about the "subjective" way news organizations were selected nationally and regionally in the United States. The networks, he said, "were easy." The five major networks all had the "same number of slots and access to all the same units." It is worth noting that they considered Fox Network one of the majors in this context. Where print was concerned, they aimed for "as wide a distribution of information as possible" and selected the top one hundred newspapers "by circulation rating." There was also a preference for putting news organizations with the units from their regions. Units were allowed to nominate preferences for national and regional representation:

This time we had 70 percent national, 20 percent foreign, and 10 percent where the media was selected by the units themselves—the local papers. The larger level units could select the media that covered them on a routine basis, the small town papers, the network affiliates, and so on. Next time I would make them more than 10 percent, because if you look at 10 percent and overall numbers, there were sometimes only five to seven slots, and for example, the 4th Infantry Division out of Texas had three different media markets—in Washington, in Colorado, and in Texas—we need enough slots to cover that.

Preference was thus given to putting national news organizations with units from the area where the organizations were based, as Major Blair explained: "If you had a national paper, but located in the Midwest, then put it with a regional unit." The allocation process follows from the policy decision that the face of the war should be America's sons and daughters, as Admiral McCreary explained:

> Once somebody decides to start a war and you start shooting, from the uniform perspective, we need the support of the American people for our troops—not for the issue, but for the troops—and what better way for people to understand that than to put the face of the troops as the face of the war, rather than one or two spokesmen up on the podium? And so you had people tied to units because— "Oh! That's my hometown unit—people are in it from here"—and you had all this face of noncommissioned officers, petty officers and junior NCOs—that really were America's sons and daughters back here—and while you may or may not agree with the war, you really support them and them coming back alive.

The results of the combined policy and allocation strategy, and the lack of any requirement to pool reports, all undoubtedly contributed to both the far greater focus in the American coverage of the war on human-interest stories related to individual members of the armed forces, and to the Pentagon team's much higher comfort levels with relatively uncontextualized reports. Moreover, unlike at the MoD, our U.S. interviewees never referred to the media in any context other than as a homogenous group that had actively subscribed to the patriotic mission of embedding from an early stage.

Conflicting Reports and Misinformation

Our analysis of media coverage of the war tells us that the reports that were of most concern in the United Kingdom—the early casualty and friendly-fire incidents, the "misreporting" or conflicting reports, the killing of unilateral journalists—were not high on the media agenda in the United States, which emphasized the hometown unit and "the soldier as the face of the war." There were clearly also not the same anxieties, politically or strategically, as were evident in the MoD interviews—about negative reports about friendly-fire incidents. Indeed, there was clearly an assumption in the Pentagon that the media would, overall, produce a version of events the Pentagon would be happy with:

> ADM. McCREARY: We've learned that we can trust the media.... I think the press have learned that we're not just whacked-out baby killers that just go off on a harebrain's notice and just shoot for the sake of pointing a gun—and quite frankly—I think there were some who believed that.

The policy was *to be seen to* just tell it like it was: that way, neither the media nor the public could claim that they did not know what the American military was doing. Thus, even when U.S. forces were caught attempting to cover up the truth of a negative story, our interviewees skipped over such attempts to embrace the idea that they were happy to see both good and bad news covered. Victoria Clarke, talking about embedding, volunteered the following in relation to the checkpoint incident near Najaf, where an embedded report contradicted the CentCom version of events:

> They did exactly what they should have done, which was open fire on the van.... It was awful.... The only bright spot was here was a tragic incident covered with accuracy and context—because there were a whole bunch of reporters—from several different news organizations. It was a problem.... Awful... it also happens to be the truth.... I don't sign the papers, but if we're willing to commit people to wars, then we ought to handle the responsibility that people get killed and injured—this was an important threshold—embedding is just as important on bad things.

Asked about the same incident, McCreary replied:

> I think that's exactly what we were expecting—that the bad stuff gets reported immediately, that there's no effort or even perception of anybody trying to conceal it. It's put in a context so they can see what the decision-making process was to make that decision to fire—and then they also see how bad people felt when they realized what the outcome was—and I think that contextual thing gets it all out there. Nobody accuses anybody of trying to spin a story—and then it's over, and you get on with the next thing, rather than try and answer it for two or three days. It worked to our advantage—bad news doesn't get better with time—if it's instantaneous, it's done.... You hang out your dirty laundry—everybody knows you've got dirty laundry—and then everybody gets over it.

Interestingly, both responses gloss over the fact that U.S. forces *did* try to "spin the story," subsequently killing the story by promising to set up an inquiry into the incident. McCreary's response was similar on friendly-fire incidents:

> We don't like them—but they happen—if you know about them right away, so much the better.... You can't say the coverage was negative—in some instances you just say the coverage was accurate. We made a mistake—it allowed us to get on with things.

These answers suggest a degree of confidence that the media will not dwell too long on negative stories, and that such stories will be overshadowed by more positive reports.

Jessica Lynch

During CentCom briefings from 2 April 2003, the now notorious story of Private First Class Jessica Lynch began to emerge. On 23 March, a convoy including the nineteen-year-old soldier from the 507th Maintenance Division took a wrong turn and found themselves in a fierce firefight near Nasiriyah. Eleven of her colleagues were killed (including the only female soldier to be killed in action), and Lynch was taken prisoner and held in an Iraqi hospital where she was treated for her injuries.

During the night of 1 April, combined U.S. Special Forces including Army Rangers and Navy Seals staged a rescue operation and recovered Lynch and the bodies of her comrades. This was announced by General Brooks the following day, accompanied by video footage filmed by a military camera team.

In the following days the story gained increasing prominence in, principally, the American media, most notably in the *Washington Post*, which ran stories claiming that Lynch had valiantly fought back despite being wounded herself. There was little mention of her colleagues, and the incident was turned into a dramatic, feel-good, above all, *human-interest* tale at a time when American forces were encountering increasing resistance.

The facts of the operation remain unclear—the level of resistance expected and encountered, the details of Private Lynch's injuries, the details of her time at the hospital have all produced conflicting information (including an official U.S. Army investigation) and considerable speculation, not least as a result of Private Lynch's subsequent celebrity status, book deal, and television movie.

This is the one incident where the Pentagon team did not give quite the same answer to our questions. Whitman had already been questioned about the accuracy of the first version of events on John Kampfner's BBC 2 *Correspondent* documentary "War Spin."[16] There the Pentagon's version of the "heroic rescue of Private Jessica" was questioned through the use of interviews with Iraqi medical personnel at the hospital, where, according to them, she was being cared for and not held prisoner. The program constructs the story as a Hollywood-type *performance* of a rescue by Special Forces, using blanks instead of bullets, for the benefit of cameras. The documentary even contains a clip from a U.S. news program in which reporter Mitchell Catlin apparently inadvertently refers to Lynch as "Private Ryan"—a clear reference to the Steven Spielberg movie *Saving Private Ryan*.

Whitman's only response to questioning about the accuracy of this story was to say that in due course the facts would be known. He has recently reiterated his views of the concerns raised: "It's inconceivable for me to believe that people honestly think there was something other to that rescue than what it really was—a valiant rescue of POWs."[17] While he did not respond to a question from us about this story, Victoria Clarke did. She pointed out that the military had corrected the "firing blanks report" and had in fact been firing "concussion weapons" designed to produce only "noise and shock"[18] and went on to argue that:

> If they could have had embeds, then we would have had a very clear unvarnished picture of what had happened. If you go back and look at our briefings, we very, very much downplayed the Jessica Lynch story.

This is only true to some extent. While statements by General Brooks and by Donald Rumsfeld were brief and ostensibly factual, the incident was repeatedly referred to over several days. In the initial briefing, Brooks refers to the mission as a "classic joint operation done by some of our nation's finest warriors who are dedicated to never leaving a comrade behind," adding, "they are loyal to a creed that they know, that they will never leave a fallen comrade and never embarrass their country."[19] Such emotive language, coupled with a steadfast refusal to either confirm or deny the facts of the operation portrayed in a heavily edited military videotape of the event, were irresistible to the media at a time when the rapid advance appeared to be slowing. It is quite possible that the Pentagon felt able to rely upon the media to play up such a story, and simply provided them with the material with which to do so.

"Militainment"

In the *Correspondent* program, Kampfner draws close parallels between the footage produced by the embeds and scenes in pro-U.S. Hollywood blockbusters, specifically *Black Hawk Down*, produced by Jerry Bruckheimer. A split-screen comparison sequence in the documentary shows the two to be strikingly similar. Of course, this should not come as a surprise, given that Bruckheimer's patriotic reputation has allowed him unprecedented access to military operations and personnel while constructing his films. Further, there is a long history of entertainment and military industries sharing their multimillion-dollar resources, in the development of training simulation environments, for example.[20]

When we inquired about allegations of Bruckheimer's involvement in the planning of the embeds process, Victoria Clarke's response was definitive—"completely untrue"—as was that from Bryan Whitman: "Absolutely ridiculous, no basis in fact at all, and just completely untrue." However, in the summer of 2002, American networks announced a raft of "feel good" reality TV–style series that seem to contradict this view. CBS screened *American Fighter Pilots*, a series documenting the training of three F-15 pilots, and VH1 had commissioned *Military Diaries*, in which sixty soldiers had been provided with digital cameras to record their activities.[21] Again, this is perhaps not surprising, given American and British public fascination with the training and activities of the military.

More compelling, however, is the primetime show *Profiles from the Front Line*. This series, shown on ABC from 27 February 2003, was produced by Jerry Bruckheimer and Bertram van Munster (producer of the successful American reality TV program *Cops*). *Profiles* involved camera crews following American troops on operations in Afghanistan, among other areas, and was given full approval by Vice President Dick Cheney and by Donald Rumsfeld. Judith Gillies (2003), writing in the *Washington Post* explains: "The series makes no attempt to discuss policy issues and whether troops should be there. Rather, it focuses on a variety of individuals, explaining who they are, what they do, and what they think and feel about their efforts." Van Munster further assures the viewer (and the Pentagon) that "obviously we're going to have a pro-military, pro-American stance. We're not going to criticize" ("Reality Show to Focus on Military Operations" 2003).

While such shows may air at any other time without comment, the timing of this particular series and the purpose of it—to demonstrate, via individual characters with whom the audience become familiar, the professionalism of American armed forces engaged in overseas operations in the war against terror—provide a clear echo of the thinking behind the embeds strategy. Vince Ogilvie, who was the Pentagon's project officer for the series, said the interactions of the film crews and military personnel provided "a prelude to the process of embedding" media representatives in military units for war coverage (Gillies 2003).

The Future of Embeds

Overall, those behind the embedding strategy, and to a large extent those directly involved with it (both military and media), seem very satisfied with the results of the coverage during the 2003 Iraq War. Whether embedding becomes the only option for future conflict reporting is less certain and will, of course, depend on the nature of individual conflicts (see, for example, Threadgold and Mosdell 2004). Victoria Clarke appears to be a firm believer in the strategy of personalizing coverage, not just of international conflict, but of domestic issues as well. Talking about the term "embedding," she referred to civilian use of this clearly successful public relations strategy:

> A couple of the power companies now have embedded reporters with their, I was going to say troops, with their workers, to go around and show them what happens when a storm hits, why it is so difficult, so to provide more context and comprehension.[22]

In response to questioning about the policy becoming a form of entertainment comparable to that of reality television, she simply replied: "Well, I don't think that there is anything more real than watching troops fighting on the streets of Baghdad."

Both Pentagon and MoD officials have expressed concerns about the coverage coming from Iraq in the postconflict period (prior to events such as the final storming of Fallujah). Both would have preferred to continue with the embed program after the narrative end of combat operations (the fall of the statue in al-Firdus [Paradise] Square). Admiral McCreary suggests that this was financially prohibitive for news companies—"We haven't stopped, it's them, it's the bean counters from the news organizations"—but also sees embedding as a natural progression of conflict reporting on behalf of both military, politicians, and pertinently, the media in the future:

> In wartime, how would you like to be the next guy that says, "Well, this time we are not going to have an embedded media"? I think you can walk the dog back in narrow circumstances, but I'm not so sure you can walk the dog back broadly.

CHAPTER FOUR

The MoD Perspective

WE INTERVIEWED SIX KEY PERSONNEL at the Ministry of Defence (MoD) who were responsible for the embedding policy from the UK military side. These were Tony Pawson, Director of Corporate Communications; David Howard; Colonel Paul Brook and Lieutenant Colonel Angus Taverner, both responsible for the strategic level of the embeds process; Squadron Leader Tom Rounds, responsible for the tactical level of placement of embeds with units; and Lieutenant Commander Steve Tatham, responsible for the Royal Navy side of the operation within theater.

The interviews took place during August 2003 in Whitehall, London. Two trips were made, the first to interview Squadron Leader Rounds, David Howard, and Colonel Brook and Lieutenant Colonel Taverner (together). On the second visit we interviewed Lieutenant Commander Tatham and Tony Pawson (with Colonel Brook in attendance). The interview schedule was similar to that described in the previous chapter.

This chapter also includes references to two MoD publications that assessed the conduct of the campaign in Iraq—*Operations in Iraq: First Reflections* (July 2003) and *Operations in Iraq: Lessons for the Future* (December 2003).

Introduction

The British military has considerable experience in what has become known as "embedding," to the extent that there exists a code of practice, the *Green Book*, which defines "working arrangements with the media in times of emergency, tension, conflict or war."[1] This document outlines the procedures for dealing with the media that the MoD should adopt during times of conflict or crisis. It arose from the report of General Sir Hugh Beach in the wake of the Falklands conflict of 1982 (during which at least a dozen UK reporters traveled with the taskforce). The *Green Book* is periodically revised, though the last update was in December 2001. A significant revamp had been considered by the MoD in the late 1990s in the light of emerging digital communications technologies, but it was decided that it would be prudent to continue with existing guidelines rather than try to preempt specific conditions for the impending conflict. Colonel Brook told us:

> If we were to be involved in Iraq, all of those things would pop out, but it was probably safer to stick with what you had, in *Green Book* terms, rather than open up Pandora's box just at the very moment people are looking for a peg in the sand.

The aims of the policy are clear: to proactively engage with the media in order to further democratic accountability; to encourage domestic support; and to demonstrate the professionalism and efficiency of British armed forces. The last two objectives, one could argue, certainly seem to have been achieved, as they often are when British forces are engaged in conflict, as demonstrated by the shift in public opinion in the UK (see Chapter 8). Indeed, during the conflict, the secretary for defence, Geoff Hoon, noted the effects of the embeds' footage in particular:

> I believe the public's understanding of what our troops are achieving is increased by the access we've given the media. The professionalism, courage, dedication, restraint of the British and coalition forces shone through. The imagery they [the embeds] broadcast is at least partially responsible for the public's change in mood, with the majority of people now saying they back the coalition.[2]

Communication between the MoD and the public via the media is also intended to emphasize the key messages of the particular campaign. In the case of Operation Telic (the UK military operation in Iraq), the publicized intention was the removal of a brutal and deceptive regime, rather than invasion and conquest. Tony Pawson explained:

Well, clearly it is important for operational news and letting be known the changes in procedures and objectives, and for letting Iraqis know that they weren't being targeted, that the regime was being targeted.

This was echoed by Lieutenant Commander Tatham:

So my primary mission out there was to what we call win the media battle space, and I had two important objectives. One was to defeat enemy propaganda, and the second was to get our information operations across. The prime one was that we are here to liberate, not conquer.

In addition to regular information briefings, a preferred technique in presenting the military to the public is to personalize it through appearances by servicemen; in this respect there are similarities with the American approach: "Our best spokesmen," Tatham stated, "are our commanding officers, our pilots, our sailors, or whoever it may be, our Royal Marines" (see Chapter 3 for the American approach; see Chapter 2 for the background to the overall information operations and communications strategy from the UK perspective).

In contrast to the American policy, however, Tatham suggested there was far less integration and political involvement from the British government in the logistics of the embed program:

It would be fair to say, certainly during the planning phase of this, we didn't talk to Downing Street, they were aware of the plans because we briefed them, but there was no input from Downing Street to say, "You must embed this amount of correspondents," or whatever.

Downing Street was certainly made aware of the progress of the media campaign, however, through daily briefings in reaction to overnight reports, press cuttings, and to organize the political response. These briefings became known as the "morning prayer meetings" and were attended by MoD media operations personnel, representatives from the three branches of the armed forces, and political advisers from the office of the defence secretary, as well as, on occasion, representatives from the Defence Intelligence Services.[3] Downing Street was clearly satisfied with the overall media strategy, at least concerning the coverage of combat operations; the director of news at the MoD, Pam Teare, has since become press secretary to Geoff Hoon.

Information Operations

American and the British forces diverged significantly in their organization and handling of the media-embedding policy, both politically and operationally. In part, this was a result of differing experience with frontline war correspondents. It was also influenced, however, by the political background to the conflict on both sides of the Atlantic. The American public, according to opinion polls, was largely in favor of military action in the Gulf and was perhaps less demanding of a political overview or justification:

> LT. COL. TAVERNER: The Americans were talking, yes, way back in September, more formally; it was, perhaps, because I think the Americans thought they were more likely to go to war than we did.

This is not to say that the UK forces were not making preparations for war, but that they did not wish to be seen to be doing so, as Tatham explained:

> The U.S. was proactive, force on mind. Daily they were taking the media out, showing jets leaving, showing troops training, they would do large fire exercises. They were saying, "If you don't come to the diplomatic table, this is what you are going to get." They were our biggest allies, and we had no media profile at all. So as a consequence, when journalists went to visit U.S. Marines who had Royal Marines embedded with them, the Royal Marines would have to hide by the tents. When the journalists went on board aircraft carriers, the Royal Naval liaison officers had to go and hide somewhere else on the ship.

Indeed, the implementation of a media operation on this scale was complicated for the MoD by the continuing attempts to arrive at a diplomatic solution to the crisis, and the necessity of avoiding a public stance that presumed inevitable military action. However, it was felt to be desirable to highlight the buildup and preparedness of troops in the region to the Iraqi regime—a technique that our interviewees referred to as "force on mind"—as an additional incentive to Iraq to consider the diplomatic routes that were, at that time, still available:

> COL. BROOK: On the one hand, we were sure that war was neither imminent nor inevitable, because clearly the diplomatic effort needed to continue, but at the same time we needed to make it absolutely crystal clear to the Iraq regime that we meant business, and that creates a dilemma. On the one hand, you want to highlight your military capability and its preparedness and its training and its efficiency, but on the other hand, you don't want to do that in a way that means back home that war is inevitable.

Tatham further illustrated this point and also commented on some of the political difficulties that were specific to the area of operations:

> We then had the practice landings, and we had them in a couple of places around the region. For us, that is a massive information operations opportunity. Coer-

cive thought—we were able to say to Saddam, "Watch this, we'll bring the media down, watch our capability, watch how well we do this, you might want to think about that diplomatic process a little bit harder than you are thinking at the moment." We weren't allowed to, because it was too "force on mind," given the profile that existed at the time, and also because there were regional sensitivities as well, because the places where we were doing these landings didn't want to be thrust into the public light at the time of Arab solidarity and so on.

In the period before combat commenced (and, to a lesser extent, since the early 1990s), both British and American forces conducted a prolonged and considerable campaign of psychological operations, designed to influence the will and morale of the Iraqi regime. American psychological operations began in October 2002 and included bombing missions in the no-fly zones, airdrops of some forty million leaflets, an e-mail and text message campaign targeting key Iraqi politicians and scientists, and flights by "Commando Solo," a modified military aircraft capable of broadcasting Arabic radio signals.[4] The Select Committee on Defence suggested that British information operations did not begin early enough in this campaign.[5] While the media operations personnel we spoke to were keen to distance themselves from the more covert information operations, the ideas of "coercive thought" expressed above perhaps represent some blurring of the two. In the case of these training displays, the mass media are delivering the force-on-mind message to the Iraqi population via internationally available television news. Some argue that using media in this way may actually constitute counterinformation: during the 1991 campaign to liberate Kuwait, similar displays of practiced beach landings were allegedly used to deliberately deceive Iraqi forces into expecting a seaborne assault. This use of media, even if to deceive the enemy, provokes controversy:

> If training, perhaps an amphibious landing even, were underway, there would be nothing wrong about inviting the media to observe the capability in action. The use of the capability would, after all, be an option. If the media then, without encouragement from military spokespersons, inaccurately speculated about the significance of the training, would that be the military's fault?[6]

While the MoD policy for media operations is one of "absolute and demonstrable truth," the overall information strategy is one of integrated media operations and information and counterinformation operations (PsyOps).[7] All of the MoD personnel we interviewed were from the media operations department, involved in the day-to-day practicalities of the operation, which forms the bulk of this chapter. It is clear, however, that this was only a part of the overall information campaign (see Chapter 2).

Embedding: Philosophy and Background

The MoD decided (according to Lt. Cdr. Tatham and Squadron Leader Rounds) that only those journalists holding British passports would be embedded with British forces. Access to footage of British military operations was possible to all through the pooling system, whereby all material that involved British forces would be available at a central location, regardless of the network association of the filing correspondents. Embeds working with American forces had exclusive rights to their footage, due in part to the differences in the scale of military operations: the American military simply had a greater capacity to accommodate a larger number of journalists.

With hindsight, the MoD concedes that the lack of representation of the Arabic networks such as al-Jazeera and Abu Dhabi TV was a weakness in the battle for the hearts and minds of the Arab "street."[8] Again, this is something of a consequence of the political situation in the area: it was simply not possible to transfer journalists from such networks through the countries of assembly and embarkation, because the governments of those countries had issues with these broadcasters. There were also some security concerns, as explained by Lt. Cdr. Tatham:

> The difficulty with al-Jazeera is that they weren't allowed into Bahrain by the Bahrain authorities, therefore they couldn't get on board any British ships who were stationed out at Bahrain. They weren't allowed into Kuwait by the Kuwait authorities, therefore they couldn't get into British units in Kuwait. We felt that we could keep reasonable control of British journalists, and if we explained to them the context under which they would be learning privileged information, then it wouldn't go further. We didn't take the same view of, say, putting a Syrian journalist on board, or a Lebanese journalist, or whoever it may be. It was an unknown quantity.

The Process of Embedding

Informal discussions between the MoD and the media began in October 2002, with an Anglo-American consultation (Exercise Internal Look) taking place in December of that year. Because there are no existing overarching organizations for broadcast news, the Ministry's representative, Squadron Leader Tom Rounds, established an adhoc committee with representatives from the main television news-gathering organizations—ITN, the BBC, and Sky—to be chaired by Ian Glover James from ITN. During the following three months, the committee established the operational details, allocating each fighting unit a maximum of five media placements. Usually only two of these would be representatives of television news—a camera operator and a reporter—the remainder being print or radio journalists. Military units provided the MoD with the number of correspondents that they could accommodate and any unique operational requirements (for example, the parachute and marine regiments elected not to have any female correspondents, on the grounds that these units operate on foot at a fast rate once deployed to theater—something of a broad assumption given the fitness levels of journalists, regardless of gender). The broadcasting organizations were then asked to fill the available positions as they saw fit. According to Rounds, the MoD steadfastly refused to be drawn into negotiations about the placement of particular organizations with particular units, since they had a strong desire to be seen as impartial:

> The number of phone calls I had, from very senior officers all the way down to reporters to editors, all trying to maneuvre to get into a better position, and senior officers saying, "So-and-so, worked with him in Bosnia two years ago, I'd like him in my unit," and I would say, "Sorry, out of my hands," and it was a deliberate ploy on our part, and a sensible one as things turned out, not to get involved in the selections, and a lot of pressure I came under, unnecessary pressure, I have to say, given the enormity of what I was dealing with here, came from people wanting a better position, a better fighting unit.

With hindsight, some at the MoD would have preferred this process to have worked differently. The importance of remaining impartial in the allocation of journalists meant that both military and media did not always achieve the placements that they felt would work best:

> LT. CDR. TATHAM: The *Sun* was a prime one, who always support British troops, who said, "We want to be with the Royal Marine Commandos," and we wanted them with the Royal Marine Commandos, but in the luck of the draw, the organization that went with the Royal Marines was the *Daily Mirror*, which was the biggest antiwar newspaper in the UK. So, not only could the *Sun* not believe it, neither could the *Mirror* believe that they had got the plum job, and the Royal Marines couldn't believe it, either. They were ringing me and saying, "This guy is antiwar, why is he with us?"

From the outset it was made clear that an embed placement was permanent. Once embedded, a correspondent could not choose to move to another unit and, although provision was made to transport those who desired to leave their units, there was to be no possibility of "reembedding," either with the same unit at a later stage or with a different one. The reason for this was not simply that it would cause inconvenience to the units, but also that the embedding program was oversubscribed from the outset:

the MoD received more than nine hundred applications. The nature of the operation meant that those who were embedded with naval units saw a great deal of the early stages—when the opening salvos and air strikes commenced, and troops and helicopters disembarked—but from then on the campaign became essentially a ground war for the British forces. Some of these embeds decided to leave to work independently in Kuwait, and a few were able to take the place of other embeds who had voluntarily left their placements. The early days of the operation were a source of frustration for those involved in the naval side of the campaign, in the media and in the MoD:

> LT. CDR. TATHAM: We then had the assault, and this was our Achilles' heel, and people say, "Well, I didn't know the navy was involved," and the reason was for fourteen hours we had complete media blackout, not just a media blackout, but also encon mission control, so all of our radios were turned off, my sonars were turned off, everything was shut off, because they were literally five miles off the coast of Iraq, flying in wave after wave after wave of Royal Marine Commandos. If we had broadcast that fact, then Saddam would have sent his missiles down and his suicide boats, so for fourteen hours we had no coverage at all, and then we did have the coverage fourteen hours later—the battle had moved ashore, and the Royal Marines were fighting around the port complex, they were fighting on gas and oil platforms. The story had moved ashore, and no one was interested in what the navy had done, and therefore now no one knows what the navy did because of that fourteen-hour blackout. The U.S. Navy didn't have that policy, because they were much farther down the Gulf launching aircraft, jet aircraft, and of course, they had journalists on board. There was no sensitivity about where they were; they were South of Bahrain, no difficulty at all.

Notably, in this case the military's desire for positive coverage was frustrated by their own operational security restrictions, imposed by their location.

Training and Placement of Embeds

Although most news organizations regularly run staff training programs for hazardous environments, the accreditation process set out in the *Green Book* requires correspondents to undergo some form of military preparation, so that they do not become an unnecessary burden on their unit. In this case, the training involved courses in first aid, mines awareness, water rationing, and so on, as well as aspects of nuclear and biological warfare pertinent to modern warfare and this conflict in particular. Additionally, all journalists were provided with the relevant protective clothing and apparatus. Scenes of veteran broadcasters—familiar to so many for bringing the evening domestic news into the living room—struggling with gas masks and NBC (Nuclear Biological & Chemical) suits are an enduring image of the 2003 Iraq War.

Formal briefings with the media began in late January 2003 and continued, alongside the training program, throughout February, with the bulk of the correspondents being dispatched to the Gulf around March 11.

> SQUADRON LEADER ROUNDS: That's how close it was, and on the 11th they left, went to theater, and they had literally a week before the whole thing kicked off. Two weeks would have been ideal, because it would have allowed them time to embed with the units that they were with, and generally get themselves settled in to how that unit works, how it fights, who the individuals are, what area the unit comes from, all of the information that you need to file reports on a fighting unit. That would have been the ideal. Of course, you can pick any date, three weeks would have been too much, and by the eight-day point they would have started to get bored, and you know that you'd end up with articles being written that we didn't necessarily want, so it was a very fine judging issue here.

There is general agreement in both the media and the MoD that this situation was not ideal, although the issue was clouded not only by the delicate political situation, but also by the logistical requirements of transporting thousands of troops and associated vehicles and equipment to the Middle East. In the event, the unwanted articles Rounds mentions did begin to emerge, to the disgruntlement of the MoD and the government, who were scathing of reports of ill-equipped troops and malfunctioning equipment.[9] Eventually, the MoD was forced to counter these reports with organized facilities showing troop buildup:

> LT. CDR. TATHAM: The media got nothing that they wanted at all. We had growing at the time a number of silly stories developing. We had the Royal Marines being called the borrowers in the press because they were taking equipment from the Americans. We had the *Sun* running their "send-a-toilet-roll-to-our-gallant-boys-in-the-forces" campaign, you know, ridiculous, so we finally, because of these ridiculous stories, convinced the powers that be that we needed to run some harder-hitting stories, and it also came at a time when the diplomatic process was clearly failing, and now was a good time to have some coercive thought. So we had another facility where we took sixty-five journalists onto Ark Royal, we steamed all of the other ships in the task force past, we had helicopters, we had Royal Marines, weapons and it looked quite tough stuff.

A further complication was the relative lack of experience of some journalists, and a lack of comprehension of the military's capacity to accommodate the amount of technical equipment the media wanted to bring into theater. This was a source of frustration for Tatham:

> No comprehension at all, and this will be a recurring theme, I suspect, in our discussion, is the complete absence of any understanding, even common-sense real-world events, with journalists. If they are defence correspondents, they know, they know it takes a long time to get on a helicopter to do this, to do that, they need to wear this and that. If you're the education correspondent, or you're the feature writer for the *Mirror* or something, they were the people selected, not by us, and you have never seen a warship before this, comes as a great mystery to you, and lack of real-world common sense was a big factor in all of this.

This contrasts starkly with the collaborative efforts between media organizations and the Pentagon, in terms of "comfort levels" and mutual technological awareness. Nonetheless, the vast majority of embeds were positioned within their respective units before the bulk of the forces moved over the border into Iraq.

Hub and Spokes

During the initial consultation period between the MoD and the media, the concept of "hub and spokes" emerged. This model, based on previous experience in the first Gulf War and the realization that this was to be a "TV-led" war (as Rounds suggested), was designed to provide the overall context for the anticipated flood of unit-specific reports from the front. The MoD and the media envisioned that material from the embedded reporters (the "spokes") would be transferred to a dedicated news center (the "hub") for two main reasons. The first concerned operational security: the hub was designed to be the press center from which the majority of broadcasts would take place, not as single pieces to camera by embeds, but as high-picture-quality packages presented by an anchor. This would involve the presence of multiple cameras and studio lighting, as well as editing facilities and the heavyweight satellite equipment required to transmit the material to the United Kingdom. A concentration of such technology emits a considerable "electronic footprint" that may interfere with military communications and would be electronically visible to Iraqi forces, something that the fighting units were obviously eager to avoid. The second reason was that the focus of embeds' reports would inevitably be "deep but narrow," as Colonel Brook eloquently put it, like "looking through a smartie tube, through a net curtain, at night."[10]

The function of the hub was to provide a platform for context, analysis, and informed speculation about the overall strategy, a place where the dramatic pictures from the front lines could be packaged with contextual material provided by the senior military commanders there and from CentCom, the American-led press center in Qatar.

The hub was officially referred to as the Forward Transmissions Unit (FTU) and traveled with the senior British military command, initially based in Kuwait and then moving forward into Iraq as the operation progressed. In addition to providing a relatively stable base for the anchors and the less mobile editing and broadcasting equipment, the FTU also afforded briefing opportunities with senior commanders and MoD spokespersons, and offered opportunities to travel to sites of particular interest around the region: a provision which led to journalists speculating that FTU stood for "Fuck the Unilaterals."[11]

In fact, this arrangement proved frustrating for both media and MoD from the outset. As the campaign progressed, the focus of reports quickly became dominated by copy from the embeds. This was a result of three factors: first, dissatisfaction with the credibility and quality of information from CentCom; second, confusion on the part of journalists at the FTU about what could and could not be reported as context (compounded as the first casualties were taken). Finally, the death of Terry Lloyd, an independent (unilateral) journalist traveling in the south of Iraq, which resulted in the withdrawal of most journalists not traveling under the protection (and ultimately the control) of the troops.

CentCom Failings

As the first bombs fell on Baghdad, in a sudden strike against a "target of opportunity,"[12] the Americans imposed a news embargo at CentCom that left the MoD bewildered:

> COL. BROOK: The first thing that happened on D-Day was that Qatar simply closed down, and they put a news blackout in place at the very moment we knew we had the world's attention in Qatar, the very moment we could use that opportunity to start setting the operational objectives in context, to start talking about what we really meant by "shock and awe," and how we wanted to target specifically the regime rather than the Iraqi people. All of those things were utterly lost, because they simply went [clicks fingers] and switched the switch off.

The American reasoning for the blackout was that any information may have revealed the intention of the ongoing operation to the regime, as well as compromising internal intelligence sources. CentCom subsequently (almost two days later) gave some details of the aims and accomplishments of this mission, but by then, as discussed later in this chapter, the story had moved on. For MoD personnel at CentCom, this approach was extremely frustrating and counter to their own intentions for the media operation at this point:

> Having lost the first skirmish, they [the US CentCom media personnel] pretty much lost the war when it came to media support. And albeit things have got better and everything came to a conclusion quite rapidly, my feeling is that they lost their initial part of the campaign and they never got on the front foot again.
>
> The media adviser here [Simon Wren, seconded from the MoD] was an expert in his field. His counterpart on the U.S. side [James Wilkinson] was evasive, was not around as much as he should have been when it came to talking to the media, and in reality what happened was you had two different styles of news media management and I feel fortunate to be, have been part of the UK one.[13]

Within hours the British had broken the embargo and were able to begin transmissions again, but the sudden commencement of hostilities meant that there was little to give the waiting media in terms of strategic announcements.

> COL. BROOK: Not only was there a blackout, but there was also inertia. Another good reason for the inertia was that nothing had happened. In the first, all there was in the first twenty-four hours was utter confusion. There was a lack of clarity on progress, lack of clarity on a whole bunch of things, and clearly if all the information that you've got in PJHQ [Permanent Joint Head Quarters] is not, gobbledygook, but it's not sorted out, you're simply not in a position to brief comprehensively and effectively, so those things put together really...I think there is an expectation in a lot of people's minds, and I think that's reflected in how the media go about their business, that we sit somewhere, and somebody looks the assembled group in the eye and says, "Gentlemen, we are at war." Nothing could be farther from the truth. Nothing could be farther than the truth.

Many of the Press Relations Officers (PROs) were regular or reserve service personnel required to perform a media relations role in addition to their regular duties (so-called double-hatters), and the MoD have also expressed concern at the lack of interpreters and trained media operations personnel on the ground.[14]

Restrictions on Information

Despite concerns expressed by journalists and commentators about the potential for military censorship associated with the embedding program, the MoD stressed that the only limitations to copy would be to avoid any compromise to operational security or regarding the issue of casualty reporting, as discussed further below. Many journalists with whom we've spoken were amazed at the amount of information that the high command and individual unit commanders gave them about the overall battle plan before the commencement of hostilities. Some were given personal briefings of the entire strategy and were encouraged to ask as many questions as they wished. Bill Neely, ITN correspondent embedded with 42 British Royal Marine Commandos, explained his feelings about this:

> So within forty-eight hours after that meeting he said, "Right, come to the back," and it was all labeled top secret, and it was tremendously impressive, and he went in, and basically there were maps laid out on a couple of tables like this, and maps on the wall, and he said, "Right, I'm going to tell you the entire battle plan," and he proceeded for the next hour to tell us not just what he and his men and we were going to do, but the entire plan for the entire invasion of Iraq. The plan to hit Baghdad fast, to bypass the main cities, not to get dragged into little fights trying to secure little towns that don't mean anything, but to go, as the jargon had it, "Why cut off the tail of the fish if you can go straight for the head?" So that was the idea. And I left that tent thinking, "Wow." Even having been in journalism since 1981, I thought, "This is a bloody heavy responsibility here. You've just been given the entire secret of the invasion, don't fuck it up."

This clearly reflects the change in strategy on the part of the MoD. Whereas in previous conflicts there was a definite system of blue-pencil censorship (even the word "censored" was censored during the Falklands campaign[15]), the emerging policy is a far more subtle one of managing a largely complicit media, brought on board and on message by apparent transparency.

For obvious security reasons, the majority of this information was for background purposes and was not permitted to be broadcast. On the whole, the MoD was satisfied with the behavior of the journalists in this respect, although in the first few days at least, there was considerable friction between the military and the media, at the FTU in particular, as to what material would not compromise future operations and what could be used as context to the initial confusion. The MoD believes that this was in part due to some self-censorship on the part of the correspondents: some not wishing to jeopardize the relationships thus far established, some feeling the weight of responsibility (as illustrated by Bill Neely) and not fully understanding the definitions of operational security. The irritability of commanders and spokespersons, who had been somewhat caught out by the sudden demand for information, didn't help the situation:

> COL. BROOK: Also, in information terms, there was a frustration in that we people, commanders particularly in those frontline units, went out of their way

to tell the journalists and the correspondents what was going on, what the plans were, and why things were as they were, which they then couldn't use, because it was almost a self-imposed, because they thought, and a lot of them, a lot of the commanders have said, "Well, why haven't you said more about this?" and the correspondents have said, "Well, you know, we thought we couldn't, and we thought we shouldn't." So there was a real amount of friction there. Yes, they were getting great information, but it wasn't great information that they could then use.

Lieutenant Colonel Taverner echoed his colleague's impressions:

> I think large numbers of them were quite surprised that they could hear the commanding officer of the unit give them contents, operation, and plan for battle, they thought, "Well, blimey." As Paul [Colonel Brook] was saying, that sort of imposed a self-censorship on them.

Casualty Reporting

The complications of operational security restrictions were further compounded by the second night of the operation, when British forces began to take casualties, not as a result of combat, but through accidents and "friendly fire" (also known as "blue-on-blue" incidents). Around midnight on 21 March 2003, a Sea Knight helicopter crashed with the loss of all on board—eight British soldiers and four American aircrew. The following night, two Sea King helicopters collided, resulting in the deaths of six British and one American servicemen. On 23 March, a tornado aircraft was downed by what turned out to be a U.S. Patriot-missile battery, resulting in the loss of the two crew members. As outlined above, the only situations in which the MoD was explicit about limitations to correspondents' reports were for reasons of operational security or during times of casualty reporting. As the *Green Book* (73) stipulates:

> The MOD is anxious to maintain close co-operation with editors during hostile operations on the question of casualties. It recognizes that casualty information is of legitimate interest to the media and the public but it faces the difficulty that reports of casualties from individual operations could be of intelligence value to an enemy.
>
> However, while there may be occasions when the MOD will be forced to delay the release of casualty information for security reasons, in general it will aim to make announcements of losses and numbers of casualties as soon as possible after they are confirmed. (For practical purposes, this might be at set times.)
>
> It may be necessary to identify an individual group, unit, or ship which has been lost and to give details of the scale of casualties and/or survivors before

next of kin have been informed—either to minimise anxiety which might be caused to families whose loved ones are not involved, or to counter enemy propaganda.

The issue of how and when to report these incidents caused considerable tension so early in the campaign, when information for an overall strategic context for the border crossing was scarce. This, coupled with the fact that these were "friendly-fire" incidents, made these casualties the first real story of the war.

> COL. BROOK: I think that the heightened awareness amongst the media and the general public is that it happened in [the first] Gulf War…and it resulted in them being aware of it, so it was almost on the media agenda, and then, lo and behold, it happened again, so they picked up on it, and also the circumstances are always pretty dire, and they are great stories.
>
> And this little vignette is blasted to strategic proportions, and if you take that against the background of news blackouts and, if you like, the fog of war, in terms of our ability to extract meaningful information and the present the picture, that's where we were in the first two or three days. The debate is whether we actually managed to catch up. I don't know.
>
> LT. CDR. TATHAM: It's worth saying that we had terrible problems with this. We have a policy that we do not release the names of those who have died until the families have been told, and the minute the aircraft went down, the BBC reported that two Sea King helicopters had collided, and it was expected that there were no survivors. I spent the best part of two hours saying to them, "You have reported Sea King helicopters, and the entire Sea King community, comprising thirty helicopters times all of their families back in the UK, is now in a state of turmoil, could you be more precise in your reporting?"

In our interview, David Howard recounts the Tornado incident in a slightly different way, but is no less disparaging toward the BBC. He received a call from theater informing him of the loss of the aircraft, and within seconds CNN was on the telephone, asking him to confirm the details, as a correspondent with American forces had actually seen the event. He claims that he then confirmed details with his commanders in the field and asked CNN's global communications director not to release the story for a few hours.

> HOWARD: He said, "Dave, we're Coalition, we're in this together," and he said, "We'll hold on to it as long as you want us to hold on to it. You know, just to make sure our boys our looked after," and I couldn't believe it. I said, "Thanks, if they hold on to it for five hours until the finish, the search and rescue" and I just knew that had that been the BBC.

Overall, though, the MoD appears to be reasonably content with the way that such incidents were dealt with over the course of the war, once the initial misunderstandings had been ironed out.

> LT. COL. TAVERNER: Broadly speaking, the embedded correspondents in particular were well aware of who had been killed, and the names of who they were, and they may have known them, and throughout that was respected, and the appropriate way in which the announcement was made, that announcement was sent through, in every case we were able to inform next of kin, and all of the necessary processes had been gone through before we made the details public, and again, that was a relationship and arrangement that worked for both sides, and we were immensely grateful to the media for staying within that, which, considering sometimes how the tabloid press particularly can break away, was remarkable.

One later casualty incident illustrates the dilemma facing MoD media operations personnel in theater with regard to the reporting of difficult stories. On 28 March, an American A-10 "tankbuster" aircraft mistakenly opened fire on a British patrol from the Household Cavalry north of Basra, destroying two armored vehicles, injuring four soldiers, and killing one. The survivors were evacuated to the hospital ship HMS Argus, where they were interviewed by a columnist from the *Times of London* newspaper. Lt. Cdr. Tatham gave us his account of the incident:

> He filed copy under the headline "U.S. cowboys murdered my mate," which subsequently went on the front page of the *Times*. This was where there was some pressure to remove, which I fought against, because he had strictly adhered to the guidelines of the *Green Book*. There was also some pressure to remove the public relations officer from the ship, which was unfair, and again I fought against that, because he had also adhered to the guidance of the *Green [Book]*, as had I, which said that you could remove matters of operational security, but you cannot remove views or opinions stated....
>
> It ended up on my e-mail machine and I thought, "This is going to be in front of the secretary of state and in front of the prime minister tomorrow, and I'm going to be in a lot of trouble over this," and you think, "I've got to send it." And it's a horrible feeling, and you send it, and you think, "I wonder how quick the phone will ring." Four minutes: "Ah, hello," and there it was. It went to the Ministry [of Defence], and it went to the prime minister, and it went to the Americans, and the president got involved, and it became a terrible issue.

> HOWARD: They were pretty critical in their comments of their American colleagues, having been shot at by them, and it was played up in the media, and it was on the television. "Cowboys," I think was the word used, a time-wasting story basically.... That interview should never have been allowed to take place. I don't blame the embed. I don't blame the soldiers at all. I just blame that fact

that they were able to carry out that interview, because it is bad, it's not fair on the soldiers, it's not even though they may have wanted to talk.

There is a certain irony about the difficulties of casualty reporting that is central to the "human face" of the embeds program. There can be no doubt that the restrictions and delays on any footage or announcements are entirely reasonable for both personal (next of kin) and operational (security) motives. However, bringing the public closer to the action by encouraging the story to be told by the individual combatants involved is somewhat diluted by the fact that the reality of their actions, either to the enemy or to themselves, can rarely be shown. When al-Jazeera broadcast footage of British soldiers allegedly executed by Iraqi forces (although this later proved to be false), Air Marshall Brian Burridge was publicly out-raged:

> The decision by al-Jazeera to broadcast such material is deplorable, and we call upon them to desist from future broadcasts of such a nature. I appreciate that all media outlets have a strong desire for "exclusive" pictures, and we have no desire to limit journalistic freedom in any way. However, all media outlets must be aware of the limits of taste and decency and be wary that they do not unwit-tingly become tools for Iraqi propaganda.[16]

A recurring metaphor in our interviews was that the frontline positions were the "tip of the spear." It seems that it is acceptable to display those at the tip of the spear, but only to show the professional way in which the spear is held, not the direct effect to which the spear is put, nor the capa-bilities of the enemy's own spear.

The Withdrawal of Unilaterals

After the uncertainty about CentCom information credibility and the boundaries of reportable material, the third major setback for the envis-aged "hub and spokes" model of embedded journalism was the death of ITN correspondent Terry Lloyd. On 22 March, the media convoy in which he was traveling near Basra came under fire, resulting in Lloyd's death and injuries to cameraman Daniel Demoustier, who later reported that the incident was a result of American military action. At the time of writing this book, two others in the convoy—cameraman Fred Nerac and translator Hussein Osman—were still missing. ITN immediately with-drew all unilateral journalists from Iraq, and many other organizations' independent representatives became understandably extremely cautious, not returning in significant numbers until the combat situation in the south of the country became more settled.

The 2003 Iraq War was a particularly dangerous one for independent journalists. At least sixteen reporters and associated cameramen and translators died during the three weeks of the major combat operations. In addition to deaths and injuries caused by accidents and natural causes, ten were killed as a result of military action. Only three were killed by the direct actions of the Iraqis—one from small-arms fire and two from artillery. None were killed by British forces. The death toll of independent journalists in the battlefield appears to be a consequence of American military policy. While the claim that the American forces deliberately targeted independent journalists is debatable—the incident at the Palestine hotel has yet to be explained beyond doubt[17]—the American military policy of maximum force, combined with an atmosphere of anxious suspicion heightened by the "asymmetric" nature of the Iraqi response (suicide bombers, allegations of combatants abandoning their uniforms for civilian clothing, allegations of fire from those apparently waving a surrender flag) clearly contributed to the dangers.

The Pentagon's policy toward unilaterals differed from the outset to that of the MoD. From their initial briefings with news chiefs, it is clear that the Americans aimed to deter independents. Some journalists to whom we have spoken suggested that forces in theater were not only unprepared to accommodate them, but in some cases were openly hostile. The MoD appeared more resigned to the presence of unilaterals in the area, but recognized that they became a serious problem as the conflict progressed, and the dangers to them became an issue for all involved.

All journalists in a theater of operations are required to register with the MoD—to become accredited. The MoD does recognize, however, that not all accredited correspondents wish to become "embedded," and the *Green Book* makes provisions in these circumstances that the military provide access to facilities and briefings, though on a more limited basis than that for those traveling with units. The most salient difference in this conflict is the provision of safety, outlined in the *Green Book*:

> Media representatives who gain access to operational areas, other than under the auspices of MOD or Allied PR staffs, should appreciate that they do so at their own risk and that neither MOD nor Allied staffs can be held responsible for their safety or assistance. (52)

After the death of Terry Lloyd, and as the casualties among independent journalists began to mount, the distinction between unilateral and embedded journalists became blurred. One of the most successful independents, Jeremy Thompson from Sky News, was able to move with relative freedom during daylight, but was also able to attach himself informally to military units at night and sometimes while traveling. This was very much a consequence of his reputation with British troops and the fact that he was able to offer them some "perks" (such as being able to pull down Sky Sports with his broadcasting equipment). All such deals were made with commanders on the ground and were frowned upon by the MoD; Press Relations Officers at the FTU had already come under considerable pressure from the embeds there over the facilities offered to groups of independents journalists compared to their relatively fixed location.

> HOWARD: The unilaterals caused a lot of problems, because we were getting a lot of pressure from various organizations to try and offer protection. What the unilaterals were doing, is going, you know, they were unilaterals by day and looking for refuge at night, that's what they were doing. And that pissed off the embeds.
>
> I don't remember any meeting where we huddled together and said, "What can we do [about] the reporting of the unilaterals?" We huddled together and said, "What can we do about the safety of the unilaterals?"

The MoD were certainly concerned about this issue. Not only do journalists begin to complain when there are differences in reporting ability, but the dangerous situation in which the unilaterals found themselves was of serious concern, and also brought pressure on active military units to divert resources to the protection of journalists on occasions (see the similar situations regarding U.S. troops referred to by Victoria Clarke in the preceding chapter). Lt. Col. Taverner suggested,

> I think it's worth speculating at this point that it may be that there is a midway house that we should examine, basically where you are not a fully accredited war correspondent, but you nevertheless enjoy some kind of protected status.

Embeds as the Focus

The immediate impact on the broadcast coverage was a dramatic shift in balance from the intended trinity of CentCom, the FTU (packaging the footage from embeds), and the unilaterals to a focus on embedded reports:

> COL. BROOK: All of a sudden, what should have been simply a part of a broader landscape, war correspondents and all the others, for a variety of reasons, they became a center of gravity, and it put an awful lot of pressure on them as

individuals, because they were having to fill twenty-four hours of programs, and it was the only story.

Now the embedded reporters began to come into their own. Broadcasters, journalists, and the MoD realized the powerful veracity of live, frontline reports that began to flow back to London in increasingly greater numbers, bypassing the FTU.

> LT. COL. TAVERNER: I think there was one other aspect, which was probably recognized, but we didn't take huge regard of, and that was the impact, well, no, the fact, that war correspondents could produce imagery in near real time, even if it was clunky videophone.

> COL. BROOK: I think the broadcasters themselves underestimated the power of that shaky videophone image.
> I think coming to grips, we've described how the embeds became the center of gravity, so you got this machine-gun-burst by machine-gun-burst coverage of the war, and the frustration here shared by ourselves and Downing Street was there seemed to be no ability or opportunity to sort of put that into context, and the war correspondents were, if you like, blamed for that by ourselves and shared over the road because the stuff was just too good. If you're an editor and you've got the choice of running gun battle in Al Nasiriya and a chap doing a briefing in Qatar, there is no contest, and that was extremely frustrating.

It is worth noting the figures from the content analysis forthcoming in Chapter 6. Footage from embeds constitutes a considerable proportion of broadcast news content, compared to very little from the official military briefings. Tumber and Palmer give similar figures from their research, suggesting that far more attention was paid to the conduct of the war than the purposes of the operations in television news bulletins (2004, 101–102). Concerns are also raised about the lack of context in *Lessons Learned* and the Select Committee on Defence (487–492) note that "the mass of tactical level detail which formed the bulk of the reports from the embedded journalists obscured the overall strategic picture and that the result was to give disproportionate importance to minor engagements."

The Impact of Twenty-Four-Hour News: Inaccuracy, Interpretation, and Information Loops

The importance and reliability of information and communications have been of considerable concern in the debates surrounding the justification, the prosecution and the reporting of the 2003 Iraq War. In the days before the war began, there were several stories regarding the mass defection of Iraqi troops and senior figures (see the *Times of London*, 18 March, 2003) that later proved to be unfounded. Both during and after the war, incorrect reporting of particular incidents has been analyzed amid claims of spin, misinformation, and even propaganda from military and media sources. The MoD argues that some of this misreporting is due to correspondents' lack of understanding of military operations, but also concedes that the pressure to feed the appetite of twenty-four-hour news coverage led to premature briefings that were not always entirely accurate.

Umm Qasr

For at least four days from 20 March onward, there were reports that Umm Qasr had been "secured" by British and American forces, yet fighting in the area continued for several days. This port town on the Faw peninsula was one of the primary objectives of the campaign, since it is Iraq's only deep-water port and was therefore crucial for resupply of the military operation and for delivery of humanitarian aid. The briefings by senior American officials certainly contributed to the inaccurate reporting. In a Department of Defense briefing on 21 March 2003, Donald Rumsfeld stated:

> The regime is starting to lose control of their country. Yesterday, the Iraqi information minister declared that the port of Umm Qasr is "completely in our hands," quote/unquote. Quote: "They [the Coalition forces] failed to capture it," unquote. In fact, Coalition forces did capture it and do control the port of Umm Qasr, and also a growing portion of the country of Iraq.[18]

Some reports from embeds, particularly those with Royal Marine Commandos, continued to reiterate claims that Umm Qasr had been taken, yet others showed fierce firefights around the town. Interviewees at the MoD suggested to us that that the media's lack of understanding of military language was partly responsible for the confusion:

> TONY PAWSON: It is going to be quite difficult to distinguish between where the media say that we got it wrong, you know, Umm Qasr was taken three times. What you actually see is somebody saying, "We are now comfortable with the security in this area," so the media say, "Umm Qasr has been taken," so you have the difference between what we actually said and what was meant with that…what was said was that pockets of resistance had been overcome, and then, to make it safe for use as a port, you have a different level of security required.

> LT. COL. TAVERNER: I was quite struck by watching the *Fighting the War* documentary [BBC] that has just been shown, because I think it was, I forget

who it was saying, "Well, we've liberated Umm Qasr and you can drive around here, but best to do it in a tank," you know, and you're still in your sixty tons of armor rather than driving round in a Volkswagen.

Others in theater were more scathing of the reports in the media, claiming that situations that demanded tactical withdrawal and regrouping or where the rapid progress of armor was halted in order to allow resupply were being wrongly reported in terms of the campaign becoming "bogged down":

> Every skirmish is presented as a "setback" for the Coalition; every casualty shows how seriously the Iraqis were underestimated and the whole thing is "bogging down". One would think the war had gone on for months and we had suffered major defeats and casualties. One reporter, embedded with a US unit that met Iraqis in a sand storm, virtually shouted, "The Americans are retreating". That they were tactically deploying and subsequently obliterated the enemy was lost.[19]

The MoD certainly believes that the misunderstood significance and the lack of context, particularly with rolling news channels, were partly responsible for the overemphasis of particular incidents. David Howard suggested in our interview:

> The context setting on the twenty-four-hour news most of the time is not going to be the strategic, it is going to be more, how important is that image, now being beamed in my screen for the fifteenth time in the last half hour of a sniper in a building twenty-five miles outside Basra, which has probably got stuff all to do with the overall war, but it is being beamed live on our screen, around the world, and everyone is looking at it, and they believe that if it has taken half an hour to get a sniper, then the whole war must have ground to a halt.

However, it was precisely the provision of strategic context that was behind the MoD's thinking when establishing the FTU and, jointly with the American high command, the CentCom press center. The sheer volume of embedded reports—the noncontextual, dramatic, "view-through-a-smartie-tube" material—placed considerable pressure on the briefing officers in theater to comment on and explain these events; something that was not always possible to achieve accurately within the timescales of the broadcast media.

> COL. BROOK: I think one of the mistakes, one of the dilemmas that we were faced with is the twenty-four-hour media vacuum cleaner, which is this sort of massive Dyson roaming around that latches onto the slightest things and sucks everything up. And for us, the temptation on the military side to feed the machine is pretty terrific, and, of course, to be fair or unfair to the correspondents,

when they file something, they want to put alongside that report the sort of language and context, bearing in mind that makes their report look pretty good, so we didn't wither on the military side. We did not do ourselves any favors in those early days by us making announcements without lots of collateral and the press picking it up and saying, "Thank you very much, we'll have that," and running it for the next half a day.

We were rather dismissive of the American approach to simply sit on their bums and say nothing for forty-eight hours, and there were many occasions when we wish we had done exactly the same thing.

Basra

Two other memorable incidents concerned events in and around Iraq's second city. On 26 March 2003, reports began to emerge of a column of up to 120 Iraqi tanks leaving the city and preparing to engage troops in the area; in the event, the actual column numbers were reduced to just three vehicles. The report appears to have originated from an embedded reporter, the BBC's Clive Myrie, with 40 Commando of the British Royal Marines, but was also corroborated, at least in part, by ITN's Bill Neely, with 42 Commando. Bill Neely has spoken about this incident at various media forums since the war and admits that he perhaps should have been more rigorous in the sourcing of the story. The ITN desk in London requested further information from Neely about the incident, who then spoke to members of the unit he was with. Although they could not confirm or deny the reports, they had no reason to believe it was not true, given that the source was fellow soldiers. The event illustrates the difficulties that reporters faced in using military sources—whether briefing officers or battlefield combatants—whom they perhaps naturally felt would be reliably informed. Bill Neely spoke to us about the difficulties of attributing the source of this information:

> I didn't think the request to do this report was unreasonable. I was in southern Iraq, I was as close to Basra as they were, it was happening in their zone, but my guys weren't saying, "This is a load of bullshit." I trusted my source [Clive Myrie], I kind of trusted the double source, as it was coming from the Marines. On ITN that night I said, "It's being reported that a column of seventy to one hundred tanks are proceeding, they're being picked off and blah blah blah...." I mean, "It's being reported that" was good enough, it's a kind of fig leaf, but in my own mind I know it wasn't good enough, really.

When questioned about such occurrences the MoD again refers to the immediacy of the coverage of the war. Although they claim to have confirmed, denied, or corrected several such incidents, the time involved in obtaining concrete information from their personnel in theater meant that the event was yesterday's news for the media.

> PAWSON: I'm just thinking of a couple of occasions where although we went back and corrected or updated and impressed on journalists to follow that up and update it, and then we could see from their agenda that they had moved on to something else, so it wasn't significant news anymore, and therefore what was the point of going back on it? One of the lessons we are pulling from this is that the media, if you don't get it right first time with them, then you've lost it. And I think that is probably right.

A second major incident in the early stages of the campaign was the reporting of a popular uprising within the city (25 March 2003). The report again appeared to emanate from British servicemen—in this case members of the Royal Scots Dragoon Guards—and was not only broadcast extensively by embedded reporters (principally GMTV's Richard Gainsford), but also given credence by senior British and American commanders. If Iraqi civilians in the city had rebelled against Saddam Hussein's regime, it would have lent considerable support to the campaign's stated objective to "liberate" the Iraqi citizens from an oppressive dictator. The fact that the Arabic news stations with correspondents inside the city refuted the claims led to allegations of the use of propaganda by the military, something Colonel Brook firmly rejected:

> It's worth saying at this point that a lot has been leveled at us for manipulation, to which we've all said, "If only we were that clever, if only we were that joined up." We certainly aim to produce a coordinated coherent public presentation base. And there are certain, if you like, master messages that we wish to make sure got into the public domain. That's perfectly reasonable stuff. Now you can call it propaganda if you like, but what we are trying to do, how we are going about the military task, where we see the, if you like, the bad guys, who are the good guys, if you like, what the rationale for any particular military activity is…those are things that quite rightly have got to come out, but the idea that somehow we would say, "Ah, if we say this now even though it hasn't happened the effect will be blah, blah, blah," it's simply, to be blunt, the media are not that gullible.

The MoD resolutely insist that those involved with the embedding policy did not engage in any such deception or manipulation, maintaining a strict distinction between Media Operations and other departments (for example, PsyOps) that were engaged in the information battle for hearts and minds of the Iraqi population:

> HOWARD: We have a very strict separation of information office to the media office, you know, information office being at the slightly more covert and de-

ception end of the market, which is absolutely nothing whatsoever to do with us. We are not here to deceive, if we're seen in that light, we wouldn't have any credibility.

Information Loops

One further impact that the live feedback from the battlefield had on the MoD was the creation of information loops. This was clearly an important element in the circulation of and response to what were relatively unsubstantiated stories. The incident of the Basra tank column described above, while of minor strategic importance, illustrates the ways in which a story that perhaps begins as innocuous speculation can rapidly assume a far greater level of significance than it actually warrants, traveling from theater to editors in London, back to other correspondents in the field, back (either through the media or through correspondents' questions) to the military, who may well feel pressured to refer to the matter during briefings, which are then reported by correspondents.

Senior figures in London could see reports from correspondents well before their commanders were able to communicate the military assessment of the operation along the chain of command and, at least to some extent, this began to set the agenda for the subsequent military briefings, as Lt. Cdr. Tatham explained:

> I did two briefs a day to the Admiral. We have what we call command briefs, where you provide the Admiral with an overnight summary of activity, and then you give him situational awareness later in the day. Then if there's a particular incident, like loss of the helicopters or something, you would brief that as well. What we didn't want is for the Admiral to be approached by somebody from the media who would say, 'What do you think about this, then, Admiral, oh, you're live on CNN,' and the Admiral would say, "I don't know what you're talking about." So I would regularly go across to the Admiral, or I would send him e-mails and say, "Sir, please look at this immediately," and it would just be a PDF document, you know, "Sky TV have just said…"

This reflects the differences in communication speed between the media and the military. Journalists' reports from the battlefield can be transmitted and received worldwide virtually instantaneously, whereas the structure of military communications follows a more linear chain of command. Lt. Col. Taverner suggested that television news reports had a direct impact on the senior military commanders in the United Kingdom:

> As a battlefield warrior you aren't plugged in to Sky, we are back here, and it does, and what I thought was interesting this time was some of that nervous-

ness about the pause, in inverted commas, even filtered into the consciousness of Chiefs of Staff here, because what you're saying was becoming true to them. They themselves thought there was a pause. I think it had them probably on the phone to PJHQ and Robin Brims and co. to find out actually if there was a pause.

It is worth noting the differences here between Victoria Clarke's somewhat relaxed approach to such occurrences (as a result of her full involvement in both the media operation and the strategic military overview) and those of the MoD personnel whom we interviewed.

There can be no doubt that all involved were touched to a greater or lesser extent by the "TV war," as Colonel Brook illustrated:

It had a fascinating effect here in Whitehall, because, of course, like the general public, we were all glued to our sets, and yet we had a machine giving us precise and detailed information. But we still chose instead to take our truth from the television.

CHAPTER FIVE

"In Bed" with the Military?
The Journalists' Perspective

IF WE ARE TO UNDERSTAND THE IMPACT of embedded reporting in the 2003 Iraq War, we need to distinguish between how the policy was conceived in the conference rooms of Washington and Whitehall, and how the policy was implemented by military personnel in the field. The emphasis on access and openness (subject to operational security restrictions) envisaged in the official Pentagon vision would mean nothing if commanders and soldiers on the ground aggressively hindered journalists or attempted to censor their reports. Additionally, while the Pentagon's news management policy had been conceived and refined at an early stage of military campaign planning as a whole, the Ministry of Defence's implementation of a news management policy could best be described as last minute. Given it was several months behind, to what extent did the MoD accept the principles behind the Pentagon's policy, taking its own distinctive institutional culture into account? And again, even if the MoD followed the Pentagon policy, how did British military personnel working under battle conditions implement it?

The best way these questions can be answered is by asking those individuals whose output this policy was intended to manage—editors and journalists working for the main news organizations covering the war—how it affected them. To what extent did editors and journalists find themselves complicit in this strategy? And to what extent were different journalists able to reconcile the situation they found themselves in with their own professional values?

For all the literature devoted to the relationship between the media and the military, there is very little based on systematic research into the conditions that journalists actually work under when reporting a war, an outstanding exception being Morrison and Tumber's definitive study of journalists reporting the Falklands conflict (1988). There is a genre of popular autobiographical books by "star" writers whose role as war correspondents put them in a position to bear witness to seismic historical events. Recent offerings on the Iraq War 2003 by John Simpson (2003) and Rageh Omaar (2004) join a longer tradition of such writing in this respect. By definition, such star correspondents' experience is not typical. Moreover, the genre does not usually allow the writer the indulgence of self-reflection on the more mundane aspects of the profession. Nevertheless, it is precisely the more mundane aspects, the aspects most journalists encountered, that we need to know. Because there were an unprecedented number of journalists deployed in the region, most of these as embeds, we need to know the common, general experience of journalists in the 2003 Iraq War.

None of these questions could be fully answered without talking to embedded correspondents themselves. This part of our research study was part of a tradition of research that examines the effects of the professional ideologies and constraints under which journalists work on their news output (Tuchman 1978; Gans 1979; Schlesinger 1978; Ericson, Baranek, and Chan 1987; 1989). Whereas many of these studies have been based on participant observation as well as interviews, for practical reasons, like Morrison and Tumber's study, our research has been based on interviews alone.

We conducted twenty-three in-depth interviews with key actors in the British television coverage of the Iraq war. Our sample included four reporters embedded with American units, three embedded with British units, four based at the Forward Transmission Unit (FTU), two unilateral correspondents and one Baghdad-based correspondent. We also interviewed nine news directors and editors responsible for policies covering the deployment of embedded reporters and the use of their reports. Finally, we interviewed five editors and journalists at al-Jazeera in Qatar.

The interviews were conducted between July and October 2003. The interviews were semistructured, our team of interviewers using a standard set of questions for each type of interviewee: news directors, embedded reporters, etc. Each set of questions was designed to address the concerns and issues raised in public and professional debates over the deployment of embedded reporters. At the same time, the questions were general enough to give interviewees the opportunity to express their own concerns about the war coverage.

Our aims in the following sections are as follows. In the first section, we discuss how the Pentagon and MoD's news management strategy impacted journalists reporting the war. In the second section, we discuss the professional concerns that editors and journalists raise about the military news management policy. In the final section, we evaluate the novelty of the news management policy as it was implemented in the 2003 Iraq War against the post-Vietnam model outlined in the introduction.

Embedded Reporting in the War Zone

The American news management policy as devised in the Pentagon was based on a vision of military personnel in the field giving journalists unprecedented access while leaving them to do their jobs—subject, of course, to operational security constraints. But to what extent was this vision realized on the ground? And to what extent did British military forces, in principle backing the policy of embedded reporting, also implement the policy as envisaged in the Pentagon?

Our interviews suggest that on the whole, particularly for those journalists embedded with U.S. military units, the policy was implemented as planned. Colin Brazier (Sky News) "was astonished by how much information we were given, how little interference or attempted interference there was. It was the most information I've ever had the privilege of dealing with." James Mates (ITV News) "considered it to be a very, very satisfactory journalistic experience.... I've rarely had such open access, to anything, let alone a war, certainly never had that level of openness and cooperation from the military who have not, in my experience, been the most open people I've ever had to deal with."

British correspondents embedded with American forces were surprised by the degree of access they were getting to the front line, and the extent of sensitive information that they were entrusted with by unit commanders. They also realized that if they broadcast any of this information before the operation had taken place, it would jeopardize their own lives. At the same time, while military personnel showed interest in their reports, most made little attempt to interfere or censor. In keeping with the Pentagon's guidelines, journalists were able to report freely as long as they did not endanger operational security. By and large, journalists accepted this operational security requirement—including restrictions on working at night ("light discipline").

It would be wrong to suggest, however, that the implementation of the strategy by the American military was entirely smooth. There seems to have been a considerable gap between the Pentagon's policy and the implementation of that policy by units on the ground, especially regarding transport arrangements and how much equipment correspondents were able to take along. The Pentagon's guidelines stipulated that "embedded media are not authorized use of their own vehicles while traveling in an embedded status."[1] The Pentagon briefing to news bureau chiefs in January 2003 advised that transport would be provided, but that reporters were limited to what they can carry. But Jonathan Baker (World News Editor, BBC) recalled that when two of their correspondents turned up at their respective units, they were told that they wouldn't be taken along if they didn't have their own vehicles. Accordingly, the BBC had to ship out two Land Rovers. When one broke down, Baker recalls trying to arrange a rescue with Bryan Whitman at the Pentagon, who maintained the line that the vehicle shouldn't have been there anyway.

James Mates's experience was somewhat different. He recalled that his unit provided him with transport for his equipment after the Pentagon blocked his vehicle:

> The Pentagon had laid down early on that no civilian vehicles were going to be allowed on the battlefield. This was clearly going to be disregarded, there were a lot of civilian vehicles.... There was ours and there was the NBC vehicle, a converted Humvee with a dish mounted on it and all the equipment inside...the regiment had agreed they were going to bring it with them. Someone from the Department of Defense got a sniff of this and sent instructions that it wasn't to come an hour before the invasion. The battalion commander said, "I'm going to take this dish." He assigned to us a seven-ton truck, which then had the dish mounted on it and a driver, and that then became our broadcast center.... This is a big difference between the Americans and the British.... He knew his guys would get great coverage.... They were thrilled to have a dish with them through which they could be seen winning the war.

However it happened, whether by being allowed their own vehicle or having one provided for them, reporters with American units recalled better transport and support for their professional equipment than many of their counterparts embedded with British units.

There was a common perception amongst our interviewees that the American networks were given special treatment by the Pentagon. They were assigned embed opportunities with the units most likely to be at the center of the action. Units went to considerable lengths to accommodate their satellite dishes. British journalists embedded alongside American network teams often benefited from being able to access some of their equipment.

However, journalists embedded with British military units presented a more mixed picture. Richard Gaisford's experience was like those of journalists embedded with U.S. units. He was provided with an armored personnel carrier by his unit and was able to take a full complement of personal and professional equipment. He was able to uplink reports direct to the London newsroom—he didn't use the Forward Transmission Unit (FTU, see Chapter 4) at all. Gaisford recalled a good working relationship with the officers and troops in his unit and no attempts at censorship other than the restriction on reporting future operations.

By contrast, ITV news correspondent Romilly Weeks described a working relationship with the commanders of her unit that started badly and got worse: "It was a constant juggling act between being able to report what we wanted to report and not upsetting the officers. I got the impression quite early on that they would have liked us to be a branch of British Forces Broadcasting." Events culminated in the most blatant military attempt at censorship reported to us, after the commander tried to forbid her from reporting the chaotic scenes following an aborted aid drop in al-Zubayr, which had seen his unit beat a hasty and undignified retreat (discussed in more detail below). Weeks did not have a satellite dish and was dependent on the military to provide her with transport back to the FTU where she could edit her reports.

The very different experiences enjoyed by Gaisford and Weeks indicates the uneven implementation of the policy on the ground by British forces. Individual unit commanders seemed to have considerable freedom to implement the policy in their own way. Bill Neely's experience was more like Gaisford's. He reported how his commander initially made it clear that he didn't want reporters there, but subsequently recalled a good working relationship. He recalled that no attempt was made to censor his material.

Juliet Bremner, on the other hand, reported having had a much more negative experience.[2] There was not enough space in the armored vehicle that was transporting her and her cameraman, so she found herself parted from edit and transmission equipment, which gave her severe logistical problems—having to go back from the front line to produce her reports. She did not feel part of the army and was not made to feel welcome.

Our interviews suggest, then, that in seeing journalists as a nuisance and often falling back on the instinct to censor, many British military personnel had not understood the basic principle behind the Pentagon's policy: support journalists in doing their job, and the big picture that emerges will be favorable. However, there was also an *institutional* sign that the British forces had not quite grasped the principle behind the policy of embedded reporting: the provision of the FTU as a conduit through which all British television pool reports were supposed to be channeled. One of the principal features of the Pentagon news management policy was to abandon the formal pool system, leaving individual journalists to send reports back to their own employers directly from the front line. By contrast, journalists embedded with British units (the "spokes" in the MoD's "hub and spokes" model) would send back reports to the FTU (the "hub") to be used by all participating British television news organizations. Here hub correspondents would edit them together and send them back to London. On the basis of these arrangements, news organizations deployed their senior correspondents at the hub, where MoD briefers were also supposed to be at hand to give regular briefings.

But our interviews indicate considerable dissatisfaction amongst journalists with this system. The method for getting tapes back to the FTU from the spoke correspondents was unreliable. Part of the problem was the distance. The FTU was a long way back from the front, starting in northern Kuwait and only moving a few miles north of the Iraqi border. Correspondents who had the technology were able to uplink reports directly back to the London newsrooms, where it was pooled. Similarly, a number of reports from the front involved two-ways between anchors and embedded correspondents using satellite or videophones. While reports from correspondents embedded with U.S. units were always intended to be relayed directly to the London newsrooms, a considerable number of reports from correspondents embedded with British units also bypassed the FTU. As a result, senior correspondents at the FTU who were supposed to be in a position to be the most well informed found that they were actually reliant on London newsrooms for a lot of information.

A major criticism from our interviewees was aimed at the MoD's performance at the FTU. Ben Brown described "a big breakdown of trust or cooperation between the journalists and the military." The criticisms were various: briefings didn't take into account the needs of a twenty-four-hour news cycle; military spokesmen were slow to confirm events (such as the Basra uprising); there was too much spin from MoD public relations people; there was not enough access to military commanders.

Jonathan Baker suggested that the problems with the briefings were partly due to the volume of information provided by the embeds:

I just don't think they were ready for this huge flood of pictures arriving in real time, and they weren't going to have the time to analyze and assess it, put it in the context of the battlefield and come up with a nice press conference.

A number of editors and journalists blamed what they saw as the MoD's lack of preparedness for the perceived failings of the embed program, a problem partly acknowledged by the Ministry itself. Meetings between ITN, BBC, and Sky and the MoD were arranged for January, which, for the news organizations, was very late. Key personnel in the MoD changed late in the day. According to journalists, the MoD had little concept of the amount of equipment that television journalists and camera operators need and therefore insufficient appreciation of the support required. Editors reported to us that one of the problems was that the MoD did not want to appear to be making arrangements for a war while politically moves were still being made to avoid war.

Overall, what we found in our interviews with embedded journalists was that when discussing working relationships with the military, they were very wary of the possibility that the military might attempt to impose direct censorship, as the military had done in previous conflicts. When, on the whole, military personnel not only did not impose direct censorship but also seemed to go out of their way to help journalists get on with their job, it clearly came as a surprise to many of our interviewees. While there was universal awareness amongst our interviewees of the dangers of getting too close to the military, nevertheless, there seemed to be a common assumption that less direct censorship equaled less manipulation.

"Embedding for Life" and the Treatment of Unilaterals

One of the key components of the Pentagon's policy was the idea of "embedding for life," as discussed in the previous chapter, whereby if journalists wanted to dis-embed they could do so, but they could not expect to re-embed with the same or any other unit. "Embedding for life" was central to the U.S. news management policy. The Pentagon wanted reporters attached to a single unit for the duration of the conflict. The idea that reporters could promiscuously dis-embed with one unit and re-embed with another was actively discouraged by Pentagon briefers. But how was the policy of embedding for life enforced in the field by military personnel?

Our interviews indicate that the line was largely followed.

JAMES MATES: It was made absolutely clear when you arrived that you can leave, but you can't come back, we're not having you dipping in and out.... They clearly from top level downward thought it was a good thing that we were there.

They wanted coverage, they thought what they were doing was right, and their only stipulation was you can come with us, you can do everything, we'll tell you everything we possibly can, we'll show you everything we possibly can, we'll put no restrictions on you. But, if you want out, we'll get you out, but we're not going to keep bringing you in and out again, so once you're gone, you're gone.

All of our respondents embedded with U.S. units stayed with their units until the fall of Baghdad, and then left.

However, some of the more experienced correspondents—either embeds or unilaterals—were able to bend the rules on the ground. So, for example, a couple of correspondents embedded with UK units recalled circumventing the formal ground rules toward the end of the war, by informally joining up with military units who were pleased to have them along. Ben Brown embedded with the 2nd Royal Tank Regiment on the way up to Basra; in Basra, he traveled with the Irish Guards, returning to the FTU to uplink reports. He recalled a high degree of cooperation from the Irish Guards.

On reaching Basra, Bill Neely described spending a couple of days investigating stories independently while still based with the Marines. This was only a problem when he encountered the Marines' Chief Press Officer, with whom he had a major row (concerning the risks he was taking)—suggesting a disparity between troops on the ground and those charged with enforcing the rules.

Jeremy Thompson's experience was significant here. His team consisted of a convoy of four vehicles initially. After meeting with hostility from Iraqi civilians and hearing what had happened to Terry Lloyd, he decided to fall in with the Desert Rats (British 7th Armored Division). He characterized the welcome from the troops as follows:

"Nice to have you along, fantastic, all the boys watch Sky, and the families are watching back home".... Nobody ever said, "Where's your pass, are you embedded or not?"... We were half embedded. We were temporarily embedded, we were treated in some ways like embeds, but we weren't nailed down with some of the restraints and restrictions of being embedded.

Once Basra had started to fall, Thompson took two of the vehicles and met up with a Sky satellite dish on the outskirts of Baghdad. He met up with a U.S. Marine colonel who "didn't ask me if I was embedded or not, he just said, 'Come on, I'll show you the war.'" Similarly, two Sky unilateral teams, who were described as "blisters," were able to move from one unit to another. Adrian Wells recalls that Ross Appleyard and Lisa Holland began with the U.S. 15th Marines and then subsequently joined up with two other American units.

Interestingly, some of our interviewees were very keen that the military should enforce the policy of "embedding for life" stringently, and expressed dismay when it broke down. Some journalists were not pleased with the treatment afforded to Sky's unilaterals, who were able to benefit from being semi-embedded whilst enjoying the advantage of being a unilateral. Richard Gaisford recalled:

> Sky had decided to take a chance and move a truck up unilaterally. We had been told that they would be offered no protection. But somebody on the airfield, and it wasn't our unit, decided to offer them protection. That caused a little bit of concern that the system was breaking down.

Andrew MacDonald at Channel 4 News was also not happy that a system that he had been led to believe would be rigidly implemented wasn't, in the end:

> One of the factors in deciding to embed was that there had been very clear signals from the British and the Americans that they would not have unilateral correspondents in the battlefield and they would simply send them back to Kuwait.

When editors and journalists were concerned about the possibility of the "embedded-for-life" system breaking down, it was because other news organizations who had flouted the rules might be able to gain a competitive advantage. Interestingly, in backing the Pentagon's rigid enforcement of this policy, they are supporting what was a key component of the Pentagon's policy in propagandist terms. In other words, the competitive ethos was more compelling than the desire for access.

The obverse of the Pentagon's encouragement of journalists to embed for life was the discouragement of journalists operating as unilaterals. Pentagon briefers said little about unilaterals, except that they had no responsibility for their safety and no duty to support them. Obviously, how military personnel treated unilateral journalists on the ground would have a major effect on the extent to which they were able to operate.

Richard Gaisford recalled that his unit treated unilaterals with courtesy and respect, while requiring them to move on. However, some of our interviewees recalled a more explicit antagonism. Romilly Weeks told us that she had met

> quite a few [unilaterals] who had made it to the air base where a lot of the British troops were camping, and they had their passes around their necks saying "unilateral," and were saying that they tried to cover [it] up...whenever they met a check point, because as soon as the troops saw that, they would be treated

very badly, and called "filthy unilaterals" and "scum" and often told to go back to Kuwait.

And whereas Jeremy Thompson might have been welcomed by the troops of the units he was with, according to Phil Wardman, Chris Vernon, a MoD official at the FTU, regarded him as a greater annoyance than Saddam Hussein. Again, it is also worth noting that the MoD felt pressure from embeds to limit access to unilaterals, a case of news personnel actually reinforcing the Pentagon's news management line.

Mark Austin was presenting the early evening ITV news bulletin from as close to the front line as possible. He described seeking assistance from military officials on a number of occasions, but found himself deliberately hindered:

> They were not happy at all about having journalists on the battlefield that they did not control, and they made that very clear. And they had their embedded journalists, and this immediately, in my view, raises an issue.... I think that the army has to rethink and reconsider the way they treat unilateral journalists, who have, for reasons of the way they operate, to be in the battlefield or in the war zone and were deliberately hindered. They were not at all set up to deal with us and not only made our job a lot more difficult, it also made our job a lot more dangerous.

However, this wasn't the case with the troops on the battlefield.

> AUSTIN: The units on the ground were positively delighted to have us with them.... The families could see what they were doing, the commander was getting on the television. The Marines were worried about the Desert Rats getting too much coverage, and so here we had a situation where we not only had embedded reporters, but they had presenters of the evening news who wanted to do the whole program from the Marine base, wherever that may be. They were delighted, they helped us, they gave us a degree of protection, you know, we set up a tented camp near where they were, and they were fantastic, but it was the press operation, the Ministry of Defence, who simply could not comprehend what we were trying to do.

In sum, the implementation of the ground rules in the field regarding unilateral reporters was mixed, with *some* troops on the ground happy to accommodate them, while others treated them with considerable hostility. Overall, the Pentagon's policies regarding embedding for life and unilateral reporters was largely implemented on the ground; what we found interesting in both cases was that many editors and journalists actually supported the Pentagon's rigorous implementation of key measures through which the military controlled the media.

News-Gathering Technology as a Constraint

The whole system of embedded reporting was dependent on the performance of news-gathering technology, able to uplink reports directly from the front line. Any shortfall in the performance of this technology would constitute a constraint on journalists' ability to report—perhaps not a constraint overtly enforced by the Pentagon, but one which could influence reporters' coverage of the war by limiting their freedom of movement and independence from military units. Our interviews suggested that the performance of the technology was mixed. Some of the public debate about reporting this war has been premised on an idealized vision of the capabilities of technology, on a vision of a war in which miniaturized, lightweight technologies would enable embeds to transmit pictures live from the front. And indeed, satellite phones and video phones did enable embedded correspondents to go live from the front to an unprecedented extent.

While this did happen, many of the correspondents recalled battling against the constraints of the technology, such as the long satellite uplink times for a short report and the adverse effects of desert conditions on cameras and phones. Power could be a problem: correspondents sometimes resorted to running equipment off the batteries of Humvees (per their training in sessions organized by the Pentagon). So the constraints of the technology did impact how journalists were able to report this war. Generally, those who had access to a number of options in terms of equipment, and particularly satellite dishes, were much more likely to be able to report stories as they wanted.

There was one overt military constraint on the use of technology. One piece of technology that was banned by the American and British military after the war began was the Thuraya phone, which has a GPS capability. The military were concerned that the use of this phone by embedded journalists could enable Iraqi forces to electronically identify the position of units. Although a number of correspondents seemed skeptical about Iraqi capability in this respect, the ban was not seen as a matter of concern.

The Demise of CentCom as an Important Source of News

Finally, with the implementation of the policy of the embedded reporting program, British news organizations were no longer as reliant on the CentCom briefing operation at Doha, Qatar, as they had been on similar facilities in previous conflicts, such as the Gulf War. With so much frontline footage available, British editors and journalists could now admit that CentCom was of little value. The BBC's Richard Sambrook felt that:

> [It] didn't really work as well as we hoped it would. The American briefing operation was not quite obstructive, but pretty close to it, they said practically nothing. The British briefing operation was better, but in the end, it didn't become the place where you could get the overview.... A lot of the embeds on the front line would know things before anyone in Doha would know it.

Jonathan Baker added that the briefings in Doha "didn't even begin to deliver. They said virtually nothing on the record and precious little off it." Stewart Purvis had no hope that it would work: "We never go big on where the spokesmen are, because we regard it as a complete farce, and it has proved to be yet again.... Anyone who complains about Qatar, to me is just naïve. What did you expect?"

British Editors' and Journalists' Views on Embedded Reporting

Many of our open-ended questions directed at editors and journalists were intended to elicit their views about the policy of embedded reporting as a central component of U.S./UK military news management strategy. Much of the criticism levelled at embedding has been aimed at the dependence of correspondents on their units for food and water, transport and safety, suggesting that this close and dependent relationship compromises the ability of correspondents to be critical of military personnel. All of our respondents expressed an awareness of this issue.

Many of the correspondents said that they could not help developing friendships with military personnel as a result of their common situation. Indeed, developing friendly relations with the troops was important for correspondents in helping them to do their job. Phil Wardman recalled how Jeremy Thompson made himself popular with the troops by downlinking Sky Sports for them. According to Wardman, Sky deliberately assigned reporters to units who would be likely to get along with the troops. At the same time, correspondents who discussed the issue denied that any friendships formed with the soldiers influenced how they reported the war.

A number of examples illustrate the potential for the position of the embedded journalist to be compromised. A number of journalists reported occasions where they were uncomfortably close to the soldiers they accompanied. Ben Brown recalled how a soldier had saved his life by shooting an Iraqi sniper:

> There was an Iraqi who had been playing dead the other side of a wall very close to us, and he had been pretending to be dead. And he jumped up with an RPG, and he was about to fire it at us, because we were just standing there, and this other Warrior just shot him with their big machine gun, and there was a big hole in his chest. That was the closest I felt to being almost too close to the troops, because me and my cameraman both felt a sense of elation that this guy was dead, which is something I've never felt before.... Because if he hadn't been, then he would have killed...afterward I sought out the gunner who had done that and shook his hand.

On another occasion, Gavin Hewitt noticed a vehicle approaching his resting unit. He saw men getting equipment out of the back. When he pointed this out to his unit, the Americans immediately opened fire. To Hewitt's relief, the truck was full of rocket-propelled grenades and exploded—the Iraqis had been about to attack.[3]

Clive Myrie was quoted in the documentary *War Spin* as recalling the following:

> There was bullets flying everywhere. We get out of the Land Rover and we hide in a ditch. One of the Marines said, "Why don't you make yourself useful? And he's throwing these flares at me. And he's throwing the flares at me, and I'm throwing them at the guy who's got to light them and send them off into the sky, and I'm thinking, Why, what am I doing here?[4]

A number of such incidents—when the independence of journalists from the soldiers they were embedded with was in danger of being compromised—emerged in our interviews. This does not mean that journalists in such a situation are incapable of filing critical reports if need be. It does mean that journalists and editors need to maintain awareness of the myriad ways in which this dependence might affect their objectivity.

Censorship

When asked whether military personnel ever tried to censor their reports, most of the correspondents we interviewed either recalled no attempts to censor or trivial requests to make minor alterations, which could easily be refused, with one significant exception. Romilly Weeks described how the commander of her unit attempted to stop her filing a report on a failed aid drop in al-Zubayr. It is worth quoting from her account at length:

> WEEKS: The town had various militia headquarters in it—it had been quite unstable, and it was by no means secured. The army was under a lot of pressure to get the aid in as quickly as possible—there was all this stuff from Kuwait which was rotting—and they went in with their convoys, and a mass of people

came out to meet them. I think there was one water lorry, maybe two trucks of food, and there were clearly too many people and too few soldiers. This was the first time that they had come into contact with Iraqi civilians, and nobody knew how they were going to react. The soldiers quickly became overpowered, and people started jumping on the trucks and grabbing the food for themselves. It was complete chaos, and people were being crushed and the soldiers were getting very frightened. It felt like it could turn into a riot…it was a really tense mood. Then the convoy and the crowd got fired at—I was told later by militia from a nearby building—and everybody fled. It was complete panic and they were climbing over each other to get out of there. There was a surge of people rushing down this road and the army retreated in complete chaos as well, not even stopping to shut the backs of the lorries so there was food spilling out of the back of the lorries.… Anyway, it was a very interesting thing to report, it was the first aid drop, it had gone badly, but not through any particular fault of the army. When we got back to base and the colonel was briefed on what had happened—it was late at night by this stage—he immediately summoned us, and he was very much of the attitude that we were under his command, that we were part of his regiment, and we should do as we were told and he said, "Right, that report won't go out." So I said, "Well, I'm afraid it has to, this is what I'm here for. It's not negative, it's balanced, I just reported what I saw," and he said, "No, I'm telling you that that report won't go out." He didn't even give a reason. It was just that I should blindly accept his word because he saw himself as the superior commanding officer. So we had this argument in front of half of the regiment and I ended by saying, "You're trying to censor us," and it sort of stopped there without any conclusion.

She then "went away and finished the report and then tried to get transport back to the hub—and of course transport couldn't be arranged that night."

To some extent, the significance of this episode is that it was unusual for this war. The blatant attempt by a military commander to censor a report that he felt would have portrayed in his unit in a poor light seems to have been unmatched by the experiences of other journalists we interviewed, although elsewhere Juliet Bremner—along with other embeds— reported that she was not allowed to report the words of General Conway in his prebattle address to the troops.[5]

It does demonstrate that not all commanders in the British army followed the principles underlying the MoD policy on embeds. It also illustrates that a reporter *could* maintain his or her independence and oppose the commander of the unit, even if—as spokes in the system—he or she were dependent on that unit for support in so doing. To draw the conclusion that there was little censorship, however, would be complacent. There may have been few attempts to "blue-pencil" reports, but many of our interviews provided documentary evidence of how the implementation of the embedded policy on the ground restricted journalists' ability to report what they wanted to report.

Firstly, there was restriction of movement. Alex Thomson told us:

> I am still amazed by people who will tell you that they weren't censored. Censorship is restricting someone's freedom of movement as much as it is restricting what someone can and cannot film.

He recalled an incident when the military tried to stop his cameraman going off to film a crashed helicopter for "security" reasons (it should be noted, though, that his cameraman did get this footage). Carl Dinnen recalls an occasion when he couldn't get to a story because he was tied to the transport provided by his unit:

> There was one location which we tried to get to where we had been told that there were a lot of dead, an Iraqi encampment that had been attacked.... We tried to get there, but weren't able to get a convoy together to go with us in time before we had to move on again, so we didn't even make it to that one.

And while the military could attempt to restrict journalists' freedom of movement to report negative stories, they could also attempt to aid journalists to report stories that would represent the case for the war in a positive light. Indeed, the ability to encourage "positive" reporting is clearly part of the Pentagon's media strategy. The following incident illustrates how this would happen:

> DINNEN: An infantry battalion put out a call to all units in the area saying that they had discovered a terrorist training camp in the north of Baghdad, and anyone who had an embedded journalist should send them down, and they would be shown it.... Our colonel was happy to put together a couple of Humvees and some men. We were shown lots of weaponry that had been stored in half-built houses. The interpretation by the unit that found it was that these houses were never intended as houses, these were intended to look like houses from the air, and in fact, they were only ever intended for storing ammunition. I was skeptical of that and didn't report it—there was no way of knowing whether it was true or not. Then they took us to a camp which had a lot of anti-Israeli and anti-Jewish murals around it, and it was obviously a military training camp of some sort.... A lot of the targets in the shooting range had Stars of David on their head and things like "Jewish filth" written in Arabic under them.... Our colonel had also discovered a huge picture of Saddam Hussein grinning sitting in front of the twin towers as they were hit by the planes on 9/11. I think all of this in his mind had made this seem like a connection between the regime and terrorists. We were slightly skeptical when we found out that his interpreter was...a former Arabic interpreter from the Israeli army, which set the alarm bells going.... A visiting general passed through to take a look, and he told us

that he didn't actually believe that it was a terrorist training camp at all.... That was the only time when I came across someone who was really trying to manipulate the media.... He also took us to see some missile warhead...and some missile parts, we had no way of assessing the significance of them. They looked pretty old, and they wouldn't have gone anywhere in forty-five minutes anyway, they were parts, really. He felt this all backed it up. I mean, we broadcast it, but we were skeptical.

Second, there was censorship through operational security restrictions. None of the correspondents we interviewed expressed any problem with restrictions in the name of operational security. If they had breached these restrictions, they would have been in contravention of the Pentagon and MoD ground rules agreement, and they may also have endangered their own safety. But a debate could be had about the point at which operational security restrictions actually inhibit a journalist's ability to convey the whole picture of the war. In discussing his role in reporting the Basra uprising (see below), Richard Gaisford revealed that:

This is the key issue I couldn't report at the time. I knew where the information inside of Basra was coming from. It wasn't just from some disaffected Iraqi, it was from British Special Forces. British Special Forces had been on the ground in the city of Basra. We knew this, we'd met them. They were staying either at the forward point in our camp or in Basra—the commanding officer confirmed this was where the information was coming from, but it was the one restriction on that night for their safety that I could not report that they were in Basra. Very little information has come out about the Special Forces throughout all of this.... It was the SAS and the SBS who had been around Basra...and this is my supposition—and anecdotally it's backed up by the soldiers—they were stirring up trouble....We weren't allowed to say it was Special Forces, because I was instructed that it would endanger their lives.

Third, there was censorship through restrictions on equipment, especially for the "spokes" trying to get reports back to the FTU. Romilly Weeks illustrates this in her account of the procedure for getting out reports:

We could have just sent the tapes back, but then I wouldn't have been in control of the editing. At the beginning, we had to go with a tank escort.... Even by the time that we left, the roads were not secure.... That was a way of controlling us. We had to behave to a certain extent, or it was difficult to get our report out.

Some of our interviewees speculated that safety concerns themselves would act as a form of censorship. According to Mark Austin, "One danger, I think, is that the MoD and the British forces start to use safety as a reason to stop journalists going into an area, and I think that is likely to happen, almost safety and fear becomes a form of censorship."

The Threat to Balance and Context

What emerged from all of our interviews with news directors, editors, and journalists was a consensual, coherent view of how reports from embedded correspondents should be used. Embedded correspondents were very valuable in providing firsthand reports from the front line, but they could only give one side of the story. The use of reports from embedded correspondents was regarded as legitimate as long as they were part of a *balanced* picture.

Our interviewees cited a number of examples of the type of story that would provide such balance. Some cited unilateral correspondents based in Baghdad and were critical of the American networks for pulling these reporters on safety grounds. According to Lindsey Hilsum:

> The Americans only saw one side of the war on television…. There were a lot
> of journalists in Baghdad, probably two hundred…everybody was there, apart
> from the Americans. Only the Americans could not see what was happening in
> Baghdad.

Others cited unilateral correspondents based in the battlefield—although a number wondered whether it was now possible to operate as a true unilateral after the death of Terry Lloyd. Other types of reports mentioned as providing a complete picture included briefings from military spokesman and reports by specialist correspondents.

At the same time, many of our respondents expressed real concerns about the way in which the United States prosecuted this war, making the battlefield much more dangerous for unilateral correspondents to operate. Many regarded the death of Lloyd as a turning point. For Richard Sambrook, from that moment, "We realized what we'd like to be able to do simply wasn't going to be possible, on safety grounds, and I fear that will be in true in future conflicts as well. I think it is unfortunate because it is an important counterbalance when you're able to do it."

Many of our interviewees regarded the deployment of roving unilateral correspondents as absolutely crucial in providing the counterbalance to the embedded correspondents. However, these unilateral correspondents need to be genuine unilaterals, not subject to controls or manipulation. Mark Austin described how some unilaterals were working in ways that reproduced the kinds of limits the embeds were under:

> You sit in the Hilton Hotel in Kuwait, you wait for daily press trips to safe, well-
> prepared areas, which everybody will go on, real media-circus operations and

you just sit there and wait until your number comes up, and off you go. In my view, this no way for a journalist to cover the war.

Romilly Weeks also recalled encountering such an expedition organized for this type of unilateral correspondent:

> A lot of the unilaterals ended up being almost as tightly controlled by the army as we were.... We went to Umm Qasr one day and were doing something about the aid stocks, and there was a day trip organized from Kuwait for unilateral journalists, who had all come on this big bus with the army, and they were being shown exactly what the army wanted them to see. So they were shown a water pipeline being turned on, which had actually been going for three days or something.

As an embedded correspondent, Weeks was in a position to know how such an expedition had been set up for the journalists. This is a very important point, because it problematizes much of the criticism of embedded reporting based on the assumption that unilateral correspondents are somehow working outside constraints. By contrast, concerns over safety amongst journalists and editors could impose different, but in many ways, *more* limiting constraints on unilateral correspondents' access to the war zone than those embedded reporters experienced.

The Portrayal of Death and Injury

One of the major professional concerns over embedded reporting in this war was the possibility of death occurring live on screen: Would live footage of military engagements transmitted from the front by embedded correspondents result in viewers witnessing deaths in real time? Jonathon Munro argued that this issue was highlighted by the coverage of 9/11 by rolling television news channels. However, there was also a very specific possibility of broadcasting live the death of a British serviceman while next of kin were watching.

In the 2003 Iraq War, this risk was less at issue, because most embedded correspondents didn't have the technology to transmit live. Indeed, the moment where death on screen could have happened was in Baghdad, when a crowd fired into reeds on the banks of the Euphrates looking for a downed aircrew—footage which did not originate from embedded reporters. Nevertheless, with improvements in technology, this issue will become more important. The interviewees who addressed it felt that some form of delay should probably be introduced, although none indicated that a delay was being used this time.

Of more concern was the wider issue of self-censorship. Many of our respondents commented on the relative absence of graphic images of people killed or injured by military action. Some interviewees suggested that camera operators were used to censoring themselves, because they knew that the more gruesome scenes that they witnessed would not be shown on British television. Roger Mosey believed that "Western crews in the field simply didn't film things which were really disturbing and horrible." Gavin Hewitt recalled that when he encountered harrowing scenes of vehicles full of casualties on entering Baghdad, his cameraman decided to shoot wide, because it was the only way in which he thought it could be shown. As a consequence, Hewitt thought that the "audience were not given a clear picture as to exactly what was happening."

Many of our interviewees felt that British television news coverage was too sanitized and would have liked to have moved the threshold in favor of more graphic coverage in some way, whilst recognizing the need to protect children from the effects of seeing such coverage. Guy Kerr contrasted the sanitized depiction of casualties on British television news with the more explicit footage shown on French, German, and Arab channels. He believed that as more British viewers become familiar with this type of coverage, they will become increasingly suspicious of mainstream British news—if it continues to be sanitized.

The issue of how casualties are represented raises a serious question about the limits of embedded reporting: the embeds are there, ostensibly, to bring viewers closer to the battlefield, and yet they are unable to show the ugly side of war. Thus, even on their own terms, the embeds cannot provide a complete or clear picture of events they are witnessing.

The Views of Iraqi Civilians

Most of the embedded correspondents we interviewed were able to gain some access to Iraqi civilians. Although embedded correspondents would not have had their own translator in the way that unilateral teams tended to, none of them reported any problems with communicating with Iraqi civilians. Many spoke English and were prepared to act as translators.

When we asked correspondents of their impressions of the views of Iraqi civilians, we got a wide range of replies—not surprisingly, as there is no reason why the views of Iraqi civilians encountered in a particular location under certain conditions should stand in for the views of the Iraqi people as a whole. Richard Gaisford recalled a surprising lack of hostility from the Iraqi civilians he encountered. By contrast, Jeremy Thompson recalled outright hostility, a response that partly convinced him to hitch up with military units. But most indicated a mixed or ambivalent response. Elsewhere, BBC Radio's Tim Franks has succinctly summarized how embedded reporters were first to be able to talk to Iraqi citizens and described their views as "subtle and fascinating":

> Few in the south suggested that they supported Saddam Hussein. But many had concerns about the invasion—about the forces will to stay, about the long-term ambitions of the American and British governments. Their lives had been shaken and sometimes steamrollered by the war: they complained of a lack of water and a lack of sleep; of Fedayeen forcing them to fight; and of injury and bereavement from the guns and bombs of the invaders.[6]

Mark Austin reported:

> You have got to remember that we were in south Iraq, where Saddam Hussein has committed some pretty appalling atrocities, and so they were clearly anti-Saddam anyway. But they were very nervous, very concerned about what was going to happen, they were very reluctant to talk, because they didn't really believe that it was the end of Saddam. But there was a huge concern about when the British and American forces were going to leave.... I remember one doctor at Basra hospital, he spoke fantastic English, I asked him to do an interview, he didn't want to do an interview, but he talked to me off camera and he said, very articulately, "We welcome you now, but you have to leave within three or four months, or else the people of Iraq will consider you occupiers." He said, "You will be seen as liberators, or the forces will be seen as liberators, but two or three months after that you will become occupiers."

Similarly, Ben Brown recalled:

> Their reaction to the troops was equivocal in Basra. There wasn't real singing and dancing and one bloke said to me, "We're not happy, but we're not unhappy." I think they were happy to be liberated but not happy to be invaded by a foreign power. There was an awful lot of looting, to be honest, it was more looting than celebrating.

Brown considered it was important to reflect that ambivalence in his reports, even at the expense of using more visually interesting footage:

> The day Basra fell, we had pictures of a jubilant crowd singing and dancing, but actually they were from a village from the north of Basra. I spent the whole day in Basra and hadn't seen anyone singing or dancing, so although pictures of them dancing were better, I didn't use them, because I felt they were unrepresentative of the mood that I'd seen.

The most broadcast event used to show the response of the Iraqi people was the demolition of the statue of Saddam Hussein in Paradise Square.

None of our embedded correspondents were at the scene, but we asked many of our interviewees what they thought of the coverage of this event, because it was so widely used to symbolize the response of the Iraqi people. Responses were divided.

On one hand, a number of our interviewees felt that although they recognized this was a staged event, and that the size of the crowd of Iraqis was by no means large, it was a legitimate expression of the Iraqi mood. Further, a couple of our interviewees argued that in their coverage, they had made the role of the Americans and the size of the crowd very clear (a claim not generally supported by our content analysis).

Others were more critical. Ben Brown felt that the coverage of the statue episode was distorted as "there was a tiny number of people, actually." He said that he would have like to have thought that he would have shown a wide shot, and criticized the way in which the formula of television news coverage of a war of liberation expects it will end in a moment of liberation.

The Baghdad correspondent for Channel 4 News, Lindsey Hilsum, was the only one of our interviewees present at the event—and as our analysis of the coverage shows, her report was conspicuously less effusive than other broadcast that day. She had been out and about reporting, and adjudged that the demolition of the statue was only of any number of events competing for headlines on that day:

> HILSUM: The statue was a tiny little thing that happened at the end.... We saw what happened, and it was an American tank recovery vehicle which pulled it down. A few Iraqis went up to it to try to get it down, and then it was the Americans who got it down, with a small crowd of Iraqis and a large crowd of journalists around it. It doesn't mean that the Iraqis weren't happy or pleased that it happened, but we took it as a small symbolic event for American television.... We did a long piece that day, maybe nine minutes, and initially the statue was the last four or five shots.... But then, interestingly, in London where they had been watching, they said, "No, you have to make that section much larger." And so they wanted to add pictures in London, so that section of the report became longer, which was fine.... But what one has to understand is that this is what the Americans did for symbolic effect.... There were a lot more interesting things that we saw that day.

Her point is an interesting one, in that it speaks to a disparity we discovered through content analysis, between reporters on the ground giving a more nuanced account of Iraqi opinion, and reports from London inclining more toward the celebratory. Significantly, in all these discussions, images of celebrating Iraqis are assumed to be "goal" pictures—a good example of how what appears to be a journalistic judgment contains clear ideological assumptions.

The Sourcing of Information

All our interviewees expressed the view that attributing information to sources is very important. Phil Wardman states that Sky had its own clear guidelines on attribution; if the army told him something, it would be, "An army spokesman said." For Nick Pollard, attributing sources was essential if viewers were to be able to judge how much they can trust what they are being told:

> I think it comes back to journalistic good practice. Tell people the source, tell people what they're saying, and to a large extent, let people make up their own mind.... I think most viewers are much smarter than people give them credit for.

However, Stewart Purvis acknowledged that there may have been problems this time in maintaining the attribution of claims down the line: "We're very good at the first announcement of saying, 'British military headquarters says this,' and then in the shorthand that goes on, that bit gets dropped." Our own content analysis indicates that this often happened, and that the failure to attribute is fairly commonplace.

The Basra Uprising

Arguably, the critics' most cited example of the weaknesses of the embeds was the reporting of an uprising in Basra that didn't happen. Richard Gaisford of GMTV did a number of phone two-ways, including ones with BBC and CNN, stating that he had been told by members of the Royal Scots Dragoon Guards that there had been a popular uprising in Basra. In a two-way with CNN, he was asked, "The British military officials are being quoted as saying that the uprising is in fact underway. How do they know? Do they have contact with people inside the city?" He replied, "That is the big question, and that is the question we've been asking here. We can only assume that they have intelligence within the city itself."[7]

So Gaisford himself was careful to identify the source of the reports. Ben Brown at the FTU then identified what happened to these reports afterward:

> He ran it, and then straight away it flashed all over the wires— "Uprising in Basra." We were trying to find senior officers to confirm it, and in

the end, they did say, yes, some sort of uprising was underway, and then it was confirmed as well, so we said, "British army are confirming." Maybe we were too accepting and not skeptical enough, but if they say it's true, you've got to run with that as long as you source it to them.

Caroline Wyatt was also at the FTU when the reports of a Basra uprising came in:

> We were told by Lieutenant Colonel Sean Tully, who was one of our press brief- ers, that Basra was revolting. The only other source for that we could find was a reporter somewhere outside Basra quoting an unnamed intelligence source, saying that they were getting indications that the people of Basra would like to rise up. We were saying to Sean, "Have you got anything stronger than that, because if that is your source, it isn't strong enough." He wouldn't say what his source was or what evidence they had. At the same time, we were coming under pressure, because it was on the wire, and it was being reported by [one of the news agencies] that the army was saying Basra has revolted. We were being asked live, "Basra has risen up, tell us more." But at that stage all we could say was, "We are being told this, but actually, there is no evidence of it," and as it turned out, that was probably about two weeks premature.

Sky editor Adrian Wells described how they reported the Basra uprising:

> He had been briefed a line...by his local liaison person in the army there, and then it had been subsequently stood up by the briefers at the hub. We had a two-source verification of it from the army.... We had no pictures, but that wasn't unusual, because no one was in the center of Basra.... So we went with it, because everybody else was going with it, and it seemed very credible.... I think with hindsight, we probably could have or should have hedged it more with "re- ports of" or "strong indications of"—slightly more hedging.

But there was "someone" in the center of Basra: a reporter working for al- Jazeera. Alex Thomson was critical of British television newsrooms for not taking advantage of Arab TV stations: "If we'd taken more notice of the Arab TV stations, we'd know that they actually had a team in Basra, who were reporting that there wasn't any uprising."

The View from Al-Jazeera

Although this report focuses predominantly on the effects of the strat- egy of deploying embedded reporters for British organizations, the wider context of the globalization of television news is impossible to ignore. One of the major developments of this globalization is the emergence of Arab rolling news channels, and in particular al-Jazeera, as major sources of news footage.

Amr El-Kahky was al-Jazeera's only reporter embedded with American forces. Unlike our interviewees from British television news organizations, he reported that the unit did not welcome his presence. He was always escorted by his unit's staff sergeant and media officer, and could not mingle with the troops. Unlike British correspondents, he was never briefed on future operations, even though he fully accepted that he could not report such information, because he knew he would be dis-embedded.

Yet at the very same time as El-Kahky was distrusted by the U.S. Marines, his life was under threat from other parties in the war. He was informed that because he was embedded with American forces, had he been captured by Iraqi troops, he would have been viewed as a spy or an infiltrator and executed. His safety was also endangered by the pro-war Arab troops. He received a death threat from the Free Iraqi forces who joined up with the unit he was with, because he worked for al-Jazeera, which they saw as a mouthpiece for Saddam Hussein. The colonel of the Marines unit refused to guarantee protection for him, and as a result, El-Kahky decided to leave.

Ibrahim Helal was the chief editor at al-Jazeera. Initially, he had agreed with the Pentagon that four reporters and four camera operators would be embedded with U.S. units. Unfortunately, the ground rules required that they join up in Kuwait and Bahrain, countries that banned al-Jazeera from operating. Despite appeals, the Pentagon refused to help by interceding with the respective governments. In the end, only El-Kahky was able to join the unit he was embedded with, and that was by using his personal contacts to travel without the knowledge of Kuwaiti authorities.

However, in the course of things, Helal didn't consider the reports that al-Jazeera's only embedded correspondent were sending back as that useful anyway. Because of the restrictions El-Kahky was working under, Helal adjudged that there was no real difference between him covering the American version of the war from the battlefield and someone covering it from CentCom in Qatar or from the Pentagon. Helal did find it significant that this was the first time an Arab reporter had witnessed firsthand the occupation of an Arab land by a foreign army, and was able to interview ordinary Iraqis who, however hostile their opinions of Saddam Hussein or other Arab leaders, spoke of feelings of bitterness and humiliation.

The different ways in which most of our British embeds were treated compared to El-Kahky does raise a number of important issues. American and British units seemed to be briefing American and British correspondents with sensitive information simply on the basis that because they were American or British, they could be trusted. To truly test the strategy of deploying embedded reporters, there should be equal treatment of professional journalists, whatever their religion, ethnicity, nationality, or race.

Embedded Reporting and the Post-Vietnam Military News Management Model

So exactly what was different about the implementation of the news management model in the 2003 Iraq War compared to previous conflicts? The concluding section of this chapter uses our interviews with editors and journalists to address this question by returning to each of the eight components of the model as set out in the introductory chapter.

1. *Reporting restrictions.* In essence, none of the reporting restrictions adopted in previous campaigns changed. Restrictions were still imposed on journalists against reporting information that could be interpreted as useful for the enemy: tactics, locations, and capability. If anything, reporting restrictions on these aspects operated more effectively on embedded journalists, because their own material security was at stake.

2. *Minders or escorts.* Public affairs officers were still deployed in the field, but the in the 2003 Iraq War they played a much more low-key role, didn't keep journalists under constant supervision (with one important exception, discussed below). Most importantly, minders/escorts didn't have a role in censoring journalists' copy.

3. *"Security review."* If there was one major qualitative difference in the 2003 Iraq War, it was the removal of prior security review. Journalists no longer had to submit their reports to minders/escorts for checking against the ground rules, and there was no chain of review going back through military channels, such as the Joint Information Bureau in the previous Gulf War. The odd clumsy attempt at censorship was committed by military commanders, not by public affairs staff.

4. *Restrictions on journalists' access to communications.* Restrictions imposed by the military on journalists' use of communications technology were indirect rather than direct. Journalists were restricted in their use of communications technology for operational security reasons: they were prevented from operating equipment at night due to light discipline, and they were prevented from using Thuraya phones at all due to fears about Iraqi capability to use such signals to pinpoint U.S. positions. Beyond that, jour-

nalists were restricted to the amount of equipment they could physically carry, which would have been well below what they needed to provide high-quality transmissions (note, however, that some American networks, despite the instructions stipulated by the Pentagon, were allowed their own vehicles and satellite dishes). The military arguably could have, but didn't, provide satellite dishes for journalists' use. Although logistical constraints did have an impact on journalists' ability to do their job, there is no evidence that restrictions were used by the military to influence the way the journalists were reporting the war. Indeed, everything else suggests that the Pentagon would have wanted embedded reporters to be sending back as much high-quality footage as possible.

5. *The pool system.* The pool system, introduced on the Falklands model by the United States in Grenada, Panama, and the Gulf War, was abandoned by the American military for the 2003 Iraq War. Indeed, within the context of the embedded system, the Pentagon now actively encouraged competition between journalists. By contrast, the United Kingdom retained the pool system, an arrangement which most UK editors and journalists were happy with, particularly the smaller broadcasting organizations unable to provide full coverage from their own resources. Arguably, the United States' removal of the pool system for the duration of the Iraq War is the second most important development after the removal of prior review. However, this cannot be described as a permanent development in U.S. military news management—the pool system could be abandoned this time because of the sheer scale of the military campaign and the number of embedded opportunities it created. For future, smaller operations, where there is not enough scope to accommodate representatives of all the media organizations wishing to report it (and most operations are likely to be smaller), the pool system is still the best mechanism. Indeed, the assault on Fallujah in November 2004 was covered by embedded journalists working under a pool system.

6. *Briefing operations.* The Pentagon and the MoD retained a briefing operation at CentCom in Doha, Qatar. This operation was singled out for particular criticism by the editors and journalists we interviewed. When asked about the reliability of the military as a source of information, many of our interviewees found them unreliable. But with the sheer quantity of reports and footage produced by embedded reporters, British editors could and did minimize their use of reports from CentCom. Fundamentally, the briefing operation at CentCom in 2003 differed little from the briefing operation at the Joint Information Bureau (JIB) in Dhahran in

1991. What had changed was the context in which it operated. Previously, editors were heavily dependent on the JIB as a source of stories about the war; now, because of embedded reporters, they were much less so. Official military sources had relinquished some of their power to define events. Yet, as we hope to have shown elsewhere in this book, this does not seem to have resulted in an overall picture any less favorable to the military. Again, the context in which official briefings operated in the 2003 Iraq War represented a relaxation of direct control.

7. *Privileged access*. With so many embedding opportunities offered, it is difficult to discuss the restrictions on places allocated to "friendly" journalists as a form of rationing. By contrast, the sole al-Jazeera embed benefitted from few of the advantages experienced by his American or British counterparts. He was not trusted with the access and the information that they received, and because of the way in which he was treated, his editor considered his reports to be of no more value than if he had been at CentCom or at the Pentagon.

8. *Exclusion of "unilaterals" from the war zone*. The death of ITN journalist Terry Lloyd along with two of his colleagues has been cited by many British editors and journalists as a defining moment, after which U.S. military action had actually made it unsafe to operate as unilaterals. However, we should remind ourselves that a deliberate attempt to exclude unilateral journalists from the war zone has been part of the dominant news management model through Grenada, Panama, and the first Gulf War. Arguably, what has changed is that editors and journalists are making the decision to exclude themselves from unilateral reporting from the front on safety grounds, rather than exclusion happening as a result of direct coercive measures on the part of the military.

So, to conclude, despite many of the claims made for the novelty of the embedded system, much of the post-Vietnam military news management model is still in place. The most radical and perhaps most permanent change has been the removal of the prior security review system (the combination of portable newsgathering technologies with the demands of the twenty-four-hour newsroom would make the reimposition of prior security review a very difficult cork to put back into the bottle). Other changes would seem to point to a more relaxed approach to news management. There were still the same type of reporting restrictions, but they were seemingly less coercively implemented. Minders were still employed, but apparently in a more enabling role, helping journalists to do their job rather than obstructing them or subjecting them to constant supervision. And while the military did impose restraints on journalists' use of communications technology for operational security and for logistical reasons, it is difficult to imagine how those restraints would help the military get their message across.

What we find in Chapters 6, 7, and 8, however, is that this more relaxed approach to news management produced a picture of the war that is no less sympathetic to the military. This is despite many British editors and journalists expressing a real awareness of the potential for being manipulated by this new approach. Our interviews indicated that embedded correspondents were conscious of the difficulties involved in maintaining objectivity. We heard a range of experiences in which reporters suggested they felt uncomfortable with the degree of closeness to the troops they were with (even if they asserted that they were able to maintain independence, and if necessary, would have been able to file reports that would have shown the armed forces in a bad light). Some journalists were concerned that restrictions on freedom of movement, the use of technology and the implementation of operational security restrictions could also effectively function as censorship. Others insisted that their position as embedded reporters enabled them to report the ambivalent or hostile views of ordinary Iraqi civilians.

Many embedded journalists were concerned that their reports would only give a partial, one-sided view of the war, but considered that embedded reporting could be justified as long as their reports were balanced by reports from other types of correspondents in the region. News chiefs and editors also stressed the importance of balance and context. Many of our interviewees consequently questioned developments in this war that threatened the ability of news organizations to maintain that balance. Some interviewees were critical of American networks for pulling out of Baghdad and not giving American television news viewers a balanced picture. A significant number were concerned that the ways in which U.S. forces had prosecuted this war had made it dangerous for unilateral correspondents to operate in the region.

We found in our interviews that there is considerable awareness of the manipulative potential of embedded reporting amongst British news personnel. Editors and journalists expressed deep professional concerns about partisanship, about balance, about censorship, and so on. And yet despite all those anxieties, as we will outline in more detail in the following chapters, their reports contributed to an overall picture that was predominantly sympathetic to the American and British governments' definition of this conflict.

One important point emerged from our interviews with editors and journalists which needs to be emphasized here. Many of our respondents commented on the relative absence of graphic images of people killed or injured by military action. As noted earlier, some interviewees pointed out that reporters and camera operators were censoring themselves, because they knew that the more gruesome scenes that they witnessed would not be shown on British television news. Again, many of our interviewees felt that British television news coverage was too sanitized and would have liked to have shown more, whilst mindful of the need to protect children from the effects of seeing such coverage. Effectively, our interviewees were admitting that they were effectively censoring themselves, albeit for well-intentioned reasons, in a way that could not help to contribute to a representation of the conflict as bloodless, as without costs to the Iraqi civilian population.

CHAPTER SIX

Broad Themes in the Coverage of the Iraq War

THUS FAR, WE HAVE EXAMINED the hopes, desires, and impressions of the American and British military and the broadcast media. These accounts provide a backdrop to the coverage, and they tell us much about what both groups wanted the coverage to achieve. But they offer only a partial glimpse of the coverage itself. The aim of the next two chapters is to provide a comprehensive analysis of that coverage. In this chapter, we focus our content analysis on British television coverage of the 2003 Iraq War. The next chapter adopts a more qualitative approach, looking at the language and narrative structure of the coverage.

While most of the data presented here is our own, we also refer to other studies of the war coverage: by the German media consultants Media Tenor; research on the BBC and ITV by Daniel Albertazzi; and research on the British Press coverage by Howard Tumber and Jerry Palmer (which also incorporates Albertazzi's research).

Media Tenor's analysis provides a comparative analysis of the way broadcasters from different countries covered the war. Their research on the representation of U.S. military action during the war found that broadcasters tended to favor the positions taken by their governments—a result that, while not surprising, goes against much vaunted notions of journalistic independence in democracies. German broadcasters were, like their government, much more likely to be critical of the American-led action, while ABC News in the United States (perhaps the least "gung ho" American network), was much more likely to be positive than negative. The BBC was, in this analysis, precisely where it would want to be, being the only broadcaster in the study to feature positive and negative portrayal in equal measure (Rettich 2003).

In other respects, however, Media Tenor found that the BBC were closer to the pro-coalition bias shown by American networks than the more skeptical German networks. So, for example, the BBC gave more coverage to coalition casualties than to Iraqi casualties (even though there were far more of the latter), though by a lesser margin than ABC News in the United States. The BBC also gave even less coverage to antiwar demonstrations than ABC News, while German broadcasters devoted a significant amount of coverage to the antiwar movement. As we shall see, these conclusions fit well with our data, which finds the BBC showing a commitment to balanced coverage but, nevertheless, tending to display a number of pro-war characteristics.

We shall refer to specific aspects of the Tumber and Palmer (2004) and Albertazzi (2003) research in what follows. Suffice it to say now that once war began, British broadcasters found themselves irresistibly drawn into the drama of the war. This left very little time for discussions about the war's purposes or outcomes—only 5 percent of ITV's reports and only 2 percent of the BBC's dealt with such issues. The great majority of reports—92 percent on the BBC and 93 percent of ITV—were simply about the progress of the war (Albertazzi 2003). The print press, who were not in a position to deliver news from the front lines with anything like the immediacy of broadcasters, spent more time covering the purposes and outcomes of the war, although the *conduct* of the war was still the main concern for all the newspapers in the Tumber and Palmer's analysis, ranging from 53 percent of coverage in the *Mirror* to 83 percent in the *Sun*. It is worth noting here the relationship between a newspaper's editorial position and the volume of coverage it gave to the progress of the war: the *Mirror*, being one of the most antiwar newspapers, focused less on the drama of war, while the narrative of war dominated coverage in the *Sun* ("the paper that supports our boys"). We shall return to this point shortly.

Our own analysis of the broadcast news coverage during the war is twofold. We begin with a fairly comprehensive quantitative analysis of the coverage by the four main television broadcasters. We then proceed, in Chapter 7, to a more focused, detailed look at how certain "key events" were reported across a wide range of broadcast outlets. In both cases, we paid particular attention to the role that embedded reporters played.

The Content Analysis

Our quantitative content analysis is based on all the wartime weekday broadcasts of *BBC News at Six*; *ITV Evening News* at 6:30 p.m.; *Channel 4 News* at 7 p.m.; and *Sky News at Ten*.[1] Each news bulletin was broken down into discrete units of analysis[2] or reports.[3]

Our coding frame involved two levels of analysis. The entire sample consisted of 1,534 reports, all of which were coded by type/authorship. The main categories of authorship used in our analysis are as follows:

- embedded reporter
- Baghdad reporter
- reporter from military briefings
- unilateral reporter
- available footage
- studio analysis
- interview with reporter
- interview with expert(s)
- anchor

The methodological task of differentiating between categories of news reporting proved difficult. This difficulty was in itself revealing about the character of television news coverage of the 2003 Iraq War. Unlike previous conflicts, this conflict produced no shortage of images to provide a sense of unfolding events. On the contrary, broadcasters had access to images from a range of sources: apart from their own embedded and non-embedded reporters, there was a steady stream of pooled reports, images from other broadcasters, and some footage provided by British and American forces. As a consequence, it was sometimes hard to identify the origins of a report.

So, for example, an embedded reporter based at the Forward Transmissions Unit (FTU) had access to a wide variety of images that could be edited together. From the viewer's perspective, the origin of these images was unclear. Was this an "embedded report" or not? And while we were sometimes reminded that embedded reporters were subject to some restrictions, it was often difficult to determine from the content of the news if a reporter was embedded or unilateral. As we suggested in our account of how journalists viewed events, this reflects a feeling articulated by many reporters on the ground, who argued that the distinction between an embed and a unilateral was, in practice, often blurred. This blurring was captured in *Sky* reporter Jeremy Thompson's description of being "half-embedded."

Where we could not positively identify the origins of stories, we coded these under the category "available footage." This category included a montage of footage from embedded reporters and unilaterals from the same news organization or through pools, news agencies, news exchanges, as well as footage from the Pentagon and the Ministry of Defence.

Who reported the news?

Table 6.1 provides an overall picture of how the war was covered, based on the 1,534 reports in our sample. Reports read by anchors constitute the largest category (48 percent—these reports may or may not include footage from the region). While we included some fairly short reports, we did not include anchor introductions or links containing no substantive news. We could positively identify 35 percent of the reports as filed by a correspondent based in the Gulf region, although a significant proportion of those—15 percent—were reports compiled from "available footage," that is, edited packages from various sources.

Table 6.1 Types of news report, by percentage (n=1,534)[4]

	BBC	ITV	C4	Sky	Total
Embedded reporters	6	13	11	7	9
Baghdad reporters	7	7	6	4	6
Reports from briefings	3	7	4	2	4
Unilateral reporter	2	2	0	0.2	1
Available footage	17	20	13	13	15
Studio analysis	8	2	4	1	4
Interview with reporter	7	4	4	9	6
Interview with expert(s)	0.3	4	8	1	3
Anchor	46	40	44	57	48
Other	5	3	7	5	5

It would be wrong to draw conclusions *only* from the percentages expressed in Table 6.1, as our method takes no account of the widely varying length of different types of reports, or the significance of their position in the running order. However, five points stand out: (1) the importance of anchors; (2) the key role of the embeds; (3) balance from Baghdad; (4) the narrow framework; and (5) the volume of reports with no clear source. We examine each below.

1. *The importance of anchors.* While the coverage from embeds on the front lines was a memorable feature of the conflict, reports delivered by anchors in the studio are still a dominant presence. Perhaps surprisingly, Sky, the one rolling news channel in the sample, carried more reports by news anchors than the other broadcasters, and fewer reports identifiably filed from the region[5]—whether by embeds or reporters from Qatar or Baghdad. Only 13 percent of Sky reports were from the region, compared with 29 percent on ITV, 21 percent on Channel 4 and 18 percent on the BBC.

As we shall see shortly, these distinctions can be significant, in that the stories told from the studio and on location can be quite different in tone or in substance. And it is clear that, despite the abundance of reports from the region, the anchors provided a key editorial voice (see Brunsdon and Morley 1978) to guide the viewer through this material.

2. *The key role of the embeds.* In previous conflicts, broadcasters have depended heavily on military briefings. During the 1991 war with Iraq, for example, military briefings from Riyadh, Dhahran, Washington, and London dominated media coverage (Taylor 1992). The coverage of the 2003 conflict, therefore, represents a significant point of departure, with less than 4 percent of reports coming from CentCom in Qatar. Indeed, as we have discussed, the lack of information coming from such briefings was a source of considerable frustration for many of the journalists stationed there. Reports from embeds, on the other hand, played a more significant role, providing 9 percent of the reports (17 percent if we exclude the anchors from the calculation), as well as much of the material included in the sizable "available footage" category.

This is an important point that illuminates some of the debate about embedded reporting. While the comparison is often made between embeds and unilaterals (e.g., Knightley 2003), the inevitable limits placed on unilateral reporters means that, in practical terms, *the more pertinent comparison is between embeds and military briefings.* Not only did the embed program thereby allow viewers to get closer to the front lines than in previous wars, it created, in effect, *more* space for independent verification of information. As a result, information about the progress of the war was *less* clearly controlled by the military.

This point is not intended to be a simple affirmation of the embed program (which is, for reasons we shall come to, highly problematic), but rather as a corrective to a romantic vision of reporters roaming around the battlefield independently. We have already outlined the dangers involved in unilateral reporting, and research on the coverage of previous wars suggests that reports from unilaterals have never played a major role in war coverage (Taylor 1992; Cook 1994). The embed program was not, therefore, a substitute for independent reporting from the front lines, because such reporting would always have been too difficult and dangerous to make a substantial contribution to day-to-day coverage.

3. *Balance from Baghdad.* Correspondents based in Baghdad (under the supervision of the Iraqi military) were also prominent in the coverage, providing 6 percent of the reports (or 11 percent of the nonanchor-based reports). The presence of these reporters in Baghdad, like the embedding program, was controversial, but for very different reasons. While the UK and U.S. governments were happy to report from the point of view of American and British troops (in a literal rather than a figurative sense), some, such as British Home Secretary David Blunkett, expressed opposition to the deployment of journalists in Baghdad, reporting, as it were, from the perspective of the "enemy" (Tumber and Palmer 2003, 31). The U.S. government also made clear that they regarded Baghdad as unsafe. While the American broadcast networks ABC, CBS, and NBC succumbed to this pressure and pulled their journalists from Baghdad, British broadcasters felt that this was an important side of the story to cover, and reports from Baghdad were a significant part of their overall mix.

On this issue, British broadcasters were critical of the American networks' capitulation and insistent that their own reporters in Baghdad were able to avoid succumbing to Iraqi propaganda. For many, the presence of reporters in Baghdad provided a necessary balance to reports alongside American and British forces; hence, as Lindsey Hilsum from Channel 4 puts it, "The Americans only saw one side of the war on television."

Indeed, this is especially notable on the part of the BBC, who—at least in the formal terms of this analysis—appear to have been assiduous in balancing reports from embeds with reports from Baghdad. The impression that the BBC's Baghdad reporter Rageh Omaar got a considerable amount of airtime is confirmed by these figures, and Omaar was, like Hilsum, committed to the importance of telling the Iraqi side of the story (Tumber and Palmer 2003, 31). Indeed, as we shall see later, British viewers not only supported the presence of reporters in Baghdad, but wanted to see more of the Iraqi perspective than the coverage provided

4. *The narrow framework.* Expert commentators were used sparingly in television coverage. We would suggest two reasons for this: first, embedded reporters made broadcasters less dependent on speculation by military experts ("armchair generals"), and second, most broadcasters decided that once the war began, wider analysis—of the reasons for war, the nongovernment organization (NGO) perspective, and so on—should be put aside.[6] This second point is bolstered by the Albertazzi (2004) and Tumber and Palmer (2003) findings, which showed that broadcasters (and, to a lesser extent, print media) focused on the progress of the war to the exclusion of discussions about purposes and outcomes.

The slight exception here was Channel 4, who were more likely to use experts, and whose format is, perhaps, better suited to news analysis. Their willingness to do so is also indicative of Channel 4's emergence (in our data) as the most questioning of the channels we looked at. Indeed, we shall explore in this and subsequent chapters the extent to which focusing on the progress of the war demonstrates impartiality.

It seems likely that the presence of embeds supplying "newsworthy" footage helped push the coverage toward a focus on the progress of the war to the exclusion of wider issues. The broadcasters had committed a number of reporters to the embed program and felt obliged to use them, limiting the space available for debate and analysis about the war.

This point is made clearer if we look at the sources of information used during the war. Tumber and Palmer's analysis suggests that "what is striking…is that…across channels: coalition official spokespersons and representatives of government dominate by a large margin in all cases" (2004, 103). If the story is simply the progress of the war, this dominance is not surprising, but it speaks to how the decision to focus on the war's progress necessarily led to the use of sources who were (in public) firmly in the pro-war camp.

Our own analysis of sources (Table 6.2) also shows the dominance of the British and American government and military (although our data suggests less imbalance between these and official Iraqi sources than the Tumber and Palmer study), although it does not reflect the greater time and credence shown British and American sources versus the degree of suspicion shown Iraqi sources. It also suggests that Channel 4 was the least reliant on these sources and most likely to broaden their coverage to include other voices.

Table 6.2 Use of on-screen sources by percentage

	BBC	ITV	C4	Sky	Total
UK/U.S government/ military	56	50	42	48	46
Official Iraqi sources	26	22	37	27	30
Other media	11	8	3	4	5
Iraqi citizens	0	11	5	8	7
Other (e.g., Red Cross)	7	8	15	13	12

5. *News from …somewhere or other.* Finally, the size of the miscellaneous category—stories with no clear origin—should give us pause. Put bluntly, if we had difficulty identifying the origins of many news reports, what chance did most viewers have? The journalists we interviewed strongly endorsed the idea that footage should always be attributed, so that the viewer is aware of its origin. As Sky's Nick Pollard, told us, attributing sources was essential if viewers were to be able to judge what they are being told: "I think it comes back to journalistic good practice. Tell people the source, tell people what they're saying and to a large extent let people make up their own mind."

This is not easy, of course—newsrooms were bombarded with images and had little time to make sense of them. It is troubling, nonetheless, that some of the footage used in these news reports came from Pentagon and Ministry of Defence camera crews and was mixed in with other images but *not* attributed. On 21 March 2003, for example, ITV and Channel 4 News used MoD footage of Iraqis surrendering in an orderly fashion with *no* indication of its origin. We explore further the question of attributing information to sources in the case studies, which make clear that what Pollard describes as "journalistic good practice" is routinely ignored.

Embeds and impartiality

Much of the criticism of embedded reporters asserts that embedding obliged journalists to become part of a military/government propaganda effort (Knightley 2003), or that, as Morrison and Tumber put it, "embeds feel an affinity with the troops, a shared determination to see the venture through to the end" (1988, 97). We have discussed the embeds' own feelings about this, but how far did the actual content of their reports suggest a bias? To test this, we looked at two long-running stories that were central to the government's case for war: claims about Iraqi possession of weapons of mass destruction (WMD); and the attitude and welfare of the Iraqi people themselves, in whose name the war was (and continues to be) often justified by the government.

We found, in total, 186 references to WMD (contained in 127 reports, or just over 8 percent of the whole sample). References to the Iraqi possession of WMD ranged from reports of U.S./UK forces discovering facilities that suggested evidence of WMD capability[7] to footage of U.S./UK forces or correspondents donning gas masks or chemical protection suits (thus implying the threat of Iraqi deployment of chemical or biological weapons). Iraqi possession of WMD was also repeatedly assessed, asserted, and speculated on by government and military sources, experts, and correspondents.

We categorized assessments of Iraqi WMD under two broad headings: those references that asserted or implied the *possible or likely* presence of chemical or biological weapons, and those references that *cast doubt* on Iraqi WMD capability. Table 6.3 shows that, overall, broadcasters were eight times more likely to make references suggesting the presence of WMD than those suggesting their absence. It also shows that the BBC made the fewest references, and while those references were 3 to 1 in favor of the government's claims about WMD, this was a little more balanced than other broadcasters. Sky, on the other hand, with a ratio of nearly 30 to 1, was both most likely to suggest the presence of WMD and least likely to cast doubt on Iraqi capability.

Table 6.3 References to Iraqi WMD capability (n= 186)[8]

	BBC	ITV	C4	Sky	Total	Total%
Implying capability	21	26	59	59	165	89
Doubting capability	6	4	9	2	21	11

If we break this down by type of report, we find that embeds were no more likely to report this issue in line with government claims than any other kind of reporter. While *all* reports about WMD were speculative, reports coming directly from embeds were a little less likely to indulge in such speculation, being responsible for 9 percent of reports on the war overall, but only 5 percent of references to WMD. By contrast, Table 6.4 shows that correspondents at the military briefings were more likely to refer to WMD, and nearly always positively (being responsible for 8 percent of references to WMD, but only 4 percent of reports on the war overall).

Table 6.4 Number of stories including one or more reference to the theme of Iraqi WMD capability against type of news report (n=127)

	Implying capability	Doubting capability	% of WMD references	% of total reports
Embedded reporters	6	1	5	9
Baghdad reporters	5	0	4	6
Reports from briefings	10	1	8	4
Unilateral reporters	1	0	0	1
Available footage	23	6	21	15
Studio analysis	10	4	10	4
Interview with reporter	11	0	8	6
Interview with expert(s)	9	3	9	3
Anchor	27	4	23	48
Other	14	0	10	5
Total	116	19		

The numbers here are small, although they do suggest that pro-government messages on WMD were more likely to come from military briefings than embedded reporters. Table 6.4 also shows that interviews with experts and reporters in the studio were also disproportionately likely to refer to WMD, although in these cases, references were a little more balanced (but still tilted in favor of the idea that Iraq had WMD). Overall, then, on the issue of WMD, there is little here to support the idea that embeds were any more responsible for reproducing a pro-government "spin" than any other type of reporter.

A more prominent theme of television war coverage was the Iraqi people: their attitude, actions, and welfare. We found 527 references to the Iraqi people in 383 reports (1 in 4 reports in total). Many of these references (45 percent) made suggestions or assertions about the Iraqi people's attitude to the U.S.-led operation. These could be divided into two main categories: those portraying the Iraqis as welcoming the troops as a liberating force (and thereby supporting the government's case), and those portraying the Iraqis as less enthusiastic or even antagonistic, displaying anything from reserve or suspicion to outright hostility.

The other main reference to the Iraqi people involved reports about casualties (30% of references). While such reports might generally be seen as detrimental to a pro-war position, most of these reports contained fairly low numbers and could also be seen to support claims about minimizing civilian deaths. Other references to the Iraqi people included images of Iraqis engaged in activities (such as shopping or looting) that did not clearly indicate how they felt about the conflict.[9]

Table 6.5 Percentage of references to the state of the Iraqi people

	BBC1 n =108	ITV n = 115	C4 n = 157	Sky n = 147	Total %
Iraqis welcoming liberation	30	31	23	32	29
Iraqis not welcoming invasion	16	17	19	13	16
Iraqi casualties	25	25	38	30	30
Other	30	27	20	25	25

It is hard to measure this against any kind of reality, as we did not know at the time how Iraqi opinion might divide. But as we have seen, as far as the broadcasters' main sources of information were concerned, the testimony of reporters on the ground suggested a very mixed response. Table 6.5 shows that broadcasters were—by a margin of around 2 to 1—more likely to portray the Iraqi people as welcoming the troops. The exception here is Channel 4 News, where the balance is only slightly tilted in favor of Iraqis welcoming the invasion, while Sky, once again, is tilted most clearly in favor of pro-war assumptions.

When we break down these figures by type of report, some interesting patterns emerge. Table 6.6 indicates that whereas the overall coverage tended to favor the government's case, *reports by embeds were much more balanced* (29 versus 27 reports). Indeed, if we exclude Sky (whose embeds gave reports slanted—by a ratio of 10 to 3—toward celebratory Iraqis), embeds for the other broadcasters gave the *least* favorable accounts of the Iraqi mood, from the government's point of view.

Table 6.6. Number of stories with references to the state of the Iraqi people, against type of news report (n=527)

	Iraqis welcoming liberation	Iraqis opposing invasion	Iraqis as casualties	Other
Embedded reporters	29	27	29	17
Baghdad reporters	16	19	21	25
Reports from briefings	3	0	4	2
Unilateral reporters	2	2	3	0
Available footage	54	25	31	47
Studio analysis	2	2	3	1
Anchor/reporter two-way	8	1	8	2
Interview with expert(s)	2	3	1	2
Anchor	34	5	56	32
Other	1	1	4	3
Totals	151	85	160	131

In short, embedded reports were notably more likely than news reports in general to portray the Iraqi people as antagonistic to or suspicious of U.S./UK military action. Put another way, of the 85 stories that included references representing the Iraqi people in this light, 32 percent were based on embedded reports—even though embedded reports constituted only 9 percent of the reports on the war overall. The notion of embeds being "in bed" with the military and government would seem, on this issue at least, to be firmly refuted.

More predictably, reports from correspondents based in Baghdad were also more balanced; they were almost as likely to include references to an Iraqi lack of enthusiasm for intervention as to an Iraqi welcome of intervention. The notable contrast here is with reports or two-ways with anchors, which had a 7 to 1 ratio of references to the Iraqi people welcoming to opposing military intervention.

Table 6.7 Number of stories with references to the state of the Iraqi people: Comparison between anchors and reporters on the ground

	Iraqis welcoming liberation	Iraqis opposing invasion
Reporters on the ground	47	48
Anchors and two-ways	42	6
Totals	89	54

This contrast (illustrated in Table 6.7) suggests an interesting pattern. Reports on the ground—whether from embeds, unilaterals, or Baghdad—presented, in roughly equal measure, a decidedly mixed picture of Iraqi reaction, one that fits with subsequent knowledge of Iraqi responses (including postwar polls, carried out in Baghdad for Channel 4 and in Iraq by Oxford Research International, which suggest that most people were happy to be rid of Saddam Hussein but unhappy with the U.S.-led occupation). The "headline" or summary reports by news anchors, by contrast, presented a *much* rosier picture of Iraqi joy at the prospect of liberation. This indicates that editorializing during the war erred heavily on the side of the government or pro-war version of Iraqi reaction, *even while* reporters on the ground were presenting a more mixed and less straightforwardly enthusiastic response. A happy Iraqi civilian, in short, was deemed more newsworthy than a disgruntled one.

Conclusions

It is clear, from our data and other research, that during the 2003 Iraq War, broadcasters concentrated their coverage on the progress of the war, rather than on broader discussions about the war or its wider implications. This emphasis may well have been accentuated by the embed program, as a result of which broadcasters devoted much of their energies to getting firsthand access to the battlefield. As a consequence, the story of the war was informed mainly by American and British government and military sources. While the coverage was balanced in many ways (with Baghdad-based reporters as well as embeds contributing), on key issues it was weighted toward the view emanating from those sources.

We found a subtle but clear bias toward two central pro-war assumptions. First, while the evidence was contradictory, broadcasters appeared to accept the argument that Iraq had a threatening WMD capability. Second, the dominant broadcast message about Iraqi responses to the invasion supported, rather than questioned, the idea that the action was welcomed by the Iraqi people.

However, in spite of criticisms that embedded reporters would serve to bolster such assumptions, little evidence emerged to support this. On the contrary, the bias toward representing Iraqi civilians as celebratory was made possible by anchors, who ignored the more balanced picture provided by embedded reporters (and by other reporters on the ground). Moreover, to compare embedded and independent reporters is, in practical terms, the wrong comparison. In practice, the embed program made military briefings—central to the coverage of previous conflicts—less significant.

There is also little evidence to support two of the main critiques of the British war coverage. First, the claim (generally aimed at the BBC) that the media were antiwar does not hold up. The first of these claims was made famously by Tony Blair's director of communications, Alastair Campbell, but was widely circulated: Matthew d'Ancona in the *Sunday Telegraph*, for example, described how "in the eyes of exasperated Blairites—the BBC whinged and whined, and did its best to sabotage the war effort" (29 June 2003). Although motivated by a desire for objectivity, the BBC, along with most other broadcasters (excepting, perhaps, Channel 4), was more likely to reflect pro-war than antiwar assumptions. At the same time, much of the countercriticism—that the media was complicit with the government and military—focused on the presence of embedded reporters as an instrument of this complicity, a focus that would appear to be misguided.

This remains a tentative conclusion, because the data presented here ignores some of the more detailed content of the coverage. So, for example, Albertazzi's (2003) data suggests both the BBC and ITV— especially the former—contained negative rather than positive evaluations of how the war was progressing. These data also offer only a glimpse into broader questions about the nature and tone of the narrative of war coverage. We consider both points in the next chapter, based on our more qualitative analysis of the broadcast war coverage.

CHAPTER SEVEN

Sources and Stories

AS WE SUGGESTED IN THE PREVIOUS CHAPTER, American and British government and military sources were the dominant sources during the 2003 Iraq War, a pattern very much in line with previous conflicts. While the use of embedded reporters brought the military and the media closer together, the practice did, to some extent, diminish the ability of government and military sources to control the flow of information. This happened in two different ways. First, there were moments when embedded reporters at the scene questioned "official" statements by military sources. So, for example, in three of the stories we examined closely (the checkpoint shooting at Najaf, the battle for Nasiriyah, and the fall of Umm Qasr), embeds gave accounts that contradicted statements made by the U.S. military.

Second, the presence of embeds disrupted the normal flow of military communications—a point we explored in our analysis of the military's role. While information from military sources has traditionally passed through a chain of command, the embeds could immediately report information coming from more local sources, thereby bypassing these procedures. This tended to increase the volume of stories that were subsequently discredited. So, for example, reports of a popular uprising in Basra and, later, of a large tank column leaving Basra, came from military sources on the ground but were given immediacy by the presence of embedded reporters who thought they had a scoop. Both stories proved unfounded.

At the same time, the network of embedded reporters helped to keep the focus on the progress of the war. As we saw in the previous chapter, this was very much the dominant narrative—especially on broadcast news—to the exclusion of other stories about the causes, contexts, and consequences of the war (or, indeed, to stories unrelated to the war in Iraq). The role of narrative was most clearly illustrated by another event we looked at in more detail: the "climactic" moment when American troops captured Baghdad, providing—or so it seemed at the time—a triumphant end to the central story.

In this chapter we explore these issues in a series of case studies, using a more detailed analysis of the coverage of a range of different news events, in order to provide a more qualitative sense of the way the war was reported and the role of embedded reporters in the development of stories. We followed, in detail, coverage of those events on:

- BBC 1 News at 10 p.m.
- ITV News at 9 p.m.
- Channel 4 News at 7 p.m.
- Sky News at 9 p.m.
- BBC News 24 News at 9 p.m.
- BBC Radio 4 News at 6 p.m.
- BBC Radio 4's *Today* Program from 7–9 a.m.
- BBC Radio 5 Live News from 5–7 p.m.

Where appropriate, we also looked at the early evening news broadcasts on ITV and the BBC, as well as the main evening ABC and NBC news broadcasts in the United States, and the Arab satellite channel al-Jazeera, to provide points of comparison.

The events themselves reflected different aspects of the reporting of the war, and we clustered them as follows:

- *The reporting of claims which proved to be unfounded*, focusing on reports of (1) the "Scud" attack on Kuwait; (2) the Basra uprising; (3) reports of the tank columns leaving Basra; and (4) the "fall" of Umm Qasr;
- *The shooting of civilians at a U.S. military checkpoint near Najaf*, an incident—witnessed by an embedded reporter—when journalistic and military accounts were at odds;

- *The battle for Nasiriyah*, which lasted for much of the second week of the conflict, and which showed U.S./UK troops meeting stiffer resistance than some had anticipated; and
- *The final stages of the war*, notably the siege of Baghdad and the toppling of the statue of Saddam Hussein by Iraqi civilians and American troops.

Reporting Claims:
"We are in a position to do nothing more than believe what they say."

We begin with a closer analysis of the way stories coming from military sources were reported on broadcast news, to see *how* information from these sources was disseminated. We will focus on what is often described as the "fog of war," in this case, four stories coming from military sources, all of which were untrue or misleading.

We examined every claim made during the coverage of the four incidents to distinguish between occasions when the stories were:

- reported without any attribution at all, i.e., simply as "factual" statements, rather than as secondhand reports;
- presented with a weak form of attribution (as in, "We're getting reports that..." or, "We've heard that...");
- attributed, either by quoting a source or by referring to specific or general sources (as in, "The military are saying that..."); or
- questioned, qualified, or overtly doubted by the reporter.

Most of the programs we have examined were broadcast within a few hours of each other, the exception being BBC Radio 4's *Today* program. Since it was broadcast the following morning, it was sometimes in a better position to examine the stories broadcast the evening before.

1. *The Scud attack.* On 20 March 2003, the U.S. military claimed that Iraq had fired Scud missiles into Kuwait. Although these reports subsequently proved unfounded, they added credence to the idea that Iraq was using "banned" weaponry—a point explicitly headlined in the British press (notably the *Express* and the *Sun*) the following day, when the incident was used as evidence that the Iraqi regime probably did have WMD and was prepared to use them.

Of thirty-seven references to this incident on the five television news channels in our sample, nearly two-thirds (24) reported the "Scud" claim without any attribution. For example:

Here in Kuwait it's been a day of scares and sirens *as Iraqi Scud missiles were fired* in retaliation for last night's attack on Baghdad. (Trevor McDonald, ITV News at 9 p.m., 20 March 2003, our emphasis)

Iraq's response to the first wave of attacks was swift.... It launched a series of missile attacks, sending Scuds over the border into Kuwait towards U.S. troops and local people. (Anna Boting, Sky News at 10 p.m., 20 March 2003)

On BBC and ITV, this pattern of nonattribution had been established during their early evening broadcasts, coupled with a sense of alarm about the potential use of WMD:

You just don't know when these Scud missiles come in whether they've got chemical or biological warheads on them.... There's a Scud shelter just to my left.... We've only just come out of it...after the eighth time. (Ben Brown, BBC News at 6 p.m., 20 March 2003)

Iraq responded to the raid on Baghdad by firing several Scud missiles into Kuwait. Two were shot down, none had chemical or biological warheads. They did, however, spark gas alerts. (Mark Austin, ITV News at 6:30 p.m., 20 March 2003)

Only three references were couched in terms of "reports" of Scud attacks; three directly attributed them to the U.S. military, and seven used cautionary language or quoted contradictory evidence (notably, Iraqi denials). All seven of these more cautionary claims came on Channel 4 News or BBC 24 News, and all came from non-embedded reporters.

Indeed, Channel 4 was conspicuously more circumspect than the other three channels. Anchor Jon Snow made three references to the Scud claim: one cited "the firing of three 'Scud-like' missiles," another elaborated that "Iraqi forces have fired at least three missiles into Kuwait, but Iraqis have denied reports that at least one is a banned Scud missile." The third reference took the form of a question to reporter Alex Thompson, who had just made two statements referring to Scud attacks:

JON SNOW: The Iraqis have been very adamant that they have fired no Scuds today, that whatever they fired were not Scuds. Why are the people at your end so convinced that they were?

ALEX THOMPSON: Because various American forces went to examine the debris where the missile fell.... They know which breed of missile they are looking at.... They saw what was lying on the ground and they told us it was a Scud.... We are in a position to do nothing more than believe what they say. (Channel 4 News, 20 March 2003)

This exchange was notable in that it revealed the source of the claim, as well as, interestingly, the high level of trust many journalists had in military sources.

The only other references in our sample that injected any doubt was on Sky News over a week later, on 1 April, when reporter Will Owen was asked: "Have we ever discovered whether Scuds were fired over towards Kuwait to the camps, or even towards the city, or was it different sort of missile that was fired?" Owen replied, "There's still considerable debate as to whether any of the attacks on Kuwait were conducted by a Scud." This was the closest any of the television news reports we examined came to a retraction of the original story.

The radio coverage was decidedly more cautious. Of eighteen references to this incident, only three reported the claim without any attribution, and one of these (on BBC Radio 5 Live) included an immediate qualification: "The Scud missiles, perhaps they weren't Scuds, the missiles which have been fired at Kuwait have been largely ineffective" (5:27 p.m., 20 March 2003). There were five references to "missiles" and six statements questioning or refuting the claim, most of these (four) coming on the BBC Radio 4 *Today* program, which included reporter Mike Williams's interview with a "local police chief," who suggested the missiles were not Scuds. However, while the original story was widely reported, such evidence debunking it was not. This accords with the evidence presented in the previous chapter, in which the potential presence of WMD was widely assumed, while the possibility that there were no WMD did not emerge as a controversial issue until much later.

This story received rather less coverage on the American networks and al-Jazeera. Interestingly, while the American networks often seemed happy to suspend objectivity,[1] in the stories we studied, the closest NBC or ABC News came to describing the missiles as Scuds was when an ABC embed referred to "Scud missiles, or what we believe were Scud missiles" (20 March 2003). Indeed, NBC was the only broadcast outlet in our study to make a point of stressing the legality of the Iraqi missiles. A report from Dana Lewis (embedded with U.S. 101st Airborne Division in Kuwait), stated, "Tonight in the Kuwaiti desert, soldiers don masks and wait in bunkers…while a Patriot missile downs the incoming *Abubeale* 100, part of Saddam's arsenal of missiles permitted under UN regulations" (21 March 2003). Al-Jazeera's only mention of Scuds was in a caption quoting Kuwaiti officials.

2. *The Basra uprising.* On 25 March, embedded reporter Richard Gaisford was told by sources in the Royal Scots Dragoon Guards of a "popular up-

rising" against Saddam Hussein in Basra. This information, according to our interviews, came from Special Forces in Basra, information that was not made public because the military did not want the presence of these Special Forces divulged. Major-General Peter Wall, Chief of Staff with British Forces, later "confirmed" this story.[2] These reports were contradicted by a unilateral reporter working for al-Jazeera, who reported that "the situation inside the city is stable and calm, except for some sounds of shelling.… The streets of Al Basra are quiet and there are no signs of violence or disobedience" (al-Jazeera News at 10 p.m., 25 March 2003).

Richard Gaisford, working for GMTV, filed his first report for ITV's twenty-four-hour news channel. The news was subsequently picked up and widely reported (every television and radio channel we monitored covered the story); Gaisford himself told us that he spent six hours on the phone to various media outlets. Most of Gaisford's early reports made attribution fairly clear, as the following extract suggests:

> My reports have been coming from the Royal Scots Dragoons Guards' battlegroup headquarters, and there they've reported this uprising, they reported an uprising amongst the public there that was being put down by Iraqi troops actually in the city center, they were firing munitions at their own people.… We are told it is a popular uprising, no one can say the size of it yet. (BBC News at 10 p.m., 25 March 2003)

In subsequent reporting, however, the language used frequently slipped away from clear attribution. Of sixty-one references to the "uprising" in our television sample, seventeen reported it without any attribution, sixteen referred to "reports," twenty-six attributed the claim directly to (or quoted) military sources, and only four cast doubt on the reports. On this occasion, both BBC channels and Channel 4 were more circumspect, while ten of fifteen references on Sky and four of eight on ITV News reported the uprising without attribution:

> It happened during a battle west of Basra, where there has since been an uprising against Saddam Hussein. (Anna Boting, Sky News at 10 p.m., 25 March 2003)

> Let's take a look at what happened in Basra today.… It began with a popular uprising against the Ba'ath party. (Chris Roberts, Sky News at 10 p.m., 25 March 2003)

> There was a popular uprising. (Richard Gaisford, Sky News at 10 p.m., 25 March 2003)

While Sky may have retracted the story in other bulletins, the first reference to a retraction on their 10 p.m. news program did not come until 2 April.

Channel 4 was, once again, the most cautious of the four channels. The following statement by Alex Thompson is fairly typical:

> Late in the day we suddenly had these reports coming out, unconfirmed, that there was a civilian uprising going on. Now I've just had an update on that from the military briefers here, they say perhaps scaling down.... They think there are some reports of something happening along those lines in the city, it's no more strongly put than that.... We have to be cautious before we get concrete evidence on what is going on in the city. (Alex Thompson, Channel 4 News, 25 March 2003)

Similarly, Jon Snow ends the broadcast with the statement: "It is still not clear if there has indeed been any uprising there."

Unlike the Scud incident (which was not "corrected" by subsequent reports), most TV broadcasters subsequently referred to the lack of the "hoped-for" uprising in Basra. Channel 4 was most explicit in rebutting the story, although in doing so it gave the impression that the story was "the work of an over-excited reporter or two on the edge of Basra" (Alex Thompson, Channel 4 News, 26 March 2003). However, the embedded reporter concerned—Richard Gaisford—made no claims to have witnessed these events and was merely passing on information from military sources. Moreover, senior military figures appeared to confirm the story.

Radio coverage of the "uprising" was considerably more in-depth, but once again, the story was generally treated with a little more caution than in television reports. Of seventy-three references to it, only five reported it without any attribution, eighteen referred to "reports," thirty-one attributed the claim directly to (or quoted) military sources and nineteen cast doubt on the reports. Radio 5 Live's coverage was particularly notable, as the story broke during their drive-time show (at 5:24 p.m.), and much of the next hour and half was spent reporting and discussing it. The show's presenters were clearly caught between the desire to speculate on something that, *if* it had happened, *would* have been a significant moment, and the awareness that there was insufficient independent information to confirm the story. This awareness was expressed far more vividly than on the television coverage, partly because reporters had more time to think aloud. The following exchange between Peter Allen and Tim Franks was unusually frank:

> PETER ALLEN ["in Kuwait City"]: Yes, I think the problem with this story, Tim, is that a lot of people would like it to be true, and we have to just remember

that it is in the interests of the coalition forces to promote this story and make sure that the whole of Iraq knows about it, too. I'm not saying it's not true, I'm only saying that we're dealing here with a matter not just of military significance, but a lot of it is psychological as well, and we have to treat these reports with caution, would you agree with that?

TIM FRANKS ["with British headquarters"]: I could not agree with you more, Peter, we absolutely have to be cautious about this, as we've had to be cautious about statements from senior politicians on both sides of the Atlantic that, for example, the port town of Umm Qasr was safe and secure when our own correspondent Adam Mynott who's been there, on the ground with the American Marines, who's been saying time and time and time again, "It's not secure," to the sound of gunfire crackling in the background. So you're right, we have to be incredibly cautious. The only thing I can say is the spokesman who we have talked to, we have been talking to over the last several days, one of the spokespeople here, he seems to be a trustworthy sort of chap, and we asked him again and again, "Are you sure of your information?" and he said, "Well, this is what divisional headquarters is telling me. The people right at the hub of the British Army intelligence operation, this is what they're telling me," and so that's what we're passing on to you, of course, as you rightly say, with all the caveats and health warnings about this, that we yet have to get independent verification. (Radio 5 Live, 25 March 2003)

While this exchange offered a clear note of caution, it also provides a glimpse of the "information loops" we described earlier. In this instance, the military spokesman was almost certainly basing his statement on the same (incorrect) intelligence that Richard Gaisford received, yet the reporters understand his statement as a form of *confirmation*, rather than simply repetition. The problem here is that regardless of whether the source "seems a trustworthy sort of chap," the capacity of military intelligence is overestimated. In short, in this case, as in many others, the military officials knew no more than the reporter.

By the time Radio 4's *Today* program went on air the following morning, the story had been denied by Iraq. We also heard a more credible denial during the broadcast from al-Jazeera (who had the only independent reporter in Basra), although Defence Secretary Geoff Hoon also appeared on the program to support the claim. Again, Hoon's statement is an example of information flows. By the time the same military intelligence Gaisford was reporting reached the Minister, a journalist on the ground was able to refute it.

Indeed, Hoon's statement that reports on the uprising came from "various sources" reveals how information can gain credibility simply by bouncing around from one source to another (as we described in our discussion of information loops). Our interviews with Richard Gaisford and others suggest the story came from one source—based on a Special Forces operation inside Basra—but that because this was seen by both the MoD and by many reporters as reliable, it was repeated in ways that seemed to confirm it.

Al-Jazeera, as the only news network with a reporter in Basra (Mohamad Abed Allah), found itself with a curious kind of "scoop." It reported the claims before interviewing its reporter, who had toured the city that day and reported he had seen no evidence at all of an uprising.

The American networks reported the claims with vague or specific attribution. Oddly, ABC continued to do so the following evening, mixing this story with another incorrect story about the Basra tank column, albeit in a modified form:

> In the southern city of Basra, where there was the beginning of a local uprising last night, Iraqi troops appeared today to be retreating. (ABC News, 26 March 2003)

3. *The Basra tank column.* On 26 March, military sources claimed a large Iraqi tank column—of "70 to 120" vehicles—was leaving Basra and being attacked by British forces.[3] This was reported by embed Clive Myrie and repeated by embedded and non-embedded reporters alike. Subsequent reports reduced the column to just three vehicles.

Of the thirty references to the story on television that evening, the majority (twenty-one) reported it without any attribution at all: five referred to "reports," and just four attributed the story. The most cautious reports came, once again, on Channel 4 and BBC 24 News, who described the incident as a report or attributed it to specific sources.

The radio coverage that evening was similarly self-assured: of the thirty-six references to the story that evening, twenty-four reported it as fact, and twelve referred to reports. BBC Radio 5 Live speculated not whether the story was true, but what it meant (in short, was this a surrender or an advance?). By the time *Today* broadcast the following morning, the MoD had scaled down the size of the convoy to just three vehicles.

On this occasion, military spokesman Colonel Chris Vernon (on Channel 4 News) and Group Captain Al Lockwood (on *Today*) specifically laid the blame for the nonexistent tank column on an "embedded journalist" (presumably Clive Myrie). As far as we can tell, this accusation appears somewhat disingenuous, since the story originated from military intelligence sources that Myrie just referenced.

In the United States, NBC reported the claim as simple fact, while on ABC, the source of the story was specifically referred to as military, although ABC's version added an even more speculative claim about the nature of the convoy: "U.S. intelligence says it's picked up what may be a large column of the Republican Guard, hundreds of vehicles, they said." Al-Jazeera's references to the incident all attributed the source to the British military.

Both Basra stories are similar in that they involve an embedded reporter passing on what turned out to be faulty military intelligence. The failure to attribute sources in these cases suggests that broadcasters placed far more faith in this information than they should have. Interestingly, when *politicians* in the British government made claims that later proved unfounded, it was treated far more tentatively. Thus, Tony Blair's claim that two British soldiers had been executed by Iraq forces was reported by most channels, but with a high degree of caution, as the following extracts suggest:

> A real show of anger, Tony Blair on what he alleged was the execution of two British soldiers... he can't give the evidence for that.... But I think what it is evidence of is a little panic, they no longer have the pictures they'd hoped for, pictures of liberated Iraqis.... Instead, they are having to make the British population angry to get them to back this war. (Nick Robinson, ITV News at 6:30 p.m., 27 March 2003)

> On the basis of the evidence offered so far by the British government, the suspicion of execution is no more than that.... What the British are saying is that two members of the Desert Rats were missing in action on Sunday, they believe those are the bodies that have been identified now. But they are saying that on the basis that they were not wearing their body armor and their helmets, and one of them appears to have been shot in the chest, that they were executed. Well, that is certainly at the best, very circumstantial evidence. (Adam Boulton, Sky News at 10 p.m., 27 March 2003)

The subsequent retraction of the story the following day was also widely reported. This indicates greater journalistic suspicion of news from politicians than that from military sources.

4. *The capture of Umm Qasr.* American forces claimed to have successfully captured the small but strategically important Iraqi port of Umm Qasr on 20, 21, 22, and 24 March. Donald Rumsfeld, for example, claimed on 21 March that "Coalition forces did capture and do control the port of Umm Qasr" (NBC News, 21 March 2003). Fighting actually continued for several days after these reports. In this case, the few more cautionary statements came mostly from embedded reporters on the ground (such as Alex Thompson and Michael Williams). Hence the presence of embeds subjected claims made by military or political figures to a degree of inde-

pendent testimony. This level of scrutiny made it more difficult to present the war as a seamless operation against a lackluster resistance.

Nonetheless, the reports by embeds did not necessarily shape the coverage: of forty-one references to the premature capture of Umm Qasr on television, sixteen reported it without any attribution, seven as "reports," and eight with attribution. Only eight cast doubt on the story (half of these being on Channel 4, while Sky offered no cautionary notes at all). Radio reports were, once again, more cautious. Of 23 references to this story in our radio sample, only two reported it as fact, one as a "report," six with attribution; the majority of references (fourteen) questioned or contradicted these reports.

In the United States, NBC's coverage involved a succession of statements that Umm Qasr *had* been captured, up until 31 March, when viewers were informed that it had not:

> American and British ground troops charged into Iraq a full day before major air strikes, quickly seizing the city of Umm Qasr. (NBC News, 21 March 2003)

> In nearby Umm Qasr, now under better control... (NBC News, 26 March 2003)

> In the south, the port town of Umm Qasr, an important link for humanitarian aid, is now under British control. (NBC News, 27 March 2003)

> Although much of the south is under coalition control, the port town of Umm Qasr remains dangerous. (NBC News, 31 March 2003)

According to the MoD, part of the problem here is semantic, with journalists assuming military statements implied a degree of absolute control. Either way, the lack of clarity on both sides makes the off-and-on "capture" of Umm Qasr a good example of the fragility of information during wartime. It is also another instance of a widespread failure to attribute information from military sources.

Quote/Unquote

All the journalists we interviewed stressed the importance of attributing information, but this would seem to be an example of journalistic good practice that is often ignored. As ITV's Stewart Purvis candidly told us: "We're very good at the first announcement of saying 'British military headquarters says this,' and then in the shorthand that goes on, that bit gets dropped." If we examine the four stories discussed above (Table 7.1), we can see that failing to attribute information to sources is fairly commonplace. Although all four stories turned out to be baseless, of 173 references to them on British television, nearly half (48.5 percent) reported these stories as fact with no attribution at all. Attribution is, at best, patchy, with less than one in four (22.5 percent) naming any source (and this includes vague references to unnamed government or military officials). Moreover, taking both attributed and nonattributed claims together, we found that nearly nine out of ten (88.5 percent) references *reinforced* the unfounded claims being made.

Table 7.1: How claims were treated on British television (n=173)

Program	As fact	As report	Source named	Claim questioned
BBC 1	20	9	6	4
ITV	23	3	3	1
C4	6	3	15	8
Sky News	24	6	8	1
BBC 24	11	9	7	6
TOTAL	84 (48.5%)	30 (16.5%)	39 (22.5%)	20 (11.5%)

The most accurate and conscientious television news source, on these criteria, was Channel 4, which attributed most of the claims made to a named source and often offered evidence questioning those claims. ITV News was the worst offender, routinely failing to supply any attribution and only once questioning a claim being made. Perhaps most striking here is that the claims made during the war that inaccuracy was a result of the rolling twenty-four-hour news services—who, with so much time to fill, were a source of rumor and speculation—are *not* borne out. Certainly Sky was as unquestioning about these stories as ITV News (although its record on attribution was similar to BBC 1's flagship news program), and yet BBC 24 News was second only to Channel 4 in attributing sources and questioning claims.

The radio news programs were, on the whole, a little more circumspect in their attribution. Of the 154 references in our sample, 23 percent made completely unattributed claims—a figure that, while higher than it should be, is less than half the percentage of nonattributed stories on television news. Radio programs overall were also more likely to question stories (as they did in 30 percent of references). Interestingly (given the scrutiny heaped upon it during the Hutton Inquiry, which criticized the

Today program's use of an attributed source), of the eight British broadcast news programs we examined, the *Today* program was most likely both to directly attribute their sources and to question them. Overall, 83 percent of references on *Today* either attributed a claim to a named source or questioned that claim—well above the average of 34 percent for television and 55 percent for radio programs. Conversely, only 3 percent of claims reported on *Today* contained no attribution, well below the average of 48.5 percent for television and 23 percent for radio. *Today*, of course, had the advantage of broadcasting the following morning (we did not include the Basra tank column story in *Today's* figures, since it was corrected by the MoD the following day), although its record does also hold up in longer-running stories, such as the "fall" of Umm Qasr.

Table 7.2: How claims were treated on radio (n = 154)

Program	As fact	As report	Source named	Claim questioned
Radio 4 News	5	8	4	7
Radio 5 Live	28	18	11	13
Today	2	8	24	26
TOTAL	35 (23%)	34 (22%)	39 (25%)	46 (30%)

Exactly why the other two radio programs did a little better than most of their television counterparts is not immediately obvious. This is particularly the case for Radio 5 Live, which operated as a rolling news channel for much of the war and broadcast at a time of maximum confusion when many of these stories were breaking. We would suggest three possible explanations: first, radio's reliance on the spoken word may lead to a greater emphasis on precision of language; second, radio programs have more time and space for questioning stories; and third, television news has a greater need to use linguistic shortcuts, making attribution seem clumsier than the use of straightforward statements. This last point may explain the poor performance of ITV and Sky News: their rather more tabloid style favors simpler, declarative language, making precise forms of attribution seem awkward, and in some cases, repetitive.

The role played by embedded reporters in these stories is mixed, overall. In the case of the two Basra stories, it is *possible* that broadcasters may have had more faith in military information when it was relayed by embedded reporters close to the action. Even if this was the case, however, it doesn't implicate the reporters or the embedded system. Rather, it simply points to the need to maintain high standards of scrutiny, caution, and careful attribution when presenting information from military sources. Indeed, in some cases, such as the battle for Umm Qasr, the presence of embedded reporters allowed broadcasters to independently verify—and correct—information from military sources.

However, the repeated failure to attribute information coming from military sources, especially on television, suggests that reporters and broadcasters place too much faith in these sources. Our analysis shows that military intelligence—regardless of its motives—is often unreliable (indeed, many of the military figures we spoke to acknowledged as much). While the individual journalists we interviewed stressed both the importance of attribution and the need to treat military sources with caution, in the day-to-day practice of reporting news in wartime, clearly, these principles get lost. There are exceptions here: audiences of Channel 4 News and the Radio 4 *Today* program would have been given far more opportunities to judge these stories on their merits.

Overall, however, it would have taken a well-informed and astute viewer to work out that these stories were speculative rather than definitive. Moreover, the majority not paying very close attention would easily have been left with the impression that these stories *were* true. As we shall see when we look at audience responses, our survey suggests that this is indeed what happened. So, for example, a quarter of our respondents were able to recall Iraq firing Scuds missiles into Kuwait, but only 15 percent of this group recalled that these claims turned out to be unfounded.

The high levels of nonattribution also suggest that journalistic reliance on military sources is much *greater* than the figures in the previous chapter suggest. Since a great deal of information coming from military sources *does not cite* those sources, a straight quantitative count of information is thus likely to underplay their significance.

Questioning the Official Version:
The Checkpoint Shooting Near Najaf

While in some of their reporting from Umm Qasr and, to some extent, Nasiriyah, embeds gave accounts that conflicted with military or government claims about the progress of the war, the checkpoint shooting at Najaf involved an explicit contradiction between an embedded reporter (William Brannigan of the *Washington Post*) and statements made by officials with U.S. forces. The coverage of the event highlights both the problem of nonattribution and the reluctance of many sections of the news media, during wartime, to be seen as questioning military information—even when there is substantive independent contradictory evidence.

On 31 March, reports emerged of the shooting of civilians in a vehicle at a U.S. Army (3rd Infantry) checkpoint near Najaf, killing at least seven women and children, and wounding others. Although the U.S. military claimed the action was justified—claiming initially that warning shots were fired, and that they shot at the vehicle as a last resort—this incident was notable because an embedded reporter witnessed the event and gave a very different account. William Brannigan reported not only that American troops failed to fire a timely warning shot, but also that an officer shouted, "You just killed a family because you didn't fire a warning shot soon enough."

While U.S. forces continued to defend their actions, Brannigan's subsequent account was difficult to dispute, and various military representatives at CentCom in Qatar shifted to more general statements about the military's right to self-defence, as well as the threat posed by vehicles at checkpoints (thereby sidestepping the misleading account they had originally offered). Three of the five TV news programs—BBC 1, ITV, and Sky—reported the shooting on 31 March, and both BBC 1 and Sky gave the U.S. military's version of events in detail, *in both cases without any attribution* (the report on ITV News was briefer):

> These details of a serious incident…involving U.S. soldiers and a civilian vehicle on the road out of Najaf at about 4:30 local time this afternoon…the vehicle was approaching a checkpoint manned by American soldiers from the 3rd Infantry Division, they signalled to the vehicle to stop, the vehicle continued, they fired warning shots, the vehicle continued, they fired shots into the engine compartment, the vehicle continued, they then fired on the passenger compartment of the vehicle. On examination they found that the vehicle contained thirteen women and children, seven of the occupants were dead, two were wounded. American soldiers of course extremely jumpy after the suicide bomb incident of two days ago, in which four American soldiers were killed…. Under instruction to exercise great caution at roadblocks, under instruction not to allow vehicles to approach too close, as a result of those circumstances, a tragic loss of civilian life. (Nicholas Witchell, BBC 1 News at 10 p.m., 31 March 2003)

> We are understanding that a vehicle approached a checkpoint that was being manned by U.S. soldiers, was asked to stop. Apparently the soldiers then, they say they fired warning shots, the vehicle then kept moving and ignored the warning shots, and according to Central Command, the soldiers then shot into the engine of the vehicle, but it continued to move towards the checkpoint, and as a last resort (this information, by the way, coming from Central Command in Qatar),

the soldiers then shot into the passenger side of the vehicle. They then examined it and they found thirteen women and children inside, seven of them dead, two wounded and four others unharmed. (Sky News at 10 p.m., 31 March 2003)

Had a reporter like Brannigan not been there, this version would have become the official history of the event (rather than the U.S. military's account of that history).

As an embedded reporter with one of the best-known American broadsheets, Brannigan's account had a great deal of credibility, and all five news programs reported Brannigan's version the following evening, although with significant differences in tone. BBC 1 played down any controversy, leading and ending the story with statements of regret from the U.S. military. This account glossed over the contradictions between the military's version (or, indeed, the BBC's version the previous evening, which told viewers, "They signalled to the vehicle to stop, the vehicle continued, they fired warning shots") and Brannigan's.

> HUW EDWARDS: Well, Matt was referring there to America's most senior military figure, General Richard Myers, who tonight expressed his regret to the families of the seven Iraqi women and children killed yesterday in a shooting at a checkpoint. He said that any loss of civilian life was tragic.
> DAVID SHUKMAN: The most serious incident came at a checkpoint yesterday near Najaf. According to the *Washington Post*, an American officer ordered his men to fire a warning shot at an approaching car. The reporter says that shot was never fired, the officer then said, "Stop him, Red One, stop him"—the soldiers did. Next the officer said, "You just killed a family because you didn't fire a warning shot soon enough." At least seven woman and children died. The Pentagon, realising the potential damage of this apologized tonight.
> GEN. RICHARD MYERS, CHAIRMAN, U.S. JOINT CHIEFS OF STAFF: I'd like to express our regrets to the families of the Iraqis killed yesterday at the checkpoint near Najaf. The loss of any innocent life is truly tragic. (BBC 1 News at 10 p.m., 31 March 2003)

At the other end of the spectrum, Channel 4 News highlighted the controversial aspects of the incident, being the only one of the five channels to report the angry response in the Arab world to the shooting.

The radio programs we looked at all picked up the story on 1 April, after Brannigan's story had been published in the *Washington Post*. Despite this, Radio 4's main evening bulletin twice repeated the military's claim that warning shots *had* been fired, simply noting that there were "conflicting accounts and an investigation is underway." Similarly, while Radio 5 Live went on to report Brannigan's account, their coverage began with a series of claims by U.S. forces that every effort was made to prevent loss of civilian life. This coverage is distinguished from the previous evening by the level of attribution: on 31 March, broadcasters were likely to accept the American military's version as an accurate account, but the following day, they were careful to stress that these were claims made by the military.

The *Today* program was conspicuously more hard hitting, taking their lead from their reporter based in Qatar, Peter Hunt, who was one of the few reporters to directly draw attention to the contradiction between the military's version and the embedded report:

> Once again clarity is sought, and clarity isn't provided during this war. They've issued a very brief statement—we only have their word for the events as they unfold, as they portray it—and they say that every effort was taken to stop this vehicle. Warning shots were fired, then they fired into the engine, then as a last resort, according to a spokesman, they fired into the vehicle with such tragic consequences—thirteen women and children inside, seven of them killed. So those are the bald facts presented by Central Command here in Qatar, talking about how they exercised considerable constraint to avoid the unnecessary loss of life. But then you have to contrast that with the report that's appeared in the *Washington Post*, appears to be from someone who's there, at the scene, and he gives a very different picture, which contradicts that official version, because he talks about one senior officer talking to a subordinate after the shooting saying, "You just killed a family because you didn't fire a warning shot soon enough." (Peter Hunt, *Today*, 1 April 2003)

Today's presenter, James Naughtie, went on to suggest, in subsequent interviews that morning, that the incident presented a problem for the credibility of U.S. forces in "winning heart and minds." The U.S. military's announcement of "an investigation" effectively ended the story, and the only reference we found to it after 1 April was on *Today*'s review of the British press the following day.

Reports on the story in the United States were brief, ABC News reporting it in the context of "increasing tension at U.S. checkpoints" while NBC simply followed the official U.S. version of events. Al-Jazeera first reported the story using footage from a CentCom briefing of the initial U.S. version. Later reports gave both the military's version and the *Washington Post* reporter's contradictory account.

This story is a clear instance of an embedded reporter forcing the U.S. military to modify an inaccurate self-justification for civilian loss of life. Without an embedded reporter to witness the event, it seems likely—particularly given the early coverage, in which the military's account was treated as authoritative—that the only version of the story to have been broadcast would have been inaccurate. And yet most news programs, apart from *Today*, were reluctant to make much of the story or its implications for the reliability of military information.

Military Sources and Trust

Perhaps the greatest problem for broadcasters during the war was simply the chaotic *volume* of information provided by the embed program, which was more difficult for broadcasters to handle than the controlled outflow from military briefings. But this does not mean that the *quality* of information about the war was impoverished. The evidence gathered here does not support the notion that "less is more." In many cases, the information coming from CentCom was less reliable than that from reporters on the ground. So, for example, we found a number of instances—such the reporting of the battles of Umm Qasr and Nasiriyah, and the checkpoint shooting near Najaf—in which embedded reporters almost certainly provided more accurate accounts than those available from official sources.

A number of commentators blamed the use of embeds by the rolling twenty-four-hour news channels for the reporting of unfounded rumors—another claim, as we noted earlier, not supported by our analysis. The television broadcast channels most likely to attribute or question information were Channel 4 and BBC 24, while Sky's poor record is comparable to ITV.

There were, of course, notable instances when embedded reporters "broke" stories that subsequently proved to be inaccurate (such as the Basra uprising and the Basra tank column stories). But our analysis suggests that, despite some attempts to apportion blame, this indicates a more general problem in covering war, rather than an indictment of the embedded reporters or the embed program.

In short, we found that all broadcasters—especially on television—failed to *attribute* or *question* information from British or American military sources as often as they should. Indeed, the research here confirms our earlier comments about "information loops" and suggests that broadcasters place more faith in military sources than is warranted. This is not simply a matter of military sources being deliberately economical with the truth, as they sometimes are, but of the limits of military information systems. As our interviews with the military made clear, these systems are simply less sophisticated or effective than journalists often assume.

Reporting Setbacks: The Battle for Nasiriya

Thus far, we have seen how, within a broad framework of impartial reporting, pro-war assumptions—about the treatment of military sources, WMD, and the mood of the Iraqis—informed the coverage. We shall return to this last issue shortly. First, we must consider one of the pro-war perspective's main criticisms: the idea that media coverage actually tended to focus on bad news (bad from an American or British perspective) rather than good.

There is certainly evidence to support this view. Tumber and Palmer's (2004) data suggests that both ITV and the BBC (especially the BBC) focused on negative rather than positive evaluations of how the war was progressing. Although it is not clear in Tumber and Palmer's account precisely how such evaluations were determined to be "good" or "bad," their figures suggest that military setbacks were seen as more newsworthy than military advances. On the BBC, for example, 60 percent of reports of the military campaign were seen as "bad news," while only 35 percent were seen as "good news." ITV was also more inclined to focus on "bad news," though to a lesser degree (43 percent of reports being "good news" and 53 percent% "bad news") (Tumber and Palmer 2004, 104–5).

The battle for Nasiriyah, which epitomized the moment in the conflict when it became clear that Iraqi forces would not simply surrender or melt away, provides a good example of this coverage. After initially claiming they had captured the town of Nasiriyah, U.S. forces met with fiercer resistance than many had expected. From 21–31 March, there were reports of fighting in and around Nasiriyah. Even when troops secured supply routes through the town across the Euphrates River, embedded reporters described how "Nasiriyah is turning into an increasingly dangerous guerilla-style conflict for American forces" (Andrew North, *Today*, 27 March 2003).

This was almost certainly a battle that received more airtime than it would have without embedded reporters. The coverage of the issue was dominated by reports from a small number of embeds, who all described the ferocity of the resistance to American forces as well as (especially during radio's coverage, where they were given more time) the unexpected scale of resistance. While there were a number of reports of fierce fighting in and around the town over several days, most of these were simply descriptive, referring to or giving details of the battle for the town, with no evaluative comments or connections made to the war in general. This was particularly the case on the rolling news channels (Sky and BBC 24 News), which offered very little in the way of analysis or comment, remaining steadfast to a "just-the-facts" approach.

When context was provided, it tended to cast events in a negative light, although the information provided was generally neither inaccurate nor speculative. News on BBC 1, ITV, Channel 4, and BBC radio all provided information that might be seen to cast the battle for Nasiriyah as a something of a setback. Lindsay Taylor on Channel 4, James Mates on ITV

News, and the BBC's David Shukman all made the point (on 24 March) that U.S. forces had prematurely claimed to have captured Nasiriyah. And reporters on BBC 1, ITV News, Channel 4 News, BBC radio, and the American networks all described the degree of resistance as "unexpected" (a view on BBC 1 and Radio 5 Live bolstered by interviews with American soldiers, who reported being told to expect little resistance).

While this kind of coverage could well be seen as negative, the accusation that this constitutes an unwarranted "wobble" on the part of broadcasters[4] is, we would suggest, an exaggeration. Only ITV News used the phrase "bogged down," and one of the few speculative comments about the possible influence Nasiriyah might have on our understanding of the progress of the war came from Robert Fox (defence correspondent for the *Evening Standard*), who suggested that the claims about "shock and awe" were "over-selling the whole game," and that "this could be a real grind" (Radio 5 Live, 27 March 2003). Indeed, we found only two reports (on Channel 4 News and Radio 5 Live) that explicitly linked the battle to Nasiriyah to wider themes about the progress of the war. The following report from Lindsay Taylor on Channel 4 News on 24 March was the most hard hitting and critical of the all the commentary offered:

> If anything is clear in this war, it is that in parts at least, Coalition forces have met much stiffer opposition than expected.... Gone are any expectations of a breeze up to Baghdad. Gone, too, are the hopes of a warm welcome. Instead, the rush is to get the dead and injured out, the objective here at least, to overcome the fierce local opposition. And tonight, with pictures emerging of the latest American wounded in the fighting near Nasiriyah, it's clear that the battle in every sense is still to be won. Again, it's not the whole picture, but it is one disturbing aspect of the difficulties of prosecuting this war.

This report was, however, very much the exception rather than the rule, and in keeping with Channel 4's generally more skeptical approach to the war in Iraq.

It is worth noting that despite its reputation, the BBC's *Today* program was fairly typical in its coverage of Nasiriyah; like other programs, it was sober and to the point. We found no examples of *Today*'s presenters or newsreaders editorializing about the significance of the battle for Nasiriyah, and the questions presenters posed to embedded reporters like Andrew North were little more than prompts to elicit information. The only possible exception to this nonevaluative use of language was a question asked by John Humphreys, who began an interview with Andrew North by referring to Nasiriyah as "the town where the American and British forces are having so much trouble."

If there was a conflict about the meaning of the events in Nasiriyah, it was between official military sources at CentCom and embedded reporters on the ground. So, for example, Peter Hunt, reporting on *Today* from a military briefing, suggested that "this (resistance) was anticipated, and everything is going according to plan," while embeds like Andrew North reported quite different perceptions among troops on the ground (reports sometimes backed up by interviews with unhappy Marines). In other words, if the scale of resistance at Nasiriyah *was* anticipated, it had not been communicated successfully with some of the troops on the ground.

It is easy to see how moments of Iraqi resistance—and subsequent battles—might be seen as more newsworthy than a steady, uneventful advance. But since news values are not neutral, to what extent might coverage of "setbacks" such as fierce resistance by Iraqi forces in the battle for Nasiriyah, be regarded as negative to the war effort? Some pro-war critics certainly adopted this view, arguing that "the BBC whinged and whined" during their war coverage. The focus on such moments was clearly, according to Albertazzi's (2003) analysis, a commonplace feature of the coverage.

The answer, we would suggest, depends on the context. Had the war become long and drawn out, a focus on "setbacks" may have undermined many of the claims made by the pro-war camp that the Iraqi people would welcome their liberators. But the fact that U.S. forces successfully captured Baghdad less than a month after the war began had the opposite effect. In this context, the moment of triumph (as it was seen at the time) was made all the more climactic because such setbacks had been—fairly quickly—overcome. In this sense, the "setbacks" actually heightened the drama of the dominant narrative. This becomes evident when we look at that moment in more detail.

The Short War Story: The Seductive Narrative of War

9 April 2003 proved to be something of a false dawn in the recent history of Iraq. On this day, U.S. troops captured Baghdad, signaling, it seemed, a triumphant end to the war. In scenes broadcast live around the world, a group of Iraqi men gleefully welcomed American troops in Baghdad's Paradise Square. The joyous crowd hugged their liberators and proceeded—with help from the troops—to tear down a statue of Saddam Hussein.

Our survey of viewers, carried out in the late summer of that year, suggested that this was by far the most memorable moment of the war. When reminded of a series of incidents (such as the bombing of a market square in Baghdad or the rescue of Private Jessica Lynch), this was the only one a majority of our respondents could remember. And not just a majority: 80 percent said they remembered it "very well," a remarkable level of recall for what was, after all, a minor demonstration in a faraway city.

Surveys that test recall of news events—especially on "hard" news stories—rarely record such high levels of preponderance in the collective memory (see, for example, Delli Carpini and Keeter 1996; Lewis 2001; Lewis and Speers 2003). So what was it about this brief, rather contrived moment—one that Robert Fisk called "the most staged photo-opportunity since Iwo Jima" (cited in Tumber and Palmer 2004, 110)—that appeared to capture the public imagination?

The glib answer to this is that the symbolism of the moment was so vivid and intense that it became instantly memorable. This begs the question of *why* the toppling of a statue of Saddam Hussein was so symbolically charged. In what follows, we will argue that the power of this particular image was deeply encoded into its media presence, both in terms of the moment itself, and, more importantly, its relationship to the narrative broadcasters told about the 2003 Iraq War. We will then consider what this tells us about war broadcasting in general, as well as the ways in which broadcasters committed to impartiality assume the innocence of news values, when those news values sometimes carry a heavy burden of ideological inflection.

The "Toppling" of Saddam Hussein

Roland Barthes's famous analysis of a black soldier saluting the French flag alerted us to the mythic power of the news image (Barthes 1988). But the image he chose was, by comparison with the "toppling of Saddam," a gentle and rather subtle invocation of an imperialist political discourse. On British television, the events in Paradise Square came replete with hyperbole, as commentators unleashed a string of superlatives. The image was, on BBC 1, "momentous," "breathtaking," and "utterly overwhelming"; on ITV News, it was "extraordinary" and "astounding"; Channel 4 News called the moment "tremendous" and "ecstatic"; and on Sky News, it was both "amazing" and "fantastic."

The significance of the image was straightforward. It showed the Iraqis "doing it for themselves," with a little help from their American friends. We saw the Iraqis greeting American troops "as liberators" and, side by side, crafting a symbolic "end to decades of Iraqi misery" (ITV News, 9 April 2003). In a single moment, it captured one of the most compelling arguments made by the pro-war camp (one that grew in importance as the chance of finding "weapons of mass destruction" receded): this was, indeed, a war of liberation, the outcome of which—the fall of Saddam—was the single, most fervent desire of the Iraqi people.

Indeed, the image was so perfect, in propagandist terms, that some have suggested that it was entirely stage-managed by the U.S. military, and that the Iraqi crowd were members of an exiled Iraqi militia flown to Baghdad by U.S. forces (Tumber and Palmer 2004, 113). Staged or not, it was certainly a "media event," one that, conveniently, took place in a square located near the hotel most used by most foreign journalists. Most Iraqis had abandoned the center of Baghdad by the time American troops arrived, and the small crowd of Iraqi men pictured clustered around the statue may have been in earnest, but they were also performing for the troops and the many journalists gathered to film and photograph it.

Indeed, there is nothing implausible about the "toppling of Saddam." While some Iraqis felt suspicious of, battered by, resentful, or hostile toward the invasion, there were undoubtedly those who welcomed it. But like many iconic images, this one held metonymic power, a small part that ended up standing for the whole. This was, in other words, the *abiding* image of the Iraqi people, the one that made the headlines and was portrayed with heavily underlined significance. It allowed discontents to be dismissed as "Saddam loyalists," mere hangovers of a despotic regime.

We analyzed the coverage of several events broadcast during the war—including the battle of Nasiriyah, which was spread over several days—but the toppling of the statue in Paradise Square in Baghdad received more coverage on television than any of them. Images of the toppling of the statue were shown a total of twenty-three times on the five main evening news programs in the United Kingdom: five times on BBC 1, six times on ITV, seven times on Channel 4, three times on Sky, and twice on BBC 24 (the rolling news channels were not necessarily being parsimonious, having already shown the image many times before their later evening bulletins).

The same scenes were replayed the following night in Kirkuk in northern Iraq, when another statue of Saddam Hussein was pulled down, with Trevor McDonald on ITV News reminding viewers: "This time it's Kirkuk, but the celebrations are the same." On this occasion, a statue was shown falling twice on BBC 1 and ITV, four times on Channel 4, four times on Sky, and twice on BBC 24—a series of images that reinforced impressions created by the previous night's coverage (and, in popular memory, may well have merged with them).

Many news reporters and editors recognized that this was a somewhat "staged" event, in which the U.S. forces had played a major role in pulling down the statue and the size of the Iraqi crowd was fairly small. The BBC's Ben Brown, for example, suggested to us in our interview that "there was a tiny number of people, actually." This observation came from seeing long shots of the event, which suggested that the event took place in a largely empty square, with a group of Iraqis in the middle, American troops to one side, and a crowd of reporters at right angles to them. Indeed, the impression created by the long shot is one of a largely deserted central Baghdad.

And yet, while longer shots of a fairly empty square made these "celebrations" seem much less impressive, there were no long shots used in *any* of the reports on the main evening reports of BBC 1, ITV, Channel 4, or Sky. Despite the length of time devoted to the story, all the footage shown on all the main channels involved closer shots, in which the frame appeared crowded by jubilant Iraqis. The impression created by these images was much more dramatic: in a textbook instance of the way in which the frame of a visual image can alter its meaning, Paradise Square seemed crowded, overflowing with jubilant Iraqi celebrants.

As we have seen, some journalists in the region questioned the use of such images. In our interview, the BBC's Ben Brown recalled rejecting such images as atypical:

> The day Basra fell, we had pictures of a jubilant crowd singing and dancing, but actually, they were from a village from the north of Basra. I spent the whole day in Basra and hadn't seen anyone singing or dancing, so although pictures of them dancing were better, I didn't use them, because I felt they were unrepresentative of the mood that I'd seen.

Brown's comment also reveals how news values can work against attempts to portray complex realities. Thus, the "pictures of them dancing" may have been unrepresentative, but he did feel, nonetheless, that they were "better" pictures.

This view was undoubtedly shared by most editors in London and New York, who, to coin the cliché, knew a good picture when they saw it. As we have seen, Lindsey Hilsum, the Baghdad correspondent for Channel 4 News, was present at the event, but like Ben Brown, felt its significance was limited. Even on Channel 4 News, the most questioning of the main television news bulletins, her editors overrode her judgment. She filed a report, which she described in her interview with us:

> The statue was a tiny little thing that happened at the end.... We saw what happened, and it was an American tank recovery vehicle which pulled it down. A few Iraqis went up to it to try to get it down, and then it was the Americans who got it down, with a small crowd of Iraqis and a large crowd of journalists around it. It doesn't mean that the Iraqis weren't happy or pleased that it happened, but we took it as a small symbolic event for American television.... We did a long piece

that day, maybe nine minutes, and initially the statue was the last four or five shots.… But then, interestingly, in London, where they had been watching, they said, "No, you have to make that section much larger." And so they wanted to add pictures in London, so that section of the report became longer.

The coverage itself thus reflected a quickly established conventional wisdom amongst news editors that this was *the* newsworthy moment of the war.

The only question about the numbers involved came from Huw Edwards on BBC 1 on 9 April, who asked Rageh Omaar in Baghdad:

> Should we point out, Rageh, that of course Baghdad is a city of millions of people, some five million, there were, maybe thousands on the streets today. What should we read into the fact that most of the Iraqi people in Baghdad certainly weren't on the streets?

He was assured by Rageh Omaar, if rather vaguely (and without supporting evidence), that there were "dozens, if not hundreds, of similar scenes" taking place in Baghdad (quite how Rageh Omaar knew this is unclear).

Huw Edwards injection of context into the coverage—a verbal equivalent of the long shot—was unusual. Most of the reporting emphasized, rather than contextualized, the significance of the moment:

> The fall of Saddam Hussein, momentous scenes as the Americans take control of central Baghdad. After three weeks of war, U.S. forces are greeted by crowds of cheering Iraqi civilians. (BBC 1 News at 10 p.m., 9 April 2003)

> Nothing could have prepared me for that moment. It was utterly overwhelming, and particularly to see the reactions of ordinary Iraqis and taking part with ordinary Iraqis and crashing down that statue. (Rageh Omaar, BBC 1 News at 10 p.m., 9 April 2003)

> "Cry freedom," the people say they've been liberated. (Sky News at 10 p.m., 9 April 2003)

> Well, that's an amazing sight isn't it, a great relief, a great sight for all the journalists here at the moment…. Live shots, of the Americans, waving to us now, fantastic, fantastic to see they're here at last, they've been so tantalisingly close for so long. No sign of any resistance as they're passing us, no sign whatsoever, now they're parking up right in front of our hotel. An amazing sight…the Americans have at last arrived, this area is being secured, this area is no longer under the control of President Saddam Hussein, we can say at last what we want and what we feel and what we like. (David Chater, Sky News at 10 p.m., 9 April 2003)

> American armored vehicles swept into the heart of Baghdad and were met by crowds of jubilant Iraqis. (BBC 24 News, 9 April 2003)

I think the main image[s] of the day are these extraordinary scenes, some of them which took place behind me in Paradise Square here. At first Iraqis were pretty cautious.... And then it was just like a dam bursting, all the pent-up emotion, the things they'd been too afraid to do and too afraid to say.... Similar scenes all over the capital...people reflecting on that tonight, and I think we're going to see bigger crowds tomorrow. (Paul Wood, BBC 24 News, 9 April 2003)

As the Iraqis gathered along the roadside to cheer their liberators into town, our correspondent John Irvine and cameraman Phil Bye were the first journalists to meet them, at the start of what was to be an extraordinary day. (ITV News, 9 April 2003)

As American tanks rolled unopposed into central Baghdad, Iraqi people rolled out to meet them, greeting them as liberators. (Ian Glover-James, ITV News, 9 April 2003)

Coverage was even more exuberant in the United States, with ABC News describing "a dream of freedom come true" and "stunning reception" given to American troops as they entered the city, while NBC opened their broadcast on 9 April thus:

Overjoyed Iraqis swarmed into the streets of Baghdad, dancing, celebrating, ripping up images of Saddam Hussein, welcoming U.S. Marines with flowers and kisses.

Of all the stories we examined, this provided the clearest point of departure between the British and independent Arab broadcasters. Al-Jazeera's coverage was far less celebratory and reported a range of different reactions—some positive, some negative. For al-Jazeera's reporter Mohamad al-Fal, the "scene history will never forget" was a moment glossed over by the British channels, when a U.S. soldier covered the falling statue of Saddam Hussein with the American flag (before later replacing it with an Iraqi flag, then with no flag at all). This, for al-Jazeera, was the key symbolic moment.

Most television channels in Britain and the United States, by contrast, repeated the same story of an Iraqi population overjoyed at liberation from a brutal regime—a simplistic assessment at best, and one that appeared to be partial, by vindicating the war itself. The only relatively sober and more nuanced television report on British television came from Lindsey Hilsum on Channel 4 News (9 April 2003):

So many complex feelings...a lot of people feel relief, they think maybe the war is over, an end to bombing and shelling and no more danger, that's one feeling. Others certainly just feel so excited, thirty years of repression gone.... They can maybe say what they think for the first time, they can talk openly. The Ba'ath Party men who controlled the neighbourhoods...they've gone. So, tremendous relief...but then, I've also met people who say, "Colonialism, we don't want to be occupied, we're Iraqis." There's a very strong patriotism and nationalism here, and I think some shame that they didn't do it themselves. So I think that people feel a complex mixture of emotions here tonight.

Of all the assessments, this was, perhaps, the most impartial and the one that has best stood the test of time.

Although the toppling of the statue was very much a television event, it also dominated radio coverage. Radio 4's news at 6 p.m. made ten references to the events in Paradise Square, and Radio 5's drive-time program twenty-three references. The only moment of dissent came from a Radio 5 listener, who e-mailed to suggest that the focus on the events in Paradise Square was propagandist (a view repeated in some of our focus groups, as the next chapter will show). Although this view was aired—a good example of citizen input into news reporting—the show's presenters suggested this concern was misplaced:

> Quick couple of emails...another cynic, Richard, suggests in a city of six million, what looks like a couple of hundred young men shouting to me doesn't seem..."Don't exaggerate and push the Blair propaganda," that from Richard. So some people not overwhelmed by what we've seen. I would say that the scenes in that center were undoubtedly very televisual, but from what we've heard, there are a lot of people in exactly that mood, in the mood to celebrate the arrival of the American troops, it's not just a few hundred we see pictured. (Peter Allen, Radio 5 Live, 9 April 2003)

On the *Today* program the following morning, the statue story was conveyed through a number of summaries of that morning's newspapers, which were also dominated by images of the "toppling of Saddam." However, a number of reports by Andrew Gilligan from Baghdad, while stressing that the widespread looting "shouldn't really be allowed to obscure the wonderfulness of yesterday," offered the kind of rounded assessment provided by Lindsey Hilsum the night before:

> JOHN HUMPHREYS: But as we speak, no resentment towards the Americans, quite the opposite, I take it?
> ANDREW GILLIGAN ["our correspondent in Baghdad"]: Well, yes, it's mixed actually, interestingly, I mean when we drove round, the pictures on the TV, as so often with TV pictures, can give you the wrong impression because they're a narrow focus snapshot, and there certainly were several hundred very jubilant Iraqis in Firdoz Square just outside our hotel the other afternoon. But equally, in the rest of the city, most people are either looting or standing on the side of the road watching you go past, or still sticking in their houses worried

about the looters, and we got a couple of cheers as we drove past in the BBC car, it felt a bit like being the Queen at one stage, but mostly people were reserving their judgment, I think, and, very interesting, a good Iraqi friend of mine went up to a U.S. soldier yesterday and said, "I'm going to exercise my right of free speech for the first time in my life, I want you to leave Iraq." (*Today*, 9 April 2003)

As widespread looting and lawlessness ensued during the next few days, we began to see a far more complex picture. For the purposes of this study, however, we should note simply that the "toppling of Saddam" was probably the most conspicuously pro-government moment of news coverage during the war, and that much of the coverage came not from the embeds, but from independent reporters in Baghdad (many of whom were understandably relieved that the most dangerous part of their assignment was over).

The incident did, however, fit well within the *limits of the narrative* embedded reporting provides. As many reporters and editors told us, the main restriction facing them was the difficulty in showing images that viewers might find too graphic or upsetting. Embeds were thus able to show exciting, frontline images of the conflict, but not the grimmer realities of war. They were also limited to an account of the progress of the war, rather than to broader issues. For the government and the military, having embedded reporters is a kind of lens, as ITV's James Mates put it, "through which they could be seen winning the war." The "toppling of Saddam" provided an irresistible climax to that narrative.

To conclude, while we found no evidence to support allegations of biased reporting by the embedded reporters, they were—as most of them acknowledged—only able to provide a partial view. The problem here is that embedded reporting, precisely *because* it provides such newsworthy reports, forces the coverage toward a simplistic narrative in which wider questions about the war are excluded. Indeed, it could be argued that the *success* of the embeds in providing objective, exciting, relatively uncensored reports made the war itself, as a story, more compelling. It is this, we would suggests, that explains the Pentagon's enthusiasm for the program. In short, if the details did not always go their way, the thrust of the coverage was very much on their terms.

So, while most of the questions surrounding the issue of embedded journalism have focused on specific aspects of their coverage to assess their objectivity and impartiality, we would suggest that the role that embedded reports played in constructing a narrative confined to the progress of the war is a more significant issue. This narrative forced wider questions about the war into the background and made the moment of victory (rather than, for example, the long-term welfare of the Iraqi people) the climax of that narrative. Thus, most British embeds were demonstrably impartial, but only within the confines of a limited perspective that focused on the progress of the war, rather than why it was being fought or what its consequences might be.

CHAPTER EIGHT

Watching War on Television

IN ORDER TO DETERMINE HOW MEMBERS of the British public responded to the media coverage we've been discussing, we carried out a nationwide survey and a series of focus groups to explore public attitudes to the war, responses to broadcast media coverage, and what people learned from that coverage. In this chapter we shall outline the findings of these surveys.

The Survey

We designed a national telephone survey based on a broadly representative sample (by education, income, gender, age, and location) of 1,002 people across Britain in August–September 2003. The survey aimed to discover people's broad attitudes to the war, their assessment of the objectivity of media coverage, their memories of the war, and what they thought they knew about it. Respondents were also asked to specify which media sources they relied upon for information, and their responses to those questions (together with all the basic sociodemographic variables and their attitude to the war) were cross-tabulated with their other responses to establish whether relationships existed between the media people use and their understanding of the Iraq war.

We included two open-ended questions in the survey: the first asked respondents who had changed their positions on the war to explain why; the second asked which images or moments were most memorable. The answers to both questions were then coded and sorted into categories.

The Focus Groups

Our monitoring of talk-back radio during the war had suggested significant gender differences in response to the war, and we also wanted to establish whether there were differences between Muslim and non-Muslim reactions. The seven focus groups were recruited randomly and allocated according to gender in four instances, and religion in two. The seventh group was mixed. Two groups were conducted in Cardiff, one all-male (n=12) and one all-female (n=11); three were conducted in Birmingham, one all-male and Muslim (n=10), one all-female and Muslim (n=9), and one mixed, non-Muslim group (n=10); two groups were conducted in London, one all-male (n=10) and one all-female (n=10). Overall, there were equal numbers of men and women, and the majority of participants were white (70.8 percent), the exception being the two Muslim groups, all of whom were Pakistani. The age group 25–44 accounted for 49 percent of the sample, with 45–59-year-olds accounting for a further 32 percent.

Our interview protocol covered several main topics of interest:

- Respondents' television news gathering and any changes in that during the war;
- Aspects of the coverage that respondents could spontaneously remember (particular reports or reporters, specific incidents);
- Memories of specific incidents prompted by video and verbal cues;
- Awareness of embedded reporting and the issues surrounding the policy;
- Views on issues of trust and impartiality concerning the government, the military, and the media reporting;
- Feelings about the motivation and justification of the war, before, during, and afterward.

We used three strategies to probe their memories of events. First, we asked respondents to recall any reports or incidents that particularly struck them during the coverage of the 2003 Iraq War. Second, we showed three video clips to the groups, with time for reactions and discussion after each. These were:

- A montage of reports taken from an ITV broadcast on 20 March 2003 dealing with the threat of Scud attacks. The clip showed several headlines from Trevor McDonald in Kuwait and reports from Romilly Weeks with British troops preparing for chemical attacks in the desert.
- A compilation of reports about the shooting of civilians by American soldiers at a checkpoint near Najaf. These were taken from BBC 1 on 31 March and from BBC 1 and ITV on 1 April, showing three reports of the incident, including graphics of the positioning of soldiers, in ITV's case, and a brief statement from General Myers at Central Command.
- BBC 1's coverage of the toppling of Saddam Hussein's statue in Paradise Square, Baghdad, based mainly on reports from Rageh Omaar.

Third, verbal prompts were given to investigate other key events and issues, if they had not already emerged during the conversation. These were:

- The Basra uprising;
- The battle for Umm Qasr;
- The battle for Nasiriyah;
- The rescue of Private Jessica Lynch;
- "Friendly-fire" incidents;
- The siege of Baghdad;
- The death of journalists;
- British soldiers who were killed (and reports of "executions");
- Weapons of mass destruction; and
- The discovery of torture facilities.

The discussions and debates provoked by the focus groups were always animated, and at times heated, and they broadly reflected the findings of the wider survey.

Findings: How Did Attitudes Change and Why?

We asked our survey respondents to say whether they supported the decision to go to war (over four months after the fall of Baghdad to U.S.-led forces), and to recall the attitude they had taken before and during the conflict. While a person's memory of the attitudes taken in the past is not always reliable (people have a tendency to want to appear to be consistent), our survey responses reflect trends found elsewhere, suggesting that clear, majority support for the war in Britain was only really achieved during the war itself and in a short period thereafter (see Figure 8.1).

Figure 8.1: Support for the war, in percentage (n = 1,002)

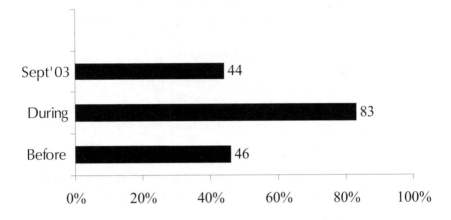

This is broadly in line with other survey data: the pollsters ICM, for example, have tracked support for a military attack on Iraq from August 2002 to October 2004 (see Table 8.1). Their findings suggest that opposition generally outweighed support for the war throughout the buildup to the conflict. There is then a dramatic turnaround in March 2003, once the conflict begins. They found clear majority support throughout the major combat phase in late March and April, peaking in mid-April, with 63 percent in support and only 23 percent opposed. Support then drops during the summer, and by September it is, once again, a minority position.

Table 8.1: Percentage of support for the military campaign in Iraq (source ICM[1])

	Approve	Disapprove	Don't know
23–25 August 2002	33	50	17
13–15 September	36	40	24
20–22 September	37	46	18
27–29 September	33	44	24
4–6 October	32	41	27
14 October	42	37	21
18–20 October	35	40	25

continued

Table 8.1—continued

25–27 October	38	40	21
1–3 November	32	41	27
21–22 November	39	40	21
13–15 December	36	44	20
17–19 January 2003	30	47	23
14–16 February	29	52	19
14–16 March	38	44	18
21–23 March	54	30	15
28–30 March	52	34	14
4–6 April	56	29	15
11–13 April	63	23	14
20–22 June	48	40	11
18–20 July	51	42	7
19–21 September	38	53	9

Our survey attempted to look behind these numbers by asking those who had changed their minds why they had done so (an open-ended question that we then categorized afterward). The responses suggest that a number of different motives were in play. The largest group of "switchers"—29 percent of the sample—were those who had *only* supported the war during the main combat stage. As Table 8.2 shows, the most common motivation for this group was a pragmatic desire to support British troops during wartime, rather than any new-found commitment to the *decision* to go to war. Of the 61 percent who had supported the war during the conflict but no longer did so after the war, around 20 percent of them told interviewers they were simply reverting to their pre-war opposition, while 80% specifically referred to the need to support British troops during wartime.

Table 8.2: Main reasons for supporting the war during, but not before or after (n=294)

Generally antiwar, and had only supported it to support the troops	61%
Felt misled about the reasons for war	16%
The bad situation in Iraq for Iraqis and/or British troops	11%
Would not say/unsure	11%
Other reasons	1%

Sympathy for British troops was also a common theme in all the focus groups, including the two Muslim groups. The London men, for example, expressed admiration for the fitness and training of the British Army, whilst the most strongly antiwar group, Cardiff women, expressed concern for their safety, such as one woman who told us, "I wanted to know what was happening to them." And while American soldiers were sometimes criticized for being too "gung ho" (London male), the British troops were never criticized. In contrast to the Americans, it was argued, as by one London woman, "Our soldiers are very professional, aren't they?"

The main other reasons for withdrawing support had more to do with subsequent events, with 16 percent stating that they felt misled by the government and/or the media about the motives for war, and 11 percent referring to the instability and bloodshed in Iraq following the war. As we might expect, these motives are more significant for a second group of "switchers" (9 percent of the total sample), who had withdrawn their support more recently. For this group, subsequent events and revelations (notably about the lack of weapons of mass destruction) tended to inform their decision (see Table 8.3).

Table 8.3: Main reasons for a more recent withdrawal of support (n=95)

Felt misled about the reasons for war	50%
The bad situation in Iraq for Iraqis and/or British troops	23%
The colonialist attitude of United States/United Kingdom	10%
Would not say/unsure	11%
Other	6%

These doubts were also expressed in the focus groups. A few expressed belief that there were WMD in Iraq:

I still think there is something there, and it will come out. (Cardiff male)

I really believed he [Blair] thought—and I think possibly they are there. (Cardiff female)

But there were more statements by respondents who believed at the time of the war that there were WMD, but have since changed their minds:

If you have got...heavily armed military coming to attack your country, and you have got to do something to defend yourself, you would use it. (Birmingham male)

I thought there might have been weapons there, but now I just think there aren't. (Cardiff female)

Indeed, we found very few people (and none outside the Muslim groups) who told us that they questioned the existence of WMD before the war, reflecting the fact that the doubts expressed, for example, by Robin Cook in his resignation speech or by former weapons inspectors like Scott Ritter, were marginal in media coverage of the issue.

Similarly, we found a number of respondents in the focus groups who argued that, while they were well rid of him, the Iraqi people led worse lives now than under Saddam Hussein. This argument centered on the shortages of daily necessities, the lack of an elected government, and on the continued armed opposition to the Americans and British. As one woman from the Cardiff sample put it, "The people are worse off over there now, they have got no heating, no water, no homes, nothing."

While the survey numbers here are small, the aftermath of the war, for some, added credence to the idea that this was a colonialist adventure in pursuit of oil. One focus group respondent specifically gave this as a reason for switching support away from the war:

> I was for the war, basically because they should have got rid of Saddam years ago.... But then when they started bringing in about the oil, my views changed. (Cardiff female)

Others referred to postwar moments that seemed to confirm their suspicions:

> One thing they had a plan for was securing the oil fields. (Cardiff female)

> Baghdad was being looted—apart from the Ministry of Oil, it was heavily defended. (Cardiff male)

Finally, those whose prewar skepticism had turned to support during the war and who still remained in support (around 7 percent of the total sample), gave a wide variety of explanations. About a third (31 percent) stressed the continuing need to support the troops; this group had a much more positive view about the consequences of the war, being much more likely to see it as a successful operation that had benefitted the Iraqi people (see Table 8.4).

Table 8.4 Main reasons for now supporting the war (n=72)

Need to support the troops	31%
The benefits to Iraqis	18%
The success of the war	7%
Would not say/unsure	11%
Other	33%

Again, we found this attitude—of viewers happy to see Iraqis liberated from the Saddam Hussein regime—in some of the focus groups:

> I believe that America has done a good deed for the Iraqis, you know, to free them. (Birmingham Muslim female)

> It is nice to see our taxpayer's money wasn't wasted, and they did appreciate it. (London male)

> I thought it was fabulous; I felt like I was celebrating with them. (Cardiff female)

The pictures of torture chambers shown during the coverage appeared to reinforce this idea. Indeed, in the focus groups we found a correlation between support for the war and unprompted recall of these pictures. Amongst the two groups in which support for the war was strongest—the non-Muslim women in Birmingham and men in London—the torture chambers were one of the first memories cited. Amongst the other groups, which were split between supporters and opponents of the war (and included many who were unsure), the torture chamber pictures did not figure at all in their lists of unprompted recollections (although, once prompted, they were recalled).

Overall, then, the surveys reveal a number of movements, the most decisive of which was pragmatic support for the troops, which overcame doubts about the *policy* of going to war with Iraq. For most of those who changed their minds for this reason, their repositioning was temporary and short lived. But there was also, for many, a feeling that they had been misled by the government and/or the media, as well as a sense of dismay at the consequences of the war. This was not a universal feeling, however; some people told us that the fact it had been a successful operation, with a positive outcome, had moved them from prewar skepticism to postwar support. In short, we find people going in opposite directions based on different perceptions of the war's aftermath.

The focus group interviews suggested that a significant current of qualification and uncertainty ran beneath these various shifts. In some ways, the main dividing line between supporters and opponents was a question of whether the end justified the means. As one respondent put it, she was "against the war but not [against] the freedom of the Iraqi people" (Cardiff female). Indeed, the question of ends and means gave the issue a complexity that made it difficult for many to hold fixed, certain positions: hence the apparent volatility of public opinion. While the survey did not find significant gender differences in those who shifted positions, in the focus groups, woman were more likely to express this uncertainty:

> I was never sure in the beginning. (London female)

> I felt very confused about it all, really. (London female)

We shall explore these shifts—in a climate where strong convictions existed alongside a great deal of uncertainty—in more detail in the next chapter, when we consider the role the media may have played in influencing public opinion.

Who Supported the War and Why?

The main sociodemographic difference between war supporters and opponents[2] is gender. Perhaps predictably, men were more likely to support the war than women, although the margins here are fairly small. Thus, by late summer, 57 percent of women said they opposed the war, compared with 48 percent of men.

The focus groups suggested that there were a number of gender differences in the way people experienced media coverage of the war, in many ways, stereotypical differences. So, for example, we found that women were more likely to dwell upon and remember news about the victims and casualties of war. In the mixed group and in all of the female-only groups, the story of Ali—the boy who lost limbs as a result of the bombardment—was often mentioned, while the only male group to mention this was the Muslim group. The following responses from women were typical:

> Images of the children, the actual children that were being burned, and I think that, even for my children, you know, to see that, it was really—that was a horrible part. What grown men do between themselves is one thing, but for all those children… (Cardiff female)

> It was the casualties and the children being hurt and that [that] I couldn't cope with. (London female)

Men, on the other hand were more likely to follow the military campaign. So, for example, male respondents gave examples of the friendly-fire incidents at the beginning of the war, prompting several discussions on the effectiveness of the American forces. Men also tended to know more of the technical details about war than women, as this exchange between men in the Cardiff group suggests:

FIRST MALE: Didn't the British come up with a very simple method of identifying the tanks? They had big yellow stripes down the side?
SECOND MALE: Inverted V. So if you saw it you didn't fire—and they
still got blown up.

Women were more likely to admit their ignorance of or lack of interest in
technical details—as this London woman did, when asked about the Scud
missile story:

I think it is because I don't really understand. I have never seen—I have never
been in the army—I don't really know—I watch these pictures, but I have no—
nothing to base it on. It's just a picture.

At the same time, all the female groups exhibited strong distaste for
graphic coverage of casualties:

No one would like it, even if the BBC did show it, they wouldn't like it. They
didn't like the dark pictures [of night air raids], did they? They didn't like the
bombing and everything. I don't know if the BBC or ITV would show them
anyway. (Birmingham Muslim female)

I think it is too much, you could see all the gruesome bits. They need to show
them with sheets over or something, or the bodies taken away and the bullet
holes. But this seemed to be just their guts hanging out and everything. (Cardiff
female)

The lone male group to discuss this issue was the London group, in which
some men wanted their children to see the death and dying so that children would know "that when you point a gun at someone, they do die"
(London male). This may suggest that women tend to be better able to
imagine the ugly side of war and sympathize with its victims, while men,
perhaps, are more inclined to get sucked into the dramatic narrative of
war, and thus need reminding of its consequences.

While these gender differences reflect various culturally learned stereotypes, we should not overstate them. As the survey suggests, many
women supported the war, and many men opposed it. But the focus groups
do show how different audiences can perceive war coverage in very different, gender-inflected terms.

There is little in the survey data to support various other stereotypes
about war supporters and opponents, both groups being broadly representative of the population as a whole. While middle-class people (social
classes A, B, and C1[3]) were a *little* more likely to oppose the war than
working-class respondents (social classes C2, D, and E), the differences
were slight, with people at the top and bottom end of the social class scale

being more likely to oppose the war overall More significant than social class was education: the higher the level of education achieved, the more oppositional people in our sample were likely to be. Thus people with less formal education tended to be war supporters, while people with post-graduate degrees were more than three to one against the war.

The survey suggested that people of all ethnic origins leaned against the war, especially British Asians (immigrants from the Indian sub-continent) although the focus groups, in which Asian Muslim viewers were well represented, and in which both men and woman were strongly opposed to the war throughout, revealed this more clearly. Those respondents most supportive of the war tended to reiterate arguments made by the American and British governments, suggesting that Saddam Hussein "was a threat" (London male) and promoted terrorism. One man put it: "He was a dangerous man, and the terrorists, he supplied them arms" (London male). As the surveys by the Program on International Policy Attitudes (PIPA) at the University of Maryland have shown, although there has never been evidence of a connection between Saddam Hussein and al Qaeda—and most experts agree that there was none—this view was also widely held in the United States and was clearly linked to support for the war (Kull 2003; 2004). In the other male groups, terrorism was also the most common reason given by those who supported the war; women, in general, emphasized the "liberation" of the Iraqi people as the main reason to support the war.

Overall, war supporters and opponents had broadly similar patterns of media use, although some notable differences did emerge. Readers of Rupert Murdoch's pro-war tabloid the *Sun* were more likely to support the war than any other group of newspaper readers. Indeed, 17 percent of war supporters were *Sun* readers, while only 7 percent of war opponents were—the biggest imbalance of any newspapers readership. This was particularly notable given the fairly even class profile of war supporters and opponents. Readers of the left-leaning broadsheets the *Guardian* and the *Independent* were most likely to be opposed, although this does not reflect a tabloid/broadsheet divide, as readers of the tabloids the *Mirror* and the *Mail* also leaned toward opposition. In this sense, *Sun* readers were clearly inline with their newspaper's strong support for the war, while readers of newspapers with a less enthusiastic (the *Mail*'s pro-war inclinations being compromised by their anti-Blair position) or oppositional approach (the *Mirror*) were more doubtful.

While we cannot assume from these correlations that the newspapers influenced their readers, it seems unlikely that these relationships can be *entirely* accounted for by readers choosing newspapers that reflected their views (especially for tabloid readers, who do not tend to choose their newspapers because of their political leanings). Moreover, the uncertainties and different patterns of recall in the focus groups indicate the degree to which the information or images in the forefront of people's minds—from the torture chambers to injured Iraqi children—might inform an opinion about the war. It is plausible, in this context, to see how media sources that emphasized positive or negative images might play an important role in opinion formation (see Lewis 2001; McCombs, Danielian, and Wanta 1995).

More interesting, perhaps, were the differences that emerged amongst broadcasters. The PIPA survey in the United States found that attitudes and assumptions were significantly related to broadcast media use (Kull 2003). We found a similar pattern in Britain, the difference being that while Fox News in the United States pursues a right-leaning (and remorselessly pro-war) agenda, British broadcasters are all obliged by—and publicly committed to—common notions of balance and impartiality.

Overall, a majority of our respondents chose BBC 1 (51.4 percent) or BBC 24 News (4.1 percent) as the news channel they most relied upon, followed by ITV (19.1 percent overall), Sky (11.6 percent) and Channel 4 (5.8 percent). As Table 8.5 shows, the most popular news providers—BBC and ITV—have viewer profiles that are fairly evenly divided (with BBC viewers a little more likely to be opposed and ITV viewers a little more likely to be supportive). Viewers of Sky and Channel 4, by contrast, are more notably partisan.

Table 8.5: The news channel war supporters and opponents watch most often

Channel	War supporters	War opponents
BBC 1 and BBC 24 News	51.4%	58.6%
ITV	22.4%	16.5%
Channel 4	3.4%	7.5%
Sky	17.4%	7.1%
Others	3.4%	10.3%

In short, Channel 4 News viewers lean heavily against the war, while Sky viewers are much more likely to be supporters. In terms of proportions supporting or opposing the war, Sky viewers break down much as *Sun* readers do, making up 17 percent of supporters and only 7 percent of opponents. War opponents are also more likely to choose other broadcast news media (such as BBC 2 and Channel 5) or to not watch much television news at all.

Again, we cannot, of course, assume causality here; indeed, while many newspapers were clearly partisan, both Channel 4 and Sky (along with other broadcasters) would claim a commitment and obligation to impartiality in a way that British newspapers do not. And yet these differences cannot be explained by sociodemographic differences. While Channel 4 viewers are a little more likely to be middle class (AB) and Sky a little more likely to be working class (social classes C2 and DE), the differences here are too small to account for these findings (quite apart from the fact that the social class was not a decisive factor in accounting for differences between war supporters and opponents).

There is, in other words, something going on here that *appears* (from this data) to relate specifically to media use. We shall explore the possible influence of the media in more detail in the next chapter, although it is worth noting, at this point, that while the broadcasters did *not* differ radically in their coverage, our content analysis suggested that Sky was, on the whole, the most likely to reflect pro-war assumptions, and Channel 4 the most likely to question those assumptions. What seems more plausible, however, is the presence of a *perception* that Sky was more in tune with a military perspective while Channel 4 was more critical. Our interviews with the Ministry of Defence, for example, suggested that Sky was their preferred broadcaster.

Media Use, Impartiality, and Trust

We found overwhelming support—92 percent to 5 percent—for the idea that broadcasters should remain impartial and objective during wartime (Figure 8.2). Existing media regulation in Britain requires news broadcasters to be impartial, but sets no limits on press bias. Support for impartiality in news is deeply held; most people would like *all* media, including the press (by 88 percent to 5 percent), to be impartial. In the focus groups, this was accompanied by widespread distaste for propaganda—although it was the government and authorities rather than the media who were usually seen as the originators of biased information.

Statements of trust in the British government were rare, and there were many strong statements of distrust across all the focus groups:

They are the biggest corrupted...the government. (Birmingham Muslim male)

They were all hiding something. (London female)

It's all just lies and deceit. (Cardiff female)

The only clear and unqualified statement of trust in the government was made by the most pro-war group of men in London: "You believe the government, don't you." However, this was not the view of the whole group, with others arguing that, "like most governments," they could not be trusted: "I wouldn't trust them as far as I could throw them" (London male).

While this abstract distrust of politicians *in general* is widespread, responses to the prime minister were a little more mixed. Some respondents made clear statements of distrust:

> Tony Blair, I do not trust him any more. (Birmingham Muslim male)

> You can't trust Tony Blair on anything. (London male)

Others judged him to be sincere, particularly on the issue of WMD:

> I really believed he thought they were there. (London female)

> Maybe it wasn't that I didn't believe Blair, but I didn't think his arguments were strong enough. (Cardiff female)

However, the media's reliance on official sources meant that this distrust also spread to the media as well, and many comments made by focus group members collapsed the media and government together.

Figure 8.2: Should TV be impartial in wartime?

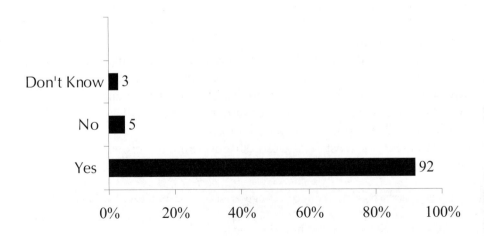

In general, those who felt that broadcast coverage *was* ob,_ impartial outnumbered those who disagreed by more than two to one. Similar findings were recorded by an Independent Television Commission (ITC) survey published in October 2003 (the exception being CNN, available to some multichannel viewers in Britian, which was widely seen as pro-war). Not surprisingly, both surveys suggested that people were less likely to have faith in the impartiality of press coverage, especially the tabloids, which are more widely read than the broadsheets but less trusted.

We should note, however (see Table 8.7), that for our survey respondents most ratings of media objectivity—for all media outlets—cluster around the middle between "very objective and impartial" and "not objective and impartial," suggesting only a modest level of endorsement for broadcasters.

Table 8.7: Perceived objectivity of media outlets

	1. Very objective	2.	3.	4.	5. Not objective	Don't know
ITV	9%	25%	37%	9%	4%	16%
BBC	14%	31%	29%	14%	5%	8%
Channel 4	8%	17%	17%	7%	2%	49%
Sky	7%	12%	10%	5%	3%	63%
Print media	6%	17%	33%	20%	10%	

Our focus groups suggest that the preference for television over print media appears to have less to do with an awareness of media regulation (which requires impartiality from broadcasters) than a sense that "seeing is believing." But the focus groups also gave us a little more insight into the degree of ambivalence suggested by the survey. In short, most people in the focus groups showed critical awareness of the way the media works, *while simultaneously* believing what they saw. In general, trust in television as a visual medium seems to override a critical media awareness. On one hand, group members expressed a certain cynicism about the media's involvement in the war on the military's terms and a concern that having reporters at the front meant the Iraq War was a "media war," not a "real" war:

> The one point that worried me, and I mean worried, I think it was on a Sunday morning, when we had a Sky reporter on the front line asking one of the American sergeants what they were going to do next, and I thought, this is a media war, not a real war. (Cardiff male)

In contrast, others believed that even if "things are being covered up and presented in a way that they want…at least you are seeing what is going on" (London male). This belief in the power of the image—that "seeing is believing"—seems to have permeated all the groups:

> What you see is true—you can't really argue… But what you are being told— that is the worrying thing. (London male)

One respondent described trust in the reporter on location in that vein:

> A lot of things are happening at the back and they [the reporters] are standing there, so you know that it's real. (London female)

Another said, "I trusted it because I saw what was happening" (London female).

Both surveys were conducted at the height of a debate about the BBC coverage of the war, with the Hutton Inquiry in full swing, and a lively public debate about allegations, broadcast on the BBC *Today* program, that the government had exaggerated the strength of military intelligence on Iraqi WMD.

Figure 8.3: Most trusted source of information about Iraq

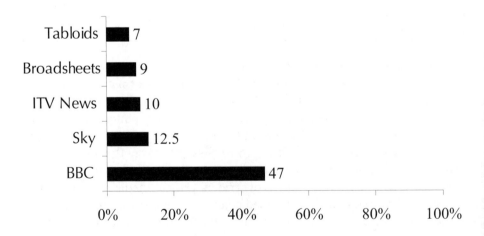

The high-profile criticisms of the BBC do not appear to have dented the public's respect for BBC news. Our survey suggested that the BBC was still widely regarded as the most trusted source of information during the war. When asked, "Which media outlet gave the best, most informed coverage?" nearly half the sample chose BBC news programs—far and away the most popular choice. This accords with ratings data, which found that BBC 1 was the most-watched news provider during the war, with Sky attracting the bulk of the audience for the rolling news. It is also worth noting here, given the criticisms leveled against it, that the BBC was the most trusted source for both war supporters and opponents alike, while Sky was three times more likely to be trusted by war supporters than opponents.

Figure 8.4: War supporters' most trusted source

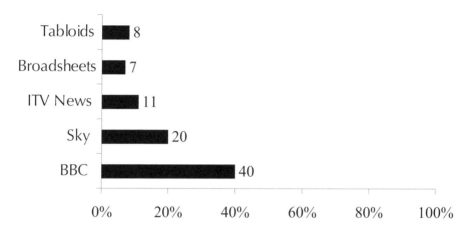

Figure 8.5: War opponents' most trusted source

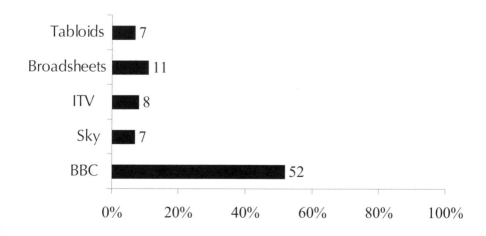

In the focus groups, statements of trust in a specific news provider are *only* made about the BBC, and in a number of different groups. While some respondents discussed criticisms of the institution, anti-BBC statements were rare. The BBC was the only outlet to garner outright declarations such as: "I trust the BBC" (Birmingham male) and "I have always trusted the BBC more" (Cardiff male). Even the Muslim female respondents, who were less trusting of television news, appeared to trust that the BBC *sought* impartiality. They were aware, for example, that the BBC did not screen Iraqi casualties due to taste and decency restrictions placed on them; as one Muslim woman in the Birmingham group put it, "If they never had a restriction, they would have shown it."

Nonetheless, we did find evidence of an anti-BBC discourse, suggesting that some of the criticism it received made an impression, albeit amongst a minority:

> I never watch the BBC, because the BBC is giving out a load of rubbish. (London male)

> The BBC was very antiwar. (London female)

> The best bit of propaganda for the Iraqis. (Birmingham male)

Since we have found no evidence to support these claims, it seems likely that this attitude reflects the presence of an anti-BBC discourse in sections of the press, rather than from a close viewing of the BBC's output. It is important to stress, however, that our survey does *not* support the notion that criticism of the BBC came only—or even mainly—from war supporters. Table 8.8 indicates that opponents of the war were as critical of a perceived BBC pro-war bias as supporters who perceived an antiwar bias (the equal balance between the two would doubtless be regarded by the BBC as a form of vindication).

Indeed, while the *high-profile* criticisms of the media coverage—from government and the press—have come from the pro-war side, been aimed at the BBC and permeated some of the focus groups, we need to stress the extent to which these criticisms were *not* reflected amongst the general population. On the contrary, our survey suggested that it was the *opponents* of the war who were, overall, more suspicious of the broadcast coverage. In our survey, only 20 percent of war supporters distrusted the information they were getting, compared with 30 percent of those who were against the war.

If we break this down by channel, we can see that war opponents were less likely to see ITV, and more particularly Sky, as objective and impartial. This is not, of course, to say that these perceptions are necessarily accurate. But it does suggest that the public debate about media bias during the war was misplaced in assuming that public discontent with media coverage came mainly from war supporters, and that the only source of unease was the BBC.

Table 8.8: Percentage of war supporters and opponents who found a news channel objective and impartial

	War supporters saying it was objective	War opponents saying it was objective
ITV	38	30
BBC	35	35
Channel 4	24	25
Sky	28	12

Indeed, the ITC survey, also suggests that broadcasters were more likely to be perceived as biased toward a pro-war, rather than antiwar, position (a perception in keeping with some aspects of our content analysis). We shall see how this unease with perceptions of the pro-war nature of media coverage manifested itself in the focus groups, when we look at what people did or did not like about the coverage.

The focus groups also suggested that definitions of "balance" and "impartiality" differ. For some focus group members, presenting two or more sides of an issue is, in fact, "antiwar." In short, there were some pro-war viewers who wanted *only* their view presented. ITV, although named as a channel some respondents watched, very rarely appeared in conversations about trust, and while the majority of respondents in all groups said they watched Sky during the war, trust is not a reason specifically given for doing so.

The other named channel in discussions on trust issues was al-Jazeera. Their coverage of Iraqi civilian casualties was criticized particularly by Muslim women: "They were trying to impress all the Muslim communities all over the world that the Americans were doing that to our Iraqi people" (Birmingham Muslim female). One respondent suggested that al-Jazeera could have faked reports (Birmingham Muslim female). Muslim male respondents, however, broadly supported al-Jazeera for showing "the Arab feeling" (Birmingham Muslim male) as part of a mix of channels: "It is better to see both sides" (Birmingham Muslim male).

Television War: What Is It Good For?

In line with the ITC survey, the majority of focus group respondents reported an increase in their television news consumption (and their reading of newspapers) for at least the first part of the war. Some respondents also reported an increase in the range of news outlets they consulted: newspapers for editorials and debate, different television channels for different perspectives, and rolling news to follow a particular event or to keep up to date with developments outside the times of scheduled terrestrial news bulletins. In all the groups, twenty-four-hour news channels were mentioned as a way to check facts and keep up with the ongoing process of the war, "because it's there all the time" and "[you can] check things" (London male). However, the use of twenty-four-hour news channels was also prompted by a desire for brevity, rather than for more news, as this woman put it:

> I watch a lot of News 24. The Sky one as well, because you can just go straight in, get the bullet points, and come straight back out again. (Cardiff female)

The range of broadcast news channels for those with satellite or cable access meant that several respondents reported seeking American channels to compare their coverage, and, in a few cases, seeking images and a generally different perspective from al-Jazeera, even though none of our respondents spoke Arabic:

> I can't really understand them, but just to see the pictures of their side, because they were showing more of Iraq, their side. (Birmingham Muslim female)

Many, however, reverted to the main evening bulletins once the initial bombardment was over and the pace of the conflict began to slow:

> At the beginning I watched it quite a lot, because my friends were watching it, so I watched it a lot, and I was really interested in what was happening. I did end up getting a bit bored with it and fed up with what was going on, all the killings, it was a bit much to watch it all the time, so I just didn't watch it anymore. I just watched the news at ten sometimes. (London female)

There were other reports of "news fatigue." As one male London group participant told us, "After a while, it gets on your nerves." Indeed, for many, the desire for news seemed to wane fairly quickly, and the coverage seemed excessive. There was a notable gender divide here, with a number of woman across a range of focus groups saying that, after a while, they tried to avoid war news altogether. The most common reasons given for this were a concern about the effect of the coverage on their children as well as a personal dislike of violence.

Similarly, the ITC survey found that most people (61 percent) felt that there had been too much coverage of the war in Iraq, with most others (37 percent) saying coverage was "about right." Opponents of the war were particularly likely to feel that the coverage was excessive. Our survey probed these attitudes by asking people *which* aspects of the war received too much or too little coverage, and there we began to see a notable divergence between journalistic and public priorities.

While the news broadcasters invested considerable resources in embedded reporters and regarded unfettered access to the front lines as of great journalistic value, our survey suggests that this was the *least* popular feature of the coverage. Over a third—35 percent—felt the reporting of "action from the front lines" was excessive, with only 8 percent wanting to see more: hardly a ringing endorsement of the kind of coverage provided by the embeds. For a significant section of the audience, it seems, *the access to the front lines provided by the embed program shaped the coverage more than it should.* It may be that, because of its apparent news value, broadcasters slightly misjudged the importance of this kind of action footage. As we have seen, there was far less coverage of military briefings in this conflict than hitherto, as the formal press conferences were eclipsed by coverage from the embeds and reporters in Baghdad. Nonetheless, more people still felt there was too much (22 percent) than too little (15 percent).

Figure 8.6: What viewers wanted more coverage of

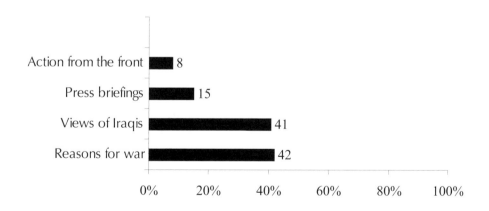

Indeed, in the focus groups, a number of negative comments about the war coverage were specifically linked to the action-focused footage provided by the embeds. One woman, during a discussion of embedded reporting, said that she "did turn it off, because I thought it was too much." A number of women noted the repetition of certain images and the broadcasting of what they regarded as "non-news"—reports that were seen as "fillers," because too much of the schedule was devoted to war coverage.

There were two aspects of the war people where a number of people said they would like to have seen more coverage (see Figure 8.6). There was fairly strong support, first of all, for more coverage of the reactions of the Iraqi people (41 percent wanted more coverage, while only 12 percent thought there was too much). In the focus groups, too, the most remarked-upon absence was the lack of news about Iraqi civilians. One Cardiff woman asked, "What happened to all the normal people?" Others were more vehement:

> I have never heard anybody say, "This many innocent people got killed".... That is the type of feelings that we have against what they show us on telly. (Cardiff female).

> They were showing you all action, they were not showing the aftermath.... To me, it is like they are hiding something. (Cardiff female)

> You killed innocent, you know, loads of innocent people they bombed. They were innocent as well, not just the people in the car. I never heard that much thing about the other civilians, just those people that they killed in the car, and that was because the reporter got it on the camera, saying, "This is what happened." (Birmingham Muslim female)

Indeed, Iraqi civilian casualties were one of the first unprompted memories of all the all-female groups, and strong expressions of sympathy and concern were expressed by all the women respondents. As we have seen, broadcasters dealt with this issue, although usually only reactively, and rarely in any depth. Given the importance of the issue—much of the political justification of the war invoked Iraqi opinion—there is clearly a case that broadcasters should have given it more serious attention during the war itself.

Perhaps more surprisingly, although the issue was well aired before the war, 42 percent of focus group respondents said they wanted more coverage and "investigation into why the war was fought and whether it was justified," with far fewer—19 percent—wanting less.[4] Here, the clearest differences emerge between war supporters and opponents: war supporters were fairly evenly divided on this question (27 percent saying they wanted more, 23 percent less), while a clear majority of war opponents (55 percent) wanted more attention paid to these matters (compared to 16 percent saying they wanted less). These figures suggest, one might argue, that *the very decision made by broadcasters to focus on the war itself, once fighting began, was not impartial.*

Attitudes toward Embedded Reporting

We must point out, first, that despite the currency of the phrase "embedded reporter" amongst broadcasters, most people—74 percent—did not know what the phrase meant, and only 20 percent were able to offer a broadly accurate definition. Although two-thirds (68 percent) assumed that reporters with American or British troops were subject to some military restrictions, 26 percent thought that they were independent and free to report what they wanted (suggesting some overestimation of the role of unilaterals). Once the concept was explained to them, most people (57 percent) were, on balance, in favor of the system, simply on the basis that it added to the information available. But over a third (36 percent) remained skeptical, feeling that the media should not get too close to the government and military, and finding that concern more critical than increased news value.

These figures are very much in line with the ITC survey, in which 52 percent of respondents believed that the embeds were able to remain impartial and 67 percent believed embedded reports added to their understanding of events. At the same time, both surveys demonstrated the limits of this support. Our survey found much higher levels of support for independent reporters free from any restrictions (65 percent thought it important to have such journalists covering the war), and for reporters in Baghdad (88 percent supported the broadcasters' decision to keep reporters in Baghdad, with only 9 percent opposed).

Figure 8.7: Important locations to have reporters, per survey respondents

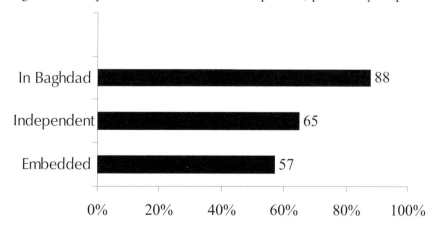

Our surveys also suggested that the debate about embedded reporters in media circles has not filtered through to the public. Just as only one in five respondents in our survey had any idea what an "embedded reporter"

was, very few focus group members, when asked if they knew the term, were able to give a definition. Those who could, appeared either to have made an effort to find out because of their involvement in the focus group, or to have seen the documentaries and press reports since the war. This is in itself a cause for concern. In short, the embed program changed the nature of war coverage without much public awareness of the special arrangements made between broadcasters and the military.

Once there had been discussion and definition of embedded reporting, people did pass opinions, many of which seemed to connect with the ongoing public and media discourse about embedding. Some respondents, echoing the comments of the military, suggested that embedded reporters were "somebody else the soldiers have to worry about" (Cardiff female), and that "they get in the way" (London male). Others reflected the journalistic perspective, that they allow viewers to "get more feedback from what is happening with the troops" (Birmingham Muslim male).

For some, embeds (and presumably, independent reporters as well) were heroic figures, endangering their lives "just to give us reports, up-to-date reports" (Birmingham Muslim female). Moreover, some felt that risk taking somehow ensured truth; as one man put it: "The more risks they take, the more the truth's going to come out" (Birmingham Muslim male). Others focused on the entertainment value of embedded reporting: "It is more exciting when you see them actually there, you are thinking, 'He is standing and that is happening there, and he is seeing it'" (Birmingham Muslim female). Skeptical participants were clearly troubled by the idea that reporters were likely to be influenced by their close proximity with military units:

> He has got to say the right things, otherwise he does not get his breakfast in the morning. (Cardiff male)

> You are going to pick up, when you are small teams in your unit, what that unit believes. (London female)

Overall, responses to the embed program were mixed, paralleling the ambivalence felt by many broadcasters, that the embed program was something of a compromise between media freedom and media control. As one woman put it, embedded reporters were "fed the information that [we] are allowed to have.... It's controlled, to a certain extent, but parts they show [us] are as near to the truth as they are allowed to get" (Birmingham female). *However, the main problem raised by the use of embeds has little to do with questions of access or censorship.* The main problem, an issue highlighted by the ITC study, which found a majority (52 percent) agreed, was that this kind of reporting can make war seem too much like fiction, and too easy to forget people are dying.

This last point endorses the concerns expressed by a number of journalists. Both editors and reporters on the ground felt constrained about showing graphic images on screen, and in trying to spare the audience's sensitivities, were not able to show the ugly side of war. For many focus group members, this gave the coverage a fictional quality. As these focus group members put it:

> For the Falklands we only had it on the radio, whereas these last two wars …you got pictures, cameramen virtually running step by step with the soldiers like, you know, a war film. (Birmingham male)

> It's like watching a film. (London male)

> I just thought it almost sort of made it a bit, glorified it—it made it more like a film rather than being—I thought it was awful, I didn't like it at all. (London female)

This comparison with fiction is worth dwelling on, particularly since the embed program, in many cases, allowed viewers to get *closer* to what was actually happening. And yet, despite the faith in "live reports," a contradiction emerges between the "reality" of these reports and the film-like or fiction-like quality of it all. This is, in many ways, the most striking feature of the focus group responses. Paradoxically, the film-like quality seems to be connected to the very images which produce the effect of truth or reality:

> It is like a mini-movie telling you a story and showing you it. If you got pictures, you take it in easier. Same as the news—when they have got pictures, it is going to hit you more, it is going to, emotionally, probably, affect you, so when you are showing pictures, it is going to stay in your head. Pictures stay in your head. (Birmingham Muslim male)

These images are clearly related, for most participants, to the genre of war movies and to Hollywood representations of war. The exclusion of the very images of death and dying seems to contribute to a sanitized, TV version of war that is, whatever the Pentagon team may argue,[5] easily conflated in the audience's mind with Hollywood.

These results also indicate a sense of the overall *narrative flow* of which embedded reporting is a part. The embeds inevitably fed into a central narrative about the progress of the war, who was winning, who was losing, and so on. The climax of this narrative is, by definition, the outcome:

hence the volume of coverage given to the triumphant scenes in Baghdad following its capture by U.S. forces. Thus, while our study suggests that the embeds were both committed to—and able to maintain—fairly high standards of objectivity, they were inevitably part of a narrative in which the war's complexity—its motives, context, and justifications—went unquestioned. The fact that this narrative dominated the coverage may account for people's unease. In other words, by focusing on "the action," the complexity of events was reduced to the cruder issue of winning and losing, a narrative in which winning itself becomes a vindication, when in fact most people felt that the debate about the war had little to do with who would win, since that was rarely in doubt.

What People Remembered

When asked an open-ended question about what they remembered from the coverage of the war, survey respondents gave a wide variety of recollections. Top of the list was the toppling of the statue of Saddam Hussein as American troops took Baghdad. In response to subsequent, more specific questions, 80 percent said they remembered this incident very well (and only 3 percent not at all), confirming the impact made by this moment. While it could be argued that this was simply a memorable moment, it seems likely that this high level of recall also reflects the volume of media coverage afforded it.

This incident was also widely referred to in the focus groups. The quote below illustrates the salience of that event, as one of the few "iconic" images of the war, giving a sense of the power of such images in an era of information overload and rolling news coverage:

> There was an awful lot—there wasn't that many iconic images, there was the guy pulling down the thing in Baghdad, the big statue, but apart from that I didn't feel, you know, there are certain, you know, the Vietnam War, you think of that photograph with the little girl and the jungle imagery... (Cardiff female)

Reactions to the image were divided. Many saw it as an accurate reflection of Iraqi joy at being liberated. Indeed, in keeping with the filmic quality of the narrative, that moment provided the proverbial happy ending:

> You can't deny like, you know, sort of be happy for them. Yes, it has brought all death and suffering, but that was going to happen anyway, at least somebody is happy at the end of it. (Cardiff female)

Watching the footage again, however, with the benefit of hindsight, prompted more critical reactions in the focus groups, casting doubt on the veracity of the "happy ending":

> I like the phrase—these pictures are being beamed live around the world—so the American troops joined in. Isn't that what the Americans wanted? I mean, you don't know how many of those people—a lot of them probably were glad to see the back of him, but in front of—faced with American tanks and American troops and Western journalists, what else are you going to do! (Cardiff female)

Thus, while some felt there was a degree of overacting for the cameras, there was also some skepticism about the size of the crowd and the tightness of the camera focus on the crowd:

> Even the way that was reported, if there was thousands and thousands of people, why wasn't there a big span back on the camera of all these people that were out and whatever? It was all just close ups and just his face and a few people behind him, a lot of it seemed staged. (Birmingham female)

Again, it needs to be stressed that these were retrospective observations: what may have *seemed* a happy ending at the time was inevitably reevaluated by ongoing fighting in Iraq. So, asked whether they thought the war was over, the majority said that it was not. And yet, this is the moment when the narrative of the media war ends, and most of the embeds went elsewhere. Indeed, there are suggestions in the focus groups that embeds did actually keep audiences informed in new ways, and that their absence from the current ongoing conflict makes a real difference:

> Are they still there? It is not shown that much any more, so how do we know that the war is over? But with the soldiers, no one is helping them now, we don't know what is going on. I don't think that the war is over. (Birmingham Muslim female)

On the other hand, there is also evidence that the audience, as well as the media, has got tired and gone home:

> Since then it has just been shootings and everything, so it has just become a sort of everyday thing, I don't really take much notice of it now. (London male)

Clearly the expense to news organizations of keeping embeds in place in Iraq made it difficult to prolong the practice (which raises questions, of course, about how sustainable the program is in anything other than a short conflict). But the media's withdrawal of embeds at precisely the moment when the "media war" had come to an iconic end (with an apparent victory for the coalition), also tells us something about the media's complicity with the embedding policy, and about the media's power to define, for audiences, what the parameters of the war would be. The complexities of what happened after the toppling of the statue would require a different story altogether, but apart from a few dramatic moments (such as the attempt to retake the city of Fallujah from insurgents in November 2004), news organizations are less prepared to invest the time or the staff to tell this longer, less straightforward tale.

There is, however, every indication in the focus groups' responses to our questions that a genuine analysis of the current situation would be welcome, along with further discussion of the reasons for and the consequences of the war. These complexities and inconsistencies in audience responses should give us serious pause when planning the involvement of embedded reporters in future conflicts. One thing clear from these focus groups is that "the public," while neither homogeneous nor consistent in its demands, was not convinced that the media coverage of the war was always appropriate, relevant, or worth watching.

The second most-recalled incident was the rescue of Private Jessica Lynch (remembered very well by 44 percent and not at all by only 19 percent); only 22 percent remembered the bombing of a market place in Baghdad (less than the 29 percent who did not remember it at all). The fact that the rather embellished "rescue" of Jessica Lynch was more memorable than incidents involving significant civilian loss of life is another reminder that when events are turned into human interest stories (as any of these stories could have been), they are more likely to capture people's attention.

Amongst our focus groups, the rescue of Private Jessica Lynch was discussed with a healthy dose of skepticism. Strong statements of distaste and disbelief were expressed—according to one woman, the whole incident was "a load of crap." A number of groups remarked on the later emergence of alternative information about the conditions in which she was held and the need for a military rescue. More significantly, this incident was linked to the "unreality" of the action images, with the comparison to Hollywood movies again being drawn.

We also looked at some of the incidents in which the original version of stories were retracted, in order to gauge how people remembered these incidents. The pattern that emerged suggests that people are much more likely to remember the original, incorrect story than the subsequent retraction. So, for example, 81 percent remembered Tony Blair's condemnation of the execution of two British prisoners of war, but of those, only 13 percent recalled that this accusation turned out to be untrue. Similarly, 25 percent were able to recall Iraq being reported as firing Scud missiles into Kuwait,[6] but only 15 percent of these recalled that these claims turned out to be unfounded. Once again, this reflects the volume of coverage, as more time was spent reporting the initial claims than on the retractions. Problematically, the coverage thereby contributes inadvertently to an apocryphal history of the war in popular memory.

CHAPTER NINE

Beyond Censorship:
Public Relations and Journalism

WHEN WARS ARE CONDUCTED by advanced democratic states, the citizens of those states need to be fully informed about the justification for war, the capability and conduct of their armed forces, the benefits and costs of military operations, and the long-term implications. Only then can citizens make informed decisions regarding the government's action in prosecuting war in their name. For the majority of people, the ability to make informed decisions about matters such as war is still largely mediated by journalism and the mass media. The quality and nature of the journalism delivering information in these contexts is thus a serious issue.

British and American television news covered the 2003 Iraq War extensively—indeed, we might say that viewers were bombarded with news coverage. But what viewers saw was a very partial picture. They saw correspondents reporting live, in full biological and chemical gear, they saw reports on the discovery of potential WMD facilities (reports that were never followed up), and they heard military sources asserting the inevitability of the discovery of such facilities in time. Yet while viewers saw a lot of coverage assuming the existence of something that we now know didn't exist, there was a lot they did not see. So, for example, viewers might well have imagined that the war was won solely through aerial bombardment and infantry movement. They would certainly not have seen the key covert role that Special Forces increasingly play.

Viewers did not see television images of American and British casualties. They did not see the more gruesome side of war, as correspondents and editors were wary of the need to produce pictures that suited norms of "taste and decency." And while British viewers did see their own correspondents reporting the war from within Baghdad, they rarely saw any footage from anywhere else in Iraq except from behind Coalition lines. They rarely heard the voice of the ordinary Iraqi citizen, in whose cause the war against Saddam Hussein was ostensibly being conducted, until, apparently spontaneously, they saw a crowd of "ordinary Iraqis" pulling down his statue to mark the symbolic end of the media war.

The sanitization of the conflict was arguably very similar to that in the Gulf War, but the context was difference. In previous conflicts, the partial nature of coverage could reasonably be attributed to the military's rigid imposition of censorship or of restrictions on movement. But in the 2003 Iraq War, there had never been so many journalists so close to the action, apparently with unprecedented freedom to report, and many with the technological capability to report straight back to the newsroom, avoiding military channels. And yet, despite the lack of censorship or restrictions like those imposed in the Falklands, in Grenada, in Panama, and in the Gulf War, this war produced a picture of the war that was as favorable to the military as ever. Given the many questions that emerged after the war in Iraq—the absence of WMD, the collapse of law and order, the increasing resentment of occupying forces—how was this possible?

Public Relations and Embedding

As we have suggested, the large network of embedded reporters changed the way the war was reported. Our own content analysis found that, on British television, most of the reports from the region came from embeds. While past war coverage has been heavily dependent upon military briefings (Taylor 1992), in 2003, reports from embeds outnumbered reports from official briefings by more than two to one. Indeed, the problem facing editors in London was not lack of reports from the front lines, but a surfeit of them.

The criticism that embedded reporters were, in effect, "in bed" with the military may be true of some of the American network coverage, but, as we have seen, our research paints a more complex picture of the British embeds. Most British reporters were acutely aware of the need to maintain a sense of distance, and few experienced many overt attempts to censor their reports. Not only did embedded reporters often provide accounts that contradicted official military claims, their reports did not differ significantly from those filed by other non-embedded reporters on the ground.

But while British broadcasters were generally committed to maintaining impartiality in their coverage of the war, our analysis of the coverage suggests that, in certain key areas, broadcasters tended to favor assumptions that were key to the pro-war case. Once the war began, the British news media tended to reproduce, rather than question, claims about weapons of mass destruction. Assessments of the Iraqi possession of such weapons were a repeated source of assertion and speculation during the war, from from government and military sources, experts, and correspondents.

Thus we found, in total, 184 references to weapons of mass destruction (contained in 127 reports, or just over 8 percent of the whole sample). Overall, British broadcasters were eight times more likely to make references suggesting the presence of chemical and biological weapons than to suggest their absence. So while no such weapons were actually found during the war, 89 percent of references *assumed* their existence, while only 11 percent cast doubt on this idea.

How far the government itself was persuaded that Iraq has such weapons remains a matter of controversy, but it was clearly successful in persuading broadcasters of their probable existence. Those who doubted the existence of WMD—like former British foreign secretary Robin Cook, or weapons inspector Scott Ritter—clearly did not have the same persuasive power. And for the many viewers uncertain about the efficacy of, or reasons for, the war, the sense implied by this coverage—that such weapons might be used against British forces—seems to have lessened doubts they may have had. This, in turn, led to the feeling expressed by people in our surveys and the focus groups, that they had been misled. As one of our focus group members put it in the previous chapter, "I thought there might have been weapons there, but now I just think there aren't."

Perhaps more significant, during the war and its aftermath, was the discourse of "liberation." Ordinary Iraqi citizens were at the center of debates about the war, with both the pro-war and antiwar camps claiming to speak on their behalf. And yet, for many, they remained something of an enigma. More than four out of ten people in our postwar survey (41 percent) said that there was too little coverage of the Iraqi people's reaction to the war, compared with 15 percent who felt there was too little coverage of military briefings, and only 8 percent who thought there was too little coverage of action from the front lines (this last response reflecting the dominant presence of embedded reporters). Again, as one woman put it, "What happened to all the normal people?"

Our analysis of the coverage uncovered little in-depth analysis of Iraqi attitudes about the war. What we found instead were brief snatches of Iraqi public opinion. As we described earlier, the pro-war account of Iraqi opinion predominated, with nearly two out of three references on British television portraying the Iraqis as welcoming the invasion. But what also emerged from our analysis is a division between reporters on the ground— both those who were embedded and those based in Baghdad— and anchors in the studio. Those reporters in a position to gauge Iraqi reaction presented a very mixed picture, with more or less equal numbers of enthusiastic and unenthusiastic Iraqi responses. What is especially notable here is that the embedded reporters (who might have been expected to err in favor of positive Iraqi reactions) and the reporters in Baghdad (who we might have assumed would have encountered more hostility) told very similar stories. *What made the headlines back in the studios in London, however, was a much more one-sided account*, with enthusiastic Iraqi responses outnumbering less enthusiastic accounts by nearly seven to one.

This clearly complicates the argument (Miller 2003; Baines and Worcester 2003) that the role of embedded reporters was a key component of the media's complicity with the government's pro-war line. In this important instance, it seems that the pro-war tilt was *in spite of* rather than *because of* embedded reporting. This is not to say that embedded reporters did not play a role in constructing a pro-war narrative, as we shall suggest shortly, but the nature of this role was more complex that most critics have implied.

The Pentagon's promotion of the embedded reporters program was based on controlling the "big picture," as framed in their Public Affairs Guidance document: "Our people in the field need to tell our story." This story was, in short, a simple tale of a military campaign, whose main characters were American and British troops. Admiral "T" McCreary, one of the key strategists behind the embed program, made this point very clearly in his interview with us:

> Once somebody decides to start a war, and you start shooting, from the uniform perspective, we need the support of the American people for our troops.... And what better way for people to understand that than to put the face of the troops as the face of the war?.... While you may or may not agree with the war, you really support them and them coming back alive.

What made this approach so appealing, from the U.S. government's perspective, was not simply its ability to create sympathy for the U.S.-led forces. They were aware that the news value of the battlefield footage the embeds provided would be compelling. While there were many more complex stories to tell—about the wider international context, the Iraqi people, the economic implications, the reaction of the Arab world, public opinion, debates about the justifications, and rationale for the war and its aftermath—these would be eclipsed *by a narrow focus on the war itself.* Our research also shows that for the United States, particularly given Victoria Clarke's public relations training and background, this was very much a public relations exercise.

The distinctions in the military between information operations, psychological operations, public diplomacy, and public affairs may indeed be blurring, but the evidence is that the development of the embeds policy and its American implementation was largely driven by a public relations agenda. Enticed by the promise of unprecedented access, the news media were complicit with this strategy. This was the case even in the United Kingdom, where the embedding policy is much older and derives from different (military, civil service, media) traditions in which the role of public relations is less well honed. As ITV's James Mates said, the embeds would become the lens "through which they [U.S. and UK forces] could be seen winning the war."

Broadcasters thereby found themselves irresistibly drawn into the action-packed drama of a war against a rarely seen enemy (if Iraqi civilians were enigmatic, the Iraqi soldiers were almost invisible—rarely seen or discussed, but generally assumed to be supportive of Saddam Hussein). Better still, from the pro-war perspective, the norms of taste and decency made it difficult for broadcasters to show the more graphic images of death and destruction, giving the narrative an almost fictional quality.

There is an irony here, of course, in which the verisimilitude of frontline reporting appears to create a sense of unreality. It explains, nonetheless, the findings of the Independent Television Commission survey in which a majority (52 percent) said that this kind of reporting can make war seem too much like fiction, and too easy to forget people are dying. This idea was echoed in our focus groups, in which people repeatedly referred to the coverage as being like a "war film" And indeed, at times it *was* a war film, as in the case of the Jessica Lynch story, or the various mooted involvements of Hollywood in the Pentagon's public affairs or psychological operations (see Chapter 3).

The pulling down of a statue of Saddam Hussein on 9 April—purportedly by Iraqis joyously greeting American troops as they arrived in Baghdad—provided an irresistible climax to this narrative. If the ugly side of war was, as we have seen, generally shot from a distance, the news value of this incident was emphasized by tighter shots in which the frame appeared crowded with celebrating Iraqis. In short, images were chosen for their drama rather than their accuracy. What made this moment so powerful was that it showed Iraqis greeting U.S. troops "as liberators," apparently emblematic of what ITV news described in its main bulletin as "an end to decades of Iraqi misery." Images of the toppling of the statue were shown a total of twenty-one times on the four main UK evening news programs, making it hard to resist, as a viewer, the impression of a city united in celebration. Sky News at 10 p.m. put it: "'Cry freedom,' the people say they've been liberated."

This iconic moment is another instance of the blurring of different modes of information management and story construction. Miller records the involvement of psychological operations (PsyOps) in the "staging" of the toppling of the statue of Saddam Hussein, arguing that this is one instance that shows that "[PsyOps] operators spend at least some of their time managing media operations which impact on domestic opinion" (2004, 94–95). Rampton and Stauber suggest that the Rendon public relations group may also have been involved in the staging of this particular incident, as it was in the construction of the "liberation" of Kuwait City at the end of the first Gulf War (2003, 5). Whatever the validity of these claims, if psychological operations and public relations were involved, what they provided seems to have simply been grist to the media mill.

When the respondents in our surveys were asked to nominate their most memorable moment of the war, the "toppling of Saddam" was, in both prompted and unprompted questions, by far the most popular choice. Most respondents—80 percent—claimed that they recalled it "very well" (compared to, for example, 22 percent who said they recalled the market place bombing in Baghdad "very well"), and only 3 percent did not recall it at all. This speaks not only to the treatment given to the incident itself, but to the way in which it provided a climactic end to the story that had dominated the news for three weeks, and to the success of a public relations strategy executed through and with media compliance.

If the victorious images from Paradise Square appear, in retrospect, rather premature, they provided broadcasters with a sense of closure. While this moment marks the beginning of a critical, rather troubled period in Iraq's history, for the embedded reporters and most of those in Baghdad, it was, "Job well done"—and time to move on. While Iraq remained a news story, the resources devoted to it, in terms of time and money, quickly dwindled. By concluding the media narrative, it provided media organizations themselves with a comfortable exit strategy. Embedding, after all, was an expensive business, and the relocation of hundreds of journalists to Iraq and away from their normal responsibilities was not, for most media organizations, sustainable in the long term.

It is worth pausing to reflect on this. The war in Iraq was, in some ways, a perfect news story. Not only was it was short enough to allow broadcasters to devote considerable resources to it, but the Pentagon and the Ministry of Defence provided journalists with front-row seats. The moral complexities that surrounded debates about the motives and justifications for war could be cast to one side to cover a battle to unseat the most demonized leader of recent times.

And yet how newsworthy was it? The United States' involvement in one-sided wars—whether in Panama, Kuwait, Kosovo, Afghanistan, or Iraq—has become a feature of the post–Cold War era. The outcome of the Iraqi conflict, as with the others, was predictable. The scale of suffering involved was far less than in other recent, less newsworthy conflicts, notably the much underreported conflict in the Congo in Africa, going on at the same time and responsible for over three million deaths. Were the battles for Basra and Baghdad so significant that there was no space left for the wider questions about the war and its ramifications?

Moreover, while there were many other factors involved, it seems likely that, in Britain at least, *the coverage of the war itself played a part in persuading a majority to support it.* This is *not*, on the whole, a simple matter of "media bias." British broadcasters were aware of the divided attitudes about the war and made efforts to be impartial. So while the American networks—following warnings from the Pentagon—pulled their teams from Baghdad, British reporters steadfastly remained. And there is little evidence that broadcast journalists were seduced by the embed program to become cheerleaders for the U.S. forces.

What the embed system did do, however, was to help bind journalists into a focus on the progress of the war, at the expense of broader contextual issues. The fact that there were no embeds with Iraqi forces (for obvious reasons) combined with traditions of taste and decency to humanize the U.S.-led forces and dehumanize the Iraqis. This war narrative, then, created its own momentum, making "liberated" Iraqis more newsworthy than the many who had, at best, mixed feelings about the war.

At the same time, journalists placed too much credence on the bipartisan consensus that Iraq possessed weapons of mass destruction. The media environment thereby shifted from a comparatively open and wide-ranging debate to one firmly situated on pro-war terrain. For someone wavering in support for the war, it became easier to support it and more difficult to summon up the arguments against it.

The media coverage and the media narrative was not, in Britain, a product of any decision to abandon impartiality, but a consequence of routine decisions about news values and practices, which raises serious questions about the media, war, and public opinion. We would argue that unless these news values and practices are also interrogated and changed, it may be that reluctant publics can be persuaded to support war simply by the act of war itself. Put another way, these decisions shift the spotlight away from difficult policy debates—including alternatives to war—toward the easier question of whether or not to support the troops.

Reporting War in an Era of Military Public Relations

The general post–Iraq 2003 consensus was that embedding had worked well, allowing journalists to produce more independent accounts of the war than in any previous conflict. This, we would argue, raises questions about the nature of institutionalized journalism (Zelizer 2004). As we pointed out in our introductory chapter, many of the issues raised by embedding were not new and were well documented (Harris 1983; Hallin 1989; Taylor 1992; Thomson 1992; MacArthur 1993; Wyatt 1993). But the lessons of the history of media and military engagements appear to have been forgotten immediately prior to Iraq 2003 (Philo and Gilmour 2004).

Even if there were some qualms, the media did not challenge the idea of embedding. They volunteered in unprecedented numbers to go to war, and then jockeyed for the best positions (more than 900 journalists from the United States and the United Kingdom applied to go to Iraq). In this environment, a competitive journalistic spirit actually served to wed journalists to the rules of embedding. As we saw in Chapter 5, embedded reporters found themselves becoming resentful of unilateral reporters shown any favors by military forces. In other words, if embeds had to obey "the rules," so should everyone else.

But criticism of the media role in the 2003 Iraq War extends beyond embedding, to the failure to comment on or investigate the development of the new forms of information warfare and political communications of which embedding was a part (Arnove 2003; Gardiner 2003; Mahajan 2003; Keeble 2003; Miller 2004a). Edwards and Cromwell (2004) aired these issues in the *Guardian*:

> The British and US governments stand accused of lying their way to war on Iraq, both at home and abroad. But while a series of what were widely regarded as nobbled inquiries have at least gone through the motions of holding them to

account, there has been no attempt to hold the media to account for its role in making the war possible....

And yet it is only by exploring these issues that we can answer the question of how it is that a free press could fail to challenge even the most transparent government deceptions in the run-up to the attack....

We would argue that the media's failure on Iraq was not really a failure at all, but rather a classic product of "balanced" professional journalism....

Built in to the new concept of neutral, professional journalism were two major biases. First, the actions and opinions of official sources were understood to form the basis of news.... Second, carrot-and-stick pressures from advertisers, business interests and political parties had the effect of steering journalists in the corporate media away from some issues and towards others. ("Balance in the service of falsehood," 2004, italics added)

Thus if the Blair and Bush governments and their information machines by early 2005 looked somewhat less comfortable than they did during the war, the question remains, how were so many constructions, based on so little evidence, believed by so many, for so long? This may well be because being embedded with public relations is actually such *a normal way of working* for journalists that it has become common sense. Our research makes it very clear that the media tend not to investigate or question the way the military/government machines work as public relations and marketing operations, and they certainly do not see themselves working as part of that operation.

Part of the problem is that journalists tend to view any problems within the media/military relationship through the lens of *censorship*. In short, suspicions of the military center on whether the military is hiding information or preventing certain truths being told. To be given access to key players or placed "close to the action" is thus widely regarded as positive, and the comparative absence of any overt censorship of embedded reporters is—as we saw in Chapter 5—regarded as *the* critical issue.

Our interview materials make equally clear that the military and government understand very well how the media works and have moved beyond this "censorship" model (even though censorship is still a key part of overall media strategy) to embrace a public relations model. This has less to do with *preventing negative* coverage than *creating positive* coverage. Our Pentagon interviews show a broad understanding that having journalists with the troops would, *most* of the time, create the kind of news story the military wanted.

Thus, both Victoria Clarke and Admiral "T" McCreary argued that "embedding" is a normal part of the everyday practice of journalism, that journalists are always "embedded" with their regular sources and "beats." Clarke spoke of the way power companies had "embedded" journalists to cover the crisis of massive power cuts in Washington, D.C. in 2003, and McCreary cited the Pentagon press corps and their regular, daily engagement with Pentagon Public Affairs as an example. The institutionalized relationship between some journalists and the press office at 10 Downing Street is a very similar instance. As Cottle puts it:

> In some areas of reporting, such as coverage of Parliament and the City, journalists appear to have become such a part of the "issue communities" they cover, they have become all but "captured" by their sources. (2003, 35)

It is in this sense that journalists can, by many traditional measures, be doing such a good job that they inadvertently become part of a military public relations effort. The journalist—embedded or otherwise—may be objective, impartial, and close to the action, seemingly epitomizing what it means to be a good journalist. The story they are telling may be compelling and truthful, and yet it also happens to be the story that the military wants told.

As a result, while journalists may be vigilant about balance and censorship, they tend not to investigate their "capture" by public relations, if it supplies them with good stories. Or, to put it another way, the temptation is to shoot first and ask questions later. This helps explain the media frenzy (Kellner 2003, 49) to join the embeds programs in both the United States and the United Kingdom. The questions asked by the more skeptical media organizations—Would embeds be censored, and could they maintain their objectivity?—are, we suggest, the wrong questions.

In the same way, our finding that many British embeds generally did maintain their objectivity should *not* be taken as a vindication of the exercise. In the future, what journalists need to ask is *why* they are being given "front-row seats" during wartime—to ask questions, in other words, *before* fixing the camera on the newsworthy shot, and to ask, crucially, what are the stories that the principal military and government sources are *not* talking about?

In this vein, Keeble (2003) has argued that just about every aspect of the Iraq War in 2003 was manufactured to provide a raison d'être for the military-industrial complexes in America and Britain. Keeble argues that the long-standing relationship between journalists and intelligence services—what he calls "close encounters of a strange kind"—produces a culture of secrecy that "feeds the myth-making" (2003, 3–5). Philo and McLaughlin (1995) have also analyzed the tendency for journalists to allow themselves to be *positioned by and within prevailing narratives* told by powerful sources. They explore, for example, the way Pentagon videos of "smart" weapons "transfixed" journalists in the context of the Gulf War, leading them to "rationalise the moral implications of high-tech war" (150), and to suggest that pictures of Iraqi civilian casualties released by the Iraqis might not be authentic (152). They comment:

> We cannot explain such absences [of television coverage of the tens of thousands of human casualties during the war] by government restrictions alone and it is not correct to see the British media as being simply forced along by politicians in the early stages of the war. Many of them, especially the popular press, were willing participants in a mood of patriotism and near euphoria. They could not resist such a "good story" and the chance to present a real war as a kind of Hollywood movie in which "our side" were the "good guys." Only later did some of them contemplate the human cost. (1995, 155)

Our research suggests that exactly the same issues were at stake again in Iraq 2003. There was no military, or public relations or psychological operations conspiracy in which the media were simply caught up. The context in which the media operated was absolutely normal, if rarely discussed. Miller (2004) is undoubtedly right that embedding was the biggest public relations coup of the war. We put forth, in this study, that it was a coup in which the media were intimately and complicitly involved—not because of any *failure* of normal media practices, but precisely because *professional journalists were carrying on with business as usual.*

Notes

Chapter One

1. In April 2004, the U.S. military requested that the al-Jazeera team based in Fallujah leave as one of the conditions for lifting the earlier siege ("U. S. forces want al-Jazeera out of Fallujah," *Islam Online.net*, 9 April 2004). In early August, the interim Iraqi government closed al-Jazeera's Baghdad offices for thirty days and then extended the ban indefinitely, because, they alleged, al-Jazeera was still covering Iraq from inside Iraq ("Iraq extends al-Jazeera ban and raids offices," *Guardian*, 6 September 2004). Bizarrely, Lieutenant Lyle Gilbert claimed that al-Jazeera was invited to embed for the Fallujah campaign along with six journalists from the Iraqi media, but simply didn't respond ("Iraqi journalists embedded with U.S. forces," *Knight-Ridder newspapers*, 4 November 2004).
2. A distinction needs to be made between the use of the word "embedded," which is new in this context, and what it denotes, which isn't. Knightley, for example, claims that the British Army had "embedded" six journalists during the First World War (2003, 531–2). The scale of the Pentagon's embedded program was significantly greater than any comparable exercise in the past.
3. "Journalists at War," debate organized by the Press Freedom Network, London, 2 May 2003; "Was Truth the Victor in Iraq?" Media Society Event, London, 10 June 2003; Media Guardian Forum on War Coverage, London, 25 June 2003.

4. See, for example, Kampfner. 2003. Correspondent: War Spin. BBC. First broadcast on BBC 2, 18 May.
5. "The Falklands provided a model of how to make sure that government policy is not undermined by the way a war is reported. The rules turned out to be fairly simple: control access to the fighting; exclude neutral correspondents; censor your own" (Knightley 2003, 484).

Chapter Two

1. http://www.publications.parliament.uk/pa/cm200304/cmselect/cmdfence/cmdfence.htm
2. House of Commons, Select Committee on Defence, Third Report (163 March 2004). http://www.publications.parliament.uk/pa/cm200304/cmselect/cmdfence/57/5702.htm
3. Available at http://www.au.af.mil/au/awc/awcgate/awcmedia.htm#dod
4. Defined by former CIA chief William Colby, http://www.psywarrior.com/psyhist.html
5. Defense Science Board, Report of the Defense Science Board Task Force on Strategic Communication, Washington, DC (2004), 78. Available at http://www.iwar.org.uk/pysops/
6. Minutes of Evidence, Select Committee on Defence Third Report, Lessons of Iraq, 16 March 2004, Volume 111, Oral and Written Evidence HC 57 –111, http://www.publications.parliament.uk/pa/cm200304/cmselect/cmdfence/cmdfence.htm.
7. For example: The Future Strategic Context for Defence: First Reflections (July 2003); Ministry of Defence, Operations in Iraq: Lessons for the Future (December 2003); House of Commons, Select Committee on Defence, Third Report (3 March 2004); House of Commons, Select Committee on Defence, Examination of Witnesses (Questions 1360–1460; 1579–1672).
8. http://www.rendon.com/rendon/layout7/wel.htm
9. Information provided by Lieutenant Colonel Angus Taverner, then Director of News Media Operations Policy, in May 2004.

Chapter Three

1. Victoria Clarke, speaking at the Brookings Institution forum, "Assessing media coverage of the war in Iraq: Press reports, Pentagon rules, and the lessons for the future," 17 June 2003. Transcript available at http://www.brookings.edu/comm/events/20030617.htm
2. Department of Defense, Public Affairs Guidance (PAG) on Embedding Media during Possible Future Operations/Deployments in the U.S. Central Commands (CENTCOM) Area of Responsibility (AOR) (10 February 2003). http://www.au.af.mil/au/awc/awcgate/awcmedia.htm#dod

3. That such programs of training in strategic response to the media are a normal part of public affairs guidance is obvious on the Pentagon website. See, for example, the Center for Army Lessons Learned (CALL) Public Affairs Guidance to "combined arms assessment team (CAAT) members when employed in actual operations or exercises." The document explains in its first paragraph that in what follows "CAAT members will come to understand the boundaries for talking to the media." http://call.army.mil/

4. The Independent Television Commission was, at the time or writing, a regulatory body for television in the UK which carried out frequent audience research. It has since become part of a new regulatory structure, OFCOM.

5. See, for example, K.T. Rhem, "Troops 'living large' in Internal Look Exercise," *American Forces Press Service*, 5 December 2002. http://www.defenselink.mil/news/Dec2002/n12052002_200212051.html

6. Ben Smith, Iraq Media Guy Rebuilds Qatar at the Garden. *New York Observer*, 27 October 2003, p. 1.

7. Michael Wolff, "I was only asking," *The Guardian*, 14 April 2003.

8. James Wilkinson, interviewed on *Correspondent: War Spin*. BBC. First broadcast on BBC 2, 18 May 2003. Transcript available at http://news.bbc.co.uk/nol/shared/spl/hi/programmes/correspondent/transcripts/18.5.031.txt

9. October, 2003. Cited in Byrne (2003), Military Examines Use of Embedded Journalists. *The Guardian*, 22 October. http://media.guardian.co.uk/broadcast/story/0,,1068363,00.html

10. Captain T. McCreary speaking at Department of Defense Briefing, *ASD PA Clarke meeting with bureau chiefs*. 14 January 2003. These are the only mentions of non-embedded journalists in the document. Note – Captain McCreary was promoted to Rear Admiral prior to our interviews. http://www.defenselink.mil/transcripts/2003/t01152003_t0114bc.html

11. Victoria Clarke speaking at Department of Defense Briefing, *ASD PA Clarke meeting with bureau chiefs*. 14 January 2003. http://www.defenselink.mil/transcripts/2003/t01152003_t0114bc.html

12. Simpson, J. 2003. Reporting under fire. *Reuters Event*, 27–28 June. http://www.newsviews.info/warcoverageiraq.html

13. Victoria Clarke speaking at Department of Defense Briefing, *ASD PA Clarke meeting with bureau chiefs*. 14 January 2003. http://www.defenselink.mil/transcripts/2003/t01152003_t0114bc.html

14. In particular, see comments from our interview with Squadron Leader Tom Rounds.

15. He had also referred to this meeting in the briefing of bureau chiefs on 14 January 2003, when asked about the lack of cigarette lighters (as power points) in the vehicles by a member of the audience.

16. *Correspondent: War Spin*. BBC. First broadcast on BBC 2, 18 May 2003. Transcript available at http://news.bbc.co.uk/nol/shared/spl/hi/programmes / correspondent/transcripts/18.5.031.txt

17. Bryan Whitman, speaking at the Newsworld International Conference in Dublin, 22 October 2003.

18. Although the use of "flash-bang" grenades is standard in such situations, it would seem incongruous for assault units in a war zone to be using anything other than live ammunition.

19. *Correspondent: War Spin*. BBC. First broadcast on BBC 2, 18 May 2003. Transcript available at http://news.bbc.co.uk/nol/shared/spl/hi/programmes / correspondent/transcripts/18.5.031.txt. And, Jim Garamone, More Details on Lynch Rescue, 11 Bodies Found. *American Forces Press Service*. 2 April 2003. http://www.defenselink.mil/news/Apr2003/n04022003_200304023. html

20. See, for example, Burston (2003).

21. Lisa de Moraes, Reality TV is marching to the Military's Tune. *Washington Post*, 19 March 2002, p. C07.

22. Prior to our interview, Washington, D.C. had suffered severe and damaging storms for several days.

Chapter Four

1. Ministry of Defence (2001). http://www.mod.uk/news/green_book/index. htm

2. Geoff Hoon in the *Times of London*, 28 March 2003, cited in Tumber and Palmer 2004, 1.

3. See also David Miller's account of the role of then Downing Street press secretary Alastair Campbell (Miller 2004a).

4. Lieutenant Colonel Steven Collins, "Mind Games," available at http://www. psywarrior.com/MindGamesSCollins.html

5. See "Information Operations," Select Committee on Defence, Third Report, Session 2003–2004. http://www.publications.parliament.uk/pa/cm200304/ cmselect/cmdfence/57/5702.htm

6. Lieutenant Colonel K. Stratford-Wright, "So, is it ok to use the media to deceive the enemy?" *HQ ARRC Journal*, April 2003. http://www.arrc.nato. int/journal/april03/media.htm

7. Ministry of Defence, Director General Corporate Communication, Operations in Iraq: Lessons for the Future (11 December 2003). http://www.mod. uk/publications/iraq_futurelessons/index.html

8. See also note 6, Operations in Iraq: Lessons for the Future.

9. The *Daily Mail* offered £10 for letters from troops who were experiencing problems, and the *Sun* launched "Operation Loo Roll," sending forty-five thousand rolls of soft toilet paper to the Gulf.

10. Smarties are candy, similar to nutless M&Ms, that are packaged in a round cardboard tube.

11. Caroline Wyatt, BBC, Journalists Handbook and Media Society Conference.

12. General Richard Myers, Department of Defense, News Briefing, Secretary Rumsfeld and Gen. Myers, 21 March 2003. http://www.defenselink.mil/transcripts/2003/t03212003_t0321sd1.html

13. Group Captain Al Lockwood, interviewed on *Correspondent: War Spin*. BBC. First broadcast on BBC 2, 18 May 2003. Transcript available at http://news.bbc.co.uk/nol/shared/spl/hi/programmes/correspondent/transcripts/18.5.031.txt

14. Ministry of Defence, Director General Corporate Communication, Operations in Iraq: Lessons Lessons for the Future (December 2003) 59. http://www.mod.uk/publications/iraq_futurelessons/index.html

15. Glasgow University Media Group, cited in McLaughlin 2002, 79.

16. Statement by Air Marshal Brian Burridge, 27 March 2003, Qatar, as part of daily briefings. http://www.operations.mod.uk/telic/burridge_27march.htm

17. See, for example, Omaar (2004).

18. Available at http://www.defenselink.mil/transcripts/2003/t032112003_t0321sd1.html

19. Major Sean Holden of the Territorial Army, "Is the press reporting fairly?" *Sandy Times*, Number 30, 9 April 2003. http://www.operations.mod.uk.telic/index.htm

Chapter Five

1. Department of Defense, Public Affairs Guidance (PAG) on Embedding Media during Possible Future Operations/Deployments in the U.S. Central Commands (CENTCOM) Area of Responsibility (AOR), 10 February 2003. http://www.au.af.mil/au/awc/awcgate/awcmedia.htm#dod

2. "Journalists at War," debate organized by the Press Freedom Network, London, 2 May 2003.

3. "Journalists at War," debate organized by the Press Freedom Network, London, 2 May 2003.

4. Kampfner, J. 2003. *Correspondent: War Spin*. BBC. First broadcast on BBC 2, 18 May.

5. "Journalists at War," debate organized by the Press Freedom Network, London, 2 May 2003.

6. Franks 2003.

7. At time of writing (October 2003) a transcript of the CNN two-way could be read on http://www.abc.net.au/am/content/2003/s816456.htm; the BBC two-way was available at http://news.bbc.co.uk/1/hi/world/middle_east/2886235.stm

Chapter Six

1. We chose the early evening news programs on BBC and ITV because they are generally the most popular, and because they were more consistent in

terms of time slot and length throughout the war than the late evening bulletins.

2. Something increasingly difficult to do in contemporary styles of broadcasting, especially when one news event dominates the news bulletin, and various reports flow into one another.

3. In this study a "report" involved an identifiable, authored segment of the news program.

4. In all tables, where percentages have been rounded up or down, totals will not add up to 100 percent.

5. By this we mean reports that originated with the reporter or the reporter's team, rather than an edited package, based on available footage, presented by the reporter on location.

6. Whether or not this second point was endorsed by viewers is, at best, debatable. Our survey (see Chapter 8) found that 42 percent of people felt that the broadcasters gave "too little coverage" to these issues, while only 19 percent said "too much."

7. For example, the reported discovery of gas masks and anti-nerve gas chemicals by U.S. troops in Nasiriyah.

8. The figures for each channel are raw numbers, while the total figure is a percentage.

9. There are, of course, arguments that images of Iraqis going about their normal business could be interpreted as adding to a pro-war case, while Iraqis looting might be seen as detrimental to that case. Both are, nonetheless, open to interpretation, hence we confined our analysis to more explicit representations of Iraqi attitudes.

Chapter Seven

1. NBC's coverage, for example, was captioned "Operation Iraqi Freedom," while reporters made liberal use of words like "we" and "us" when referring to American forces.

2. From our piecing together of the timeline here, Wall's confirmation—presumably based on the same intelligence as Gaisford's reports—appeared to come just as evidence from an al-Jazeera reporter was contradicting it.

3. In the United States, ABC News stated that they were under attack by "U.S. forces."

4. Broadcasters were accused of moving from overly optimistic coverage in the first week of the war, to overly pessimistic coverage in the second week.

Chapter Eight

1. See http://www.icmresearch.co.uk

2. These figures refer to attitudes expressed about the war in late summer, where opinion overall was 53 percent to 44 percent against the war.

3. A,B,C1,C2, D, and E are the commonly used categories in British sociological analysis.

4. As our analysis of the coverage suggested, there was, in fact, very little coverage of this aspect of the war once it started. It may be that the 19 percent who thought there was too much were remembering the great deal of coverage this issue received before the war.

5. Blair, McCreary, and Whitman were prepared in interview to concede that the coverage could sometimes be read this way, but Victoria Clarke insisted on the "reality" of it: "Boy, I don't think there's anything more real than watching troops fighting in the streets of Baghdad." She refused the possibility that audiences could react as these audiences do.

6. We asked respondents to provide the name of the missile.

References

Albertazzi, D. 2003. "Framing Gulf War 2: A preliminary assessment of the coverage of the Iraq War in British television reporting." Paper presented at MeCCSA Annual Conference, Sussex University, UK.

Arnove, A. 2003. *Iraq under siege: The deadly impact of sanctions and war.* London: Pluto Press.

Baines, P. and Worcester, R. 2003. "When the British "Tommy" went to war, public opinion followed." World Association of Public Opinion Research, Prague, 17–19 September 2003.

Balance in the service of falsehood. 2004. http://www.medialens.org/pun. 15 December.

Barthes, R. 1988. *Mythologies.* New York: Noonday Press.

Brown, R. 2003. Spinning the war: Political communications, information operations and public diplomacy in the war on terrorism. In *War and the media: Reporting conflict 24/7*, ed. D. Thussu and D. Freedman, 87–100. London: Sage.

Brunsdon, C. and Morley, D. 1978. *Everyday television – Nationwide.* London: British Film Institute

Burston, J. 2003. War and the entertainment industry: New research priorities in an era of cyber-patriotism. In *War and the media: Reporting conflict 24/7*, ed. D. Thussu and D. Freedman, 163–175. London: Sage.

Carruthers, S. 2000. *The media at war.* Basingstoke, UK: Macmillan.

Cook, T. 1994. Washington newsbeats and network news after the Iraqi invasion of Kuwait. In *Taken by storm: The media public opinion and U.S. foreign policy in the Gulf War,* ed. W. Bennett and D. Paletz, 105-30. Chicago: University of Chicago Press.

Cottle, S., ed. 2003. *News, public relations and power.* London: Sage.

Curtis, M. 2004. Psychological warfare against the public: Iraq and beyond. In *Tell me lies: Propaganda and media distortion in the attack on Iraq,* ed. D. Miller, 70–79, London: Pluto Press.

Davis, A. 2000. Public relations, news production and changing patterns of source access in the British national media. *Media, Culture and Society* 22: 39–59.

Defense Science Board. 2004. *Report of the Defense Science Board Task Force on strategic communication.* http://www.iwar.org.uk/psyops/

Delli Carpini, M. and S. Keeter. 1996. *What Americans know about politics and why it matters.* New Haven, CT: Yale University Press.

Department of Defense. 2003. *Public affairs guidance (PAG) on embedding media during possible future operations/deployments in the U.S. Central Commands (CENTCOM) area of responsibility (AOR).* 10 February. http://www.au.af.mil/au/awc/awcgate/awcmedia.htm#dod

Dorril, S. 2004. Spies and lies. In *Tell me lies: propaganda and media distortion in the attack on Iraq,* ed. D. Miller, 108–114. London: Pluto Press.

Ericson R., Baranek, P. and Chan, J. 1987. *Visualising deviance: A study of news organizations.* Toronto: University of Toronto Press.

Ericson R., Baranek, P. and Chan, J. 1989. *Negotiating control: A study of news sources.* Toronto: University of Toronto Press.

Franks, T. 2003. Not war reporting—just reporting. *British Journalism Review* 14 (2): 15–19.

Gans, H. 1979. *Deciding what's news.* New York: Pantheon.

Gardiner, S. 2003. *Truth from these podia: Summary of a study of strategic influence, perception management, strategic information warfare and strategic psychological operations in Gulf II.* http://www.usnews.com/usnews/politics/whispers/documents/truth.pdf

Gilles, J. 2003. Putting a Face on Those Who Serve. *Washington Post,* 9 March.

Glasgow University Media Group. 1985. *Bad news.* In *The war correspondent,* ed. G. McLaughlin, 79. London: Pluto Press, 2002.

Hallin, D. 1989. *The "Uncensored War": The media and Vietnam.* Berkeley and Los Angeles: University of California Press.

Harris, R. 1983. *Gotcha! The media, the government and the Falklands crisis.* London: Faber and Faber.

Hickey, N. 2002. Access denied. *Columbia Journalism Review* January/February: 26–31.

House of Commons. 2004. Select Committee on Defence. *Third Report*. 3 March. http://www.publications.parliament.uk/pa/cm200304/cmselect/cmdfence/57/5702.htm

Hutton, Maj. J. E. Center for Army Lessons Learned (CALL) *Public Affairs Guidance*. http://call.army.mil/ (Accessed August 2003)

Joint Chiefs of Staff. 2003. *Doctrine for joint psychological operations*. Joint Publication 3–53. http://www.au.af.mil/au/awc/awcgate/awcmedia.htm#dod

Kampfner, J. 2003. *Correspondent: War Spin*. BBC. First broadcast on BBC 2, 18 May. Transcript available at http://news.bbc.co.uk/nol/shared/spl/hi/programmes/correspondent/transcripts/18.5.031.txt

Kampfner, J. 2004. *Blair's wars*. London: Free Press.

Katovsky, B. and T. Carlson. 2003. *Embedded. The media at war in Iraq*. Guilford, CT: Lyons Press.

Keeble, R. 1997. *Secret state, silent press: New militarism, the Gulf and the modern image of warfare*. Luton, UK: University of Luton Press.

Keeble, R. 2003. The myth of Gulf War II. Inaugural lecture at University of Lincoln. http://www.Anti-Spin.com (Accessed 29/03/05)

Kellner, D. 2003. *From 9/11 to terror war: The dangers of the Bush legacy*. Lanham, MD: Rowman and Littlefield Publishers.

Knightley, P. 2003. *The first casualty*, 3rd ed. London: Andre Deutsch.

Knightley, P. 2004. History or bunkum? In *Tell me lies: Propaganda and media distortion in the attack on Iraq*, ed. D. Miller 100–107. London: Pluto Press.

Kull, S. 2003. *Misperceptions: The media and the Iraq War*. Program on International Policy Attitudes at the University of Maryland. http://www.pipa.org

Kull, S. 2004. *Public perceptions of the foreign policy positions of the presidential candidates*. Program on International Policy Attitudes at the University of Maryland. http://www.pipa.org

Lewis, J. 2001. *Constructing public opinion: How elites do what they like and why we seem to go along with it*. New York: Columbia University Press.

Lewis, J. 2003. Biased broadcasting corporation? *Guardian*, 4 July, p. 27.

Lewis, J. 2004. Television, public opinion and the war in Iraq: The case of Britain. *International Journal of Public Opinion Research* 16 (3): 295–310.

Lewis, J. and R. Brookes. 2004a. Reporting the war on British television. In *Tell me lies: Propaganda and media distortion in the attack on Iraq*, ed. D. Miller, 132–43. London: Pluto Press.

Lewis, J. and R. Brookes. 2004b. How British television news represented the case for the war in Iraq. In *Reporting war: Journalism in wartime*, ed. S. Allan and B. Zelizer, 283–300. London: Routledge.

Lewis, J. and T. Speers. 2003. MMR: Misleading media reporting? *Nature Reviews Immunology* Vol 3 no 11, pp. 913–918.

Lewis, J. et al. 2004. *Too close for comfort: The role of embedded reporters during the 2003 Iraq War*. Cardiff, UK: Cardiff School of Journalism Media and Cultural Studies.

MacArthur, J. 1993. *Second front: Censorship and propaganda in the Gulf War*. Berkeley: University of California Press.

Mahajan, R. 2003. *Full spectrum dominance: US power in Iraq and beyond*. New York: Seven Stories Press.

Maltese, J. A. 1992. *Spin control: The White House Office of Communications and the management of presidential news*. Chapel Hill and London: University of North Carolina Press.

Manning, P. 2001. *News and news sources: A critical introduction*. London: Sage.

McCombs, M., Danielian, M. and Wanta, W. 1995. Issues in the News and the Public Agenda. In *Public opinion and the communication of consent*, eds. C. Salmon and T. Glasser. New York: Guilford Press.

Miller, D., ed. 2004a. *Tell me lies: Propaganda and media distortion in the attack on Iraq*. London: Pluto Press.

Miller, D. 2004b. Information dominance: The philosophy of total propaganda control. *ColdType*. http://www.coldtype.net (Accessed January 2004)

Miller, D. 2004c. Information dominance: The philosophy of total propaganda control? In *War, media and propaganda: A global perspective*, ed. Y. R. Kamalipour and N. Snow, 7–16, Lanham, MD: Rowman and Littlefield Publishers.

Miller, D. 2004d. The propaganda machine. In *Tell me lies: Propaganda and media distortion in the attack on Iraq*, ed. D. Miller, 80–99. London: Pluto Press.

Ministry of Defence. 1983. *The handling of press and public information during the Falklands conflict: Observations presented to the Secretary of State for Defence on the First Report from the Defence Committee*. House of Commons Papers 17-1-11 1982-3.

Ministry of Defence. 2001. *The Green Book*. http://www.mod.uk/news/green_book/index.htm

Ministry of Defence. 2003a. *Operations in Iraq: First reflections*. Director General Corporate Communication, 7 July. http://www.mod.uk/publications/iraq_lessons/index.html

Ministry of Defence. 2003b. *Operations in Iraq: Lessons for the future.* Directorate General Corporate Communication, 11 December. http://www.mod.uk/publications/iraq_futurelessons/index.html

Morrison, D. and H. Tumber. 1988. *Journalists at war.* London: Sage.

Omaar, R. 2004. *Revolution day: The human story of the battle for Iraq.* London: Viking.

Philo, G., ed. 1995. *Industry, economy, war and politics. Glasgow Media Group reader,* vol. 2. London: Routledge.

Philo, G. and M. Gilmour. 2004. Black holes of history: Public understanding and the shaping of our past. In *Tell me lies: Propaganda and media distortion in the attack on Iraq,* ed. D. Miller, 232–42. London: Pluto Press.

Philo, G. and G. McLaughlin. 1995. The British media and the Gulf War. In *Industry, Economy, War and Politics. Glasgow Media Group reader,* ed. G. Philo, vol. 2, 146–58. London: Routledge.

Pilger, J., ed. 2004. *Tell me no lies: Investigative journalism and its triumphs.* London: Jonathan Cape.

Rampton, S. and J. Stauber. 2003. *Weapons of mass deception: The uses of propaganda in Bush's war on Iraq.* London: Robinson.

Reality Show to Focus on Military Operations. 21 February, 2003 *Army Times.*

Rettich, M. 2003. The war on TV: "Better" is not good enough. *Media Tenor* 2: 39–43.

Rouse, Major E. 2004. *Psychological operations/warfare.* http://www.pipeline.com/~psywarrior/

Sancho, J. and J. Glover. 2003. *Conflict around the clock: Audience reactions to media coverage of the 2003 Iraq War.* London: Independent Television Commission.

Schanker, T. and E. Schmitt. 2004. Pentagon weighs use of deception in a broad arena. *Settle Post-Intelligencer.* http://www.commondreams.org (Accessed 3 January 2005)

Schechter, D. 2003. *Embedded: Weapons of mass deception. How the media failed to cover the war in Iraq.* Amherst, NY: Prometheus.

Schlesinger, P. 1978. *Putting "reality" together.* London: Constable.

Short, C. 2004. *An honourable deception? New Labour, Iraq and the misuse of power.* London: Free Press.

Simpson, J. 2003. *The wars against Saddam: Taking the hard road to Baghdad.* London: Macmillan.

Snow, N. 2002. *Propaganda inc.: Selling America's culture to the world.* New York: Seven Stories Press.

Snow, N. 2003. *Information war: American propaganda, free speech and opinion control since 9-11.* New York: Seven Stories Press.

Stratford-Wright, Lieutenant Colonel K. 2003. So, is it ok to use the media to deceive the enemy? *HQ ARRC Journal.* April. http://www.arrc. nato.int/journal/april03/media.htm

Taylor, P. M. 1990. *Munitions of the mind: War propaganda from the ancient world to the nuclear age.* Northamptonshire, UK: Patrick Stephens.

Taylor, P. M. 1992. *War and the media: Propaganda and persuasion in the Gulf War.* Manchester, UK: Manchester University Press.

Taylor, P. M. 2003. "We know where you are": Psychological operations media during Enduring Freedom. In *War and the media: Reporting conflict 24/7,* ed. D. Thussu and D. Freedman, 101–114. London: Sage.

Threadgold, T. and N. Mosdell. 2004. Embedded reporting: Lessons learned. *Defence Management Journal* 25: 12–16.

Thussu, D. 2003. Live TV and bloodless deaths: War, infotainment, and 24/7 news. In *War and the media: Reporting conflict 24/7,* ed. D. Thussu and D. Freedman, 117–32. London: Sage.

Thomson, A. 1992. *Smokescreen: The media—the censors—the Gulf.* Tunbridge Wells, UK: Laburnam and Spellmount, Ltd.

Tuchman, G. 1978. *Making news.* New York: Free Press.

Tumber, H. and J. Palmer. 2004. *Media at war: The Iraq crisis.* London: Sage.

Williams, P. 1992. Ground rules and guidelines for Desert Shield. In *The media and the Gulf War,* ed. H. Smith. Washington, DC: Seven Locks.

Wyatt, C. R. 1993. *Paper soldiers: The American press and the Vietnam War.* Chicago: Chicago University Press.

Young, P. and P. Jesser. 1997. *The media and the military: From the Crimea to Desert Strike.* Basingstoke, UK: Macmillan.

Zelizer, B. 2004. *Taking journalism seriously: News and the academy.* London: Sage.

Sut Jhally & Justin Lewis
General Editors

This series publishes works on media and culture, focusing on research embracing a variety of critical perspectives. The series is particularly interested in promoting theoretically informed empirical work using both quantitative and qualitative approaches. Although the focus is on scholarly research, the series aims to speak beyond a narrow, specialist audience.